Rebuilding the Financial System in Central and Eastern Europe, 1918–1994

Rebuilding the Financial System in Central and Eastern Europe, 1918–1994

Edited by

PHILIP L. COTTRELL

Routledge
Taylor & Francis Group
LONDON AND NEW YORK

First published 1997 by Ashgate Publishing

Published 2016 by Routledge
2 Park Square, Milton Park, Abingdon, Oxfordshire OX14 4RN
711 Third Avenue, New York, NY 10017, USA

First issued in paperback 2016

Routledge is an imprint of the Taylor & Francis Group, an informa business

British Library Cataloguing-in-Publication Data

Cottrell, P. L.
Rebuilding the Financial System in Central and Eastern Europe, 1918-1994
1. Financial institutions — Europe. 2. Finance — Europe. 3. Financial institutions — Europe — History — 20th century. 4. Finance — Europe — History — 20th century. I. Title II. European Banking History Association
332'.0943'0904

Library of Congress Cataloging-in-Publication Data

Cottrell, P. L.
Rebuilding the Financial System in Central and Eastern Europe, 1918-1994 / Philip L. Cottrell
p. cm.
1. Banks and banking — Europe, Eastern — History. 2. Banks and banking — Europe, Central — History. 3. Finance — Europe, Eastern — History. 4. Finance — Europe, Central — History. I. Title.
HG2980.7.A6C67 1997
332.1'0943 — dc21 96-40378
CIP

ISBN 13: 978-1-138-26909-5 (pbk)
ISBN 13: 978-1-85928-413-1 (hbk)

Contents

List of tables

Preface

This collection of essays, written by former bankers, practising central bankers, government advisers and historians, celebrates the seventieth anniversary of the foundation of the National Bank of Hungary in 1994. From a range of view points, each contribution considers the monetary and financial history of the past century and, in particular, explores in varying ways possible parallelisms between experiences of the collapse of the Habsburg Monarchy in 1918 and of contemporary changes since 1989. Part I, comprising four essays, concentrates upon central banking, especially the development of the National Bank of Hungary since 1878 and the establishment of the Bank of Poland. Commercial banking is the theme of Part II, where continuities and discontinuities are reviewed and analysed with respect to Austria, Czechoslovakia, Romania, Slovenia and Yugoslavia.

This collection has a catholic approach and, deliberately so, in order to capitalize upon the greatest possible benefits that might arise when a variety of unfettered views are solicited. Consequently, in his introduction, Péter Bod takes issue with the possibility of there being historical parallels. Rather, he maintains that a process of creation, as opposed to re-creation, is taking place in eastern Europe during the 1990s since the tradition of the market economy within this region has faded into the distant past. He receives some support from Daniel Daianu, who considers that the post-communist transition is an exceptional experience, involving a modernization that has to start from scratch. However, Daianu also points to central and eastern Europe being particularly subject to path-dependency, so that bring about economic and societal change involves having to address structures that are a legacy of backwardness - and a legacy bequeathed by centuries as opposed to decades or half-centuries.

Despite the old adage, history seldom repeats itself exactly and what emerges from these contributions is that the events of 1918/19 within eastern Europe comprised less of a discontinuity than those that have unfolded since 1989. With the national revolutions of 1918, the major financial problem that had to be resolved was currency reform, posed by wartime and post-war inflation and hyperinflation. In the case of commercial banking, there was greater continuity with the further development of 'universal' banking out of its pre-war mould of the Austrian/German model, albeit after 1918 within new national frameworks for financial systems.

In Part I, there is an over-riding emphasis on central banks being continuously engaged in 'a struggle for good money', to use the phrase of Tamás Bácskai. None the less, Daianu shows that, in the case of at least the National Bank of Romania, the central bank could be expected to discharge a range of other functions, from supporting industrialization since the bank's very foundation in the 1880s to refinancing commercial banks during the inflation of the early 1920s to conducting commercial policy over the 1930s and to being an 'institutional builder' during both the interwar period and the post-communist transition. Maintaining the value of the currency through the unrestricted conduct of monetary policy was a delicate task for central bankers, which could bring them into collusion with government. Both Bácskai and György Szapáry show how the independent position of the National Bank of Hungary was undermined by the state's policies, first in 1933 due to reactions to the Great Depression and then in 1938 with the Györ war programme. Similarly, as Landau argues, the Bank of Poland's freedom for manoeuvre was progressively affected and reduced by Pilsudski's coup d'état of May 1926, the 1927 Polish stabilization plan, the requirement to provide state loans from 1931, the imposition of foreign exchange controls from 1936 and the expansion of the currency from 1938.

The National Bank of Hungary benefited from the prior experience of the senior staff of the Austro-Hungarian Bank and there is some agreement among the contributors that the development of central banking is a learning process, involving the building of a tradition. However, like Poland itself, the Bank of Poland had to be created almost *de novo* but its first president, Karpinski, had a very clear view of his institution's role as a private joint stock bank despite having previously favoured, when Minster of Finance, the establishment of a state-owned central bank. His views chimed very much with those of Montagu Norman, developed over the winter of 1920/1, and which were to play a such significant part in the creation of new, independent central banks in central and eastern Europe. None the less, despite Norman's stress upon the need for an apolitical, unconstrained approach to what he considered to be technical questions of currency and financial structures, ultimately he too proved to be a servant of the British state. Although objecting to the League of Nations' monetary reconstruction scheme for Hungary because of the continuing reparation charges that it entailed, when asked by the Chancellor of the Exchequer, Norman put his considerable energies to ensuring the success of the issue of the 1924 Hungarian stabilization loan.

Commercial banking in Part II is treated from a wide range of approaches: the anatomy of capitalism, the impact of political change, economic autonomy, and its part within modernization. Peter Eigner analyses the relatively late development of 'universal banking' within Cisleithania from the mid-1890s, but then demonstrates its persistence, and its ultimate advantage to the Nazi regime in 1938. He argues that the process of nostrification within the successor states was not the crux of the crisis that Austrian banks faced between 1924 and 1934, whereas his demonstration of the maintenance of bank-industry relationships is also alluded to in the studies of Czechoslovakia and Slovenia. The continuing links of major Slovene financial institutions with Vienna, pointed out by Franjo Štiblar, acted as a transmission mechanism for the 1931 crisis to spread south. Indeed, the complete retreat of the Viennese banks from the area of the former 'imperial' economy only took place during the 1930s through a process aptly dubbed 'Austrification'.

The contributions in both Part I and Part II indicate in various ways the relationship between financial institutions and demands for national autonomy. Beginning in the late eighteenth century, Magyars agitated for a national bank, the Czechs began to develop their own financial institutions from the 1830s, whereas the Viennese banks only established branches in Slovenia during the 1900s in response to the success of locally-founded 'universal' banks. The new currencies after 1918 assisted the development of national institutions, while the post-war inflations induced mushroom-like increases in the sizes of financial sectors. As Vlastislav Lacina indicates in his survey, the number of Czechoslovak banks rose by sixteen during the relatively mild inflation experienced by this economy over the early 1920s, whereas there was a considerably more marked financial expansion in both Romania and Slovenia. However, this increase in the number of banks was transitory, a product of inflation, to be largely cut back by the introduction of stabilization policies. Only one new Czechoslovak bank of the early 1920s proved to be of any enduring importance.

Post-war inflation, while posing a critical problem for the region's central bankers, enabled reconstruction to the extent that Štiblar considers the early 1920s to be an important period in Slovenia's industrial development. Comparable developments took place within Romania. However, differing views are taken of the stabilization crisis of the mid- and late 1920s, with it being put forward that this led to a consolidation of banking in Romania and Slovenia, so placing these financial systems on a firmer foundation - to make them better fitted to absorb the shocks of the Great Depression. Eigner draws a very different interpretation of Austrian banking developments after hyper-inflation, in which senior Viennese bankers continued with misguided policies, not heeding, let alone positively responding to, the clear warning signs of the financial sector's developing implosion.

Some of the new banks of the 1920s were established by savings institutions, as in Slovenia, replicating a development path that had begun during the 1860s with the creation of the Živnostenská banka in the Czech Crown Lands. Secondary and tertiary financial institutions have played a significant role in the historical development of banking in eastern Europe and some acknowledgement of this is made by both Lacina and Štiblar. A largely new factor during the 1920s was the sizeable involvement of western European capital through participations in both major banks and significant industrial companies and which, in some respects, paralleled the international dimensions of the decade's monetary reform programmes. Particular aspects of the engagement of western capital in Austria during the 1920s are discussed in detail by Eigner, whereas the significance of foreign investment in Czechoslovakia, Romania and Yugoslavia is indicated in the other studies. Such inflows were assisted by the predominance of 'universal banking' at the top tiers of financial sectors but Daianu raises the question in his wide-ranging review of the efficacy of this institutional type for the post-communist transition.

The production of this volume was aided by many, including Brigitte Hatke-Beck who assisted in the preparations for the Colloquium, Emma Johnston who co-ordinated the assembly of the revised papers, and Gillian Austen who undertook the arduous task of preparing the camera-ready copy. However, the greatest thanks must go to the National Bank of Hungary for its kind invitation to the European Association for Banking History to participate in its seventieth-birthday celebrations. The Bank's senior staff greatly aided the planning for the Colloquium and were the most hospitable of hosts. The then Governor, Péter Bod, took a continuing active interest and, generous of his time, opened the Colloquium in Budapest which was attended by 120 delegates from eastern Europe, western Europe and further afield. The vigorous debate on the day between practising bankers and financial historians more than fulfilled the aims of the European Association for Banking History and, it is to be hoped, was a fitting tribute to our kind hosts.

Frankfurt-am-Main, Leicester P. L. Cottrell

INTRODUCTION

Rebuilding the financial system in central and eastern Europe

Péter Á. Bod

The National Bank of Hungary takes great pleasure in hosting this academic seminar of the European Association for Banking History. Our bank became a member of the association in 1993 and, while the selection of Budapest as the venue for this meeting might be a polite gesture - an appreciation of a new member's enthusiasm - there must be more involved, and in particular the recognition of the whole of this region's significance. Currently, all the countries of east central Europe, the former Soviet Union, the Balkans and the Baltic are experiencing historic changes. Some, including Hungary, are undergoing the painful process of returning to the market economy. Elsewhere, new structures and institutions of the nation state, and in particular of the national economy, are being resurrected. However, in some cases, it is clearly difficult to talk about the revival of the market economy as its tradition has faded into the distant past. Therefore, the key task today is to *create*, as opposed to *re-create*.

Efforts towards economic reconstruction are not unprecedented within the region as, unfortunately, past centuries have witnessed several failed attempts and re-starts. As an example, there is the remarkable financial culture of medieval Hungary which subsequently, for 150 years, was stymied by Ottoman-Turkish conquest. Hungary, weakened economically, militarily and demographically, was unable to break away from the Turkish empire by its own efforts. As a result, the country had no choice but, from the seventeenth century, to become a part of the Austrian Empire. Within the framework of this empire the Hungarian reform period started to germinate during the first three decades of the nineteenth century - an age of reform which culminated in the civic revolution and fight for independence of 1848-49. That revolution called for the country's sovereignty, liberty and freedom of trade.

One of the demands which had an economic nature, the ninth of the famous *Twelve Demands of March 1848*, put it most succinctly: *'A National Bank'*. The creation of national financial institutions - fought for politically if necessary - was unquestionably the leading condition for civic development. Without financial intermediation, the concentration of capital, so vital for economic development, could not have been achieved and, moreover, the physical and legal infrastructure of civic society created. By the same token, the National Bank carries a symbolic meaning. Not incidentally, during the 1866/7 talks between the Austrian Empire and the Hungarians leading to the creation of the Austro-Hungarian Monarchy, the royal court proved much more amenable on the issues of defence and foreign policy or even fiscal matters than on the question of Hungary's own central bank. Thus, well after the *Compromise of 1867*, the Austrian

National Bank continued to discharge central bank functions on the territory of the Kingdom of Hungary. It was only after the fall of the Monarchy and the First World War that it was possible to establish the National Bank of Hungary, some 70 years ago.

Being conscious of the hardship of this process provides a much better position for understanding why new states have always considered the creation of an independent currency and central bank as one of the tasks of utmost importance. In general, the recent developments of the late twentieth century in the region are looked at with greater empathy from Budapest, where banking in the modern sense spans a mere 150 years, where the independent central bank can boast only 70 years of existence and where the once flourishing commodity and stock exchanges were condemned to shut their doors in 1948 for four decades, only to re-open at the beginning of the 1990s.

Recent re-starts gives particular topicality to banking history studies concerned with earlier reconstruction attempts in the region. The external conditions of the present restart, however, are very different from those at a time when the Austro-Hungarian Monarchy collapsed and the new national financial systems were created. In comparison with the isolation following the First World War, commodity and capital markets currently display a high level of mobility. Furthermore, a process of integration has been underway for several decades within western Europe. Factor mobility brings with it fierce competition, rapid capital flows and a high degree of liberalization for the new, 'emerging' or 're-emerging', market economies. Moreover, European integration requires its members to surrender part of their economic sovereignty and comply with common legal standards, while, for other nations, who wish to be integrated, this adaption is all the more compelling, regardless of the fact that they are only candidates for admission.

Yet, the history of European banking reminds us that, despite the dynamic process of integration since the early 1950s, European countries are still characterized by a variety of institutions and financial structures. It seems that efficiency and international compatibility *can* be achieved under widely differing national institutional systems. True, national autonomy has its boundaries; competition, cultural influences and EU directives all move in one direction - *harmonisation*. However, the fact that European development has tested a vast number of institutional systems is instructive for emerging economies while they are in the process of rebuilding their financial systems.

Europe has experimented with various national models in the relationships between: central bank and government; bank capital and industrial capital; and insurers, savings and building societies, and commercial banks.

Hic et nunc, this meeting has special importance, beyond and above due respect to banking history since the contributors will present papers concerned with history when, here and now, historic events are taking place. Recognizing the particular significance of this moment, I am convinced that the conference will prove to be successful both as a banking history colloquium and as a reminder for present-day policy-makers.

PART I
CENTRAL BANKING

CHAPTER ONE

Currency reform and the establishment of the National Bank of Hungary

Tamás Bácskai

This contribution must begin with an apology to professional historians since it comprises the reflections of an economist who was for a long time a central banker. Furthermore, this experience has led to the personal belief that an institution's history is contained and sustained as much in and by its staff, whose experience, traditions and esprit de corps is inherited by successive generations, as in its archives and written history - if ever they are consulted. I am proud of the training that I received from such custodians of tradition as Janos Baracs, who was for a considerable period the chief economist of the National Bank of Hungary and then became an important staff expert with Maxwell Stamp, London; Bela Szajani of the Bank's Economics Division; and the Bank's General Director Ferenc Jeszenszky, as well as from former officials of the Treasury concerned with credit, such as György Matyasfalvy and Bela Csikos-Nagy.

Traditions, both good and bad, persist side by side, while the personal evaluation of what is good and what is bad may differ according to past experience and current situations. Yet, central bankers, although hailing from different times or different places, share one common aim: maintaining the relative stability of the value, or the purchasing power, of the currency for which they are responsible.

The monetary history of central and eastern Europe is marked by a greater frequency of currency reform - either manifest or implicit - than that of western Europe. This is shown in the changing names of the region's currencies and by the volatility of either their past silver and gold values or their exchange rates since the Second World War. Very recently, a considerable number of new, or rather re-newed, currency names and central banks have emerged in the successor states to the former Soviet Union, Yugoslavia and Czechoslovakia (although solely with regard to the monetary authorities in the case of the latter). It is further to the point that this has occurred for the third time during the historically brief period comprising the years since the end of the First World War.

When reviewing the era characterised by a more or less modern financial system and financial policy in the Habsburg empire, it is apparent that brief spells of monetary stability were preceded and followed by inflations. These, involving currency debasement and other unwelcome monetary phenomena, disorganised the economy and provoked attempts, often futile, to stabilize. The Empire's monetary authorities, whatever their name or official title, were engaged in a relentless struggle with their fiscal counterparts in order to safeguard the values of the various currencies, by name, that they managed. In most cases, it was not their fault if they were unable to persuade others of the strength of the arguments that they made as governments were involved almost continuously in wars that undermined the value of money. In this sense, there was continuity in the attitudes of the monetary authorities in charge of the Empire, including Hungary (the latter as an object or, after 1867, as a subject of monetary matters), who established a positive tradition involving at least a struggle for good money.

This era also had periods of central banking victory, even glory, as with the currency reform of 1892. A special sort of the gold standard - a 'limping' standard - was introduced by this legislation which had been framed by Sándor Wekerie, the Hungarian Minister of Finance, and then was executed under Gyula Kautz, a newly-appointed Hungarian Governor of the Bank. Kautz was an experienced central banker as well as an eminent scholar, with his *The History of Economic Thought and its Impact on Public Affairs in Hungary* being even favourably mentioned by Marx, who generally was not well disposed to Kautz's colleagues.[1]

It is clear that the region's monetary authorities were forced by circumstances to be almost permanent crisis managers so that their leaders and staff became experts in what has come to be called across the Atlantic 'specialist trouble-shooting'. This skill played an important part in resolving the enormous problems posed by the monetary consequences of the dissolution of the Empire in 1918. Equally and unfortunately, they came to the fore again in the stabilization and the creation of a new currency in Hungary after the Second World War. Most probably, it was an asset then that the introduction of some sort of a gold standard was still, after only 22 years, retained in living memory. This expertise was also sought in the difficult processes of returning to a market economy and parliamentary democracy during the late 1980s. These latter developments need separate mention because they required transparency, whereas, for about 40 years previously, monetary policy, especially the financing of the budget, had been clad in a cloak of secrecy.[2]

If it is possible to put to one side the brief episode between 17 June 1848 and 8 July 1849 when, with the revolution, the Pesti Magyar Kereskedelmi Bank [Hungarian Commercial Bank of Pest] issued notes,[3] then an autonomous and separate Hungarian bank of issue was established rather late - in 1924 - in terms of the historical development of such institutions. This took place in conjunction with monetary stabilization and the introduction of a new currency: the Pengö. As a result, in the first volume of the history of the National Bank of Hungary concerned with the period 1816 to 1924[4], the chief 'actor' in the story - the National Bank - appears at the very end, like Fortinbras in Shakespeare's *Hamlet.*

Someone may challenge the use here of 'late' with regard to the foundation of a Hungarian central bank and not without justification since there were only 18 such institutions at the opening of the twentieth century. With the dissolution of empires, that number increased, leading to 80 countries by 1960, and 157 countries in the mid-1990s,[5] with a central bank. However, 'late' can be justified by the centuries that had elapsed since 1661, when the then four-year old Stockholms Banco of Johan Palmstruch (indeed, an infant!), became Europe's and the world's first bank of issue through having the right to circulate Swedish notes convertible into coin, or specie. Palmstruch's initiative produced an episode in the proto-history of central banking that started gloriously but finished ignominiously. Palmstruch issued more notes than he could redeem, with the result that the bank closed, he was sent to jail and the government founded a state-owned bank in 1668 that was the pro-genitor of the Sveriges Riksbank. Unfortunately, central banking is a learning process, involving trial and error, and the errors of the central banks are trials for the holders of their bank notes. Fortunately or unfortunately, central banks have been experimenting ever since 1661.

With such a late emergence, historically, of a Hungarian central bank, is it possible to maintain that there was a discontinuity, a discreet change in the sphere of the monetary authority, so that the National Bank of Hungary sprang, like Pallas Athenae from Zeus's head, as a new and complete entity? Or was it that the duration of the learning process was too short? The answer is in the negative, since there had been monetary authorities operating for centuries on Hungarian soil, continually either causing or fighting inflation. The phenomenon, called in medieval Latin *renovatio monetae* or *mutatio monetae*, can be first detected in a constitutional document drawn up during the reign of Andras I. Subsequently in 1222, the Golden Bull, granted by King Endre II, gave the assurance that the sovereign would not debase the currency. But the 1231 version of the Bull displays a more realistic attitude as its provisions stipulated that the king would have recourse to debasement only once a year! Later, under King Carlobertus, a descendant of the House of Anjou who reigned between 1308 and 1342, a comprehensive monetary reform aimed at stabilization was successfully carried out in c.1328/9.[6]

Furthermore, from the end of the eighteenth century, the Hungarian political élite took up the conception of an autonomous Hungarian bank of issue and then campaigned for its establishment. This institution also embodied the country's economic sovereignty in that its supporters considered the National Bank of Austria to be an *Austrian* as well as a *private* banking institution, instead of the *Hungarian* and *state-owned* body controlling the system of money flows within Hungary that they sought. Some politicians equally maintained that the shortage of capital within Hungary was due to the lack of a central bank belonging solely to Hungary. They voiced a view that resembled the thoughts of John Law by mixing the notion of money with that of capital. In any case, the primitive state of financial institutions in Hungary was one of several reasons for the backwardness of the country and, therefore, it is not surprising that the ninth of the twelve demands ('points') of 15 March 1848 revolution concerned the establishment of a national bank.

What seems to be puzzling is that, when there was a possibility of creating a separate bank of issue during the negotiations for the Compromise of 1867, a separate National Bank of Hungary failed to emerge. The Compromise had placed Hungary on an equal footing with Austria within the framework of the Dual Monarchy. Rather, it was the protracted negotiations in 1878 for the renewal of the Compromise, that is eleven years later than those that had produced the other Dualist institutions, which led to creation of the *Austro-Hungarian* Bank. This had statutes based on the principle of parity between the two halves of the Monarchy. How was that possible, given the recent consideration of Forrest Capie, Charles Goodhart and Norbert Schnadt that 'setting up an independent central bank is a key ingredient in establishing national autonomy - slightly below the design of the flag, but above the establishment of a national airline'?[7] The constraint put on Hungarian national aspirations in 1878 was certainly wise from an economic point of view, but failed to calm the storm of political discontent within Hungarian, or Austrian or Bohemian-Moravian circles. These were reflected in the heated debates of the so-called banking conferences that took place with each decennial negotiation of the renewal of the Compromise. Yet, the very idea of limiting national sovereignty in monetary affairs, through the transfer of powers to an empire, or to a region, or to a semi-continent or even to a continent, is a modern, late-twentieth century conception. It might be interpreted as a symbolic gesture that, in Alexandre Lamfalussy, a person of Hungarian origin has been given charge of the seed germ for the future European central bank.

Most probably, the domestic operations of the independent central bank within the Dual Monarchy, involving a currency with an empire-wide value, should have been no more than shadow-boxing - keeping a monetary parity constant between Transleithania and Cisleithania. Then, with the collapse of the Dual Monarchy in 1918, previous monetary disputes within the Empire were transformed into the tasks of separating out the monetary systems of the successor states, creating the necessary and stable monetary instruments and institutions for each new republic and, last but not least, the liquidation of the Austro-Hungarian Bank. These took more than five years to be completed. They were repeated, fully or partially, when the Soviet Union, Czechoslovakia and Yugoslavia were dissolved. They raise, in turn, the question as to what extent the experience of the post-1918 period was taken into consideration? Yet it must be understood that the tasks of the late 1980s and early 1990s have also involved the return to a market economy and necessitated a reorganisation of the monobank system[8] into a two-level banking system, in turn, involving the re-establishment of central banks of the classical type and shaped primarily by the example of the Old Lady of

Threadneedle Street.

Why did the founding fathers of the National Bank of Hungary during the early 1920s also choose the Bank of England as a model to emulate? Their peers had previously granted the privilege of note issuing to the Pest Magyar Kereskedelmi Bank, which undertook this function in 1848-9, and they also had the example of the Magyar Általános Hitelbank [Hungarian General Credit Bank], an institution partly owned by the Rothschilds and which had been banker to the government from 1880. Why did those creating the monetary institutions of Hungary during the mid-1920s select the Bank of England as their model?[9] This Bank had begun as a private corporation, chartered in 1694, to fund the government's war costs, to stabilize chaotic financial conditions and to manage the public debt with, in exchange, receiving a monopoly of issuing notes. It is clear that they most certainly chose the Bank of England in its guise between 1844 and 1924 (and which was to be maintained until 1945) - a period when its governors and directors refined and honed the tools of central banking. Yet, during the early 1920s the Bank of England was not the only model for emulation.[10] There was the Banque de France, the central bank of another victorious country in the war; the Sveriges Riksbank of neutral Sweden and which had the greatest longevity; or the Swiss National Bank, responsible for a currency unblemished by the consequences of the Great War and located in Zürich, the financial centre where the bulk of international payments for central and eastern Europe was transacted. It is clear that the staff of the Austro-Hungarian Bank had admired the British central bank while, moreover, the influences of Peel's 1844 Act and associated legislation can be traced in the provisions of the Austro-Hungarian Bank's statutes, albeit sometimes in somewhat distorted forms.

What needs to be emphasized is the continuity of monetary experience, skills and learning within the newly-established central bank of Hungary, as well as amongst the leading politicians of the 1920s. This, undisrupted by the brief existence of a Soviet Republic in 1919, had permeated the State Issuing Institute which had acted as the central bank until the National Bank was founded. Seen in this perspective, the National Bank of Hungary came out of the womb of the Austro-Hungarian Bank, especially as its most important human capital resources were drawn from the most senior posts of its 'mother' bank. It is almost symbolic of this continuity that Sándor Popovics, the first President of the National Bank of Hungary, had been a President of the Austro-Hungarian Bank. However, he also had over many decades a continuous close personal relationship with Montagu Norman of the Bank of England, who played an important part in Hungarian stabilization and the establishment of the National Bank of Hungary. The Bank of England provided the exemplar for the outstanding senior central bankers of the Austro-Hungarian Bank, while for Sándor Popovics there was also a personal bond. As Péteri[11] has shown, between 1924 and 1931, that is until the outbreak of the liquidity crisis, the money supply in Hungary followed, with a lag of three months, changes in specie (including foreign exchange) holdings of the National Bank as if Peel's 1844 Act had been in force.

Continuity is the most outstanding feature of the development of the National Bank. This was due to its inherited collective memory arising from the way that succesive generations of its staff had replaced each other in manner of relay runners passing the baton. Such a bequest was augmented by their experience and the written record contained in the archives, while, the National Bank was permeated by the esprit de corps of its progenitor institution. Equally, the senior management of the Bank have successively displayed the same propensity for using unorthodox methods when coping with unusual situations. One novel, even precocious, solution conceived by the Austro-Hungarian Bank's staff was the introduction of a gold exchange standard in the midst of the classic gold standard era. They had conceived of a foreign exchange rate regime which was only to gain wide use during the 1920s. In the case of Hungary alone, an original solution was the establishment of the Penzintezeti Kozpont [Central Corporation of Banking Companies] during the First World War. This was a precursor of state banking supervision, as well as an early type of institution designed to avoid bank bankruptcies or, *in extremis*, to mitigate the consequences of bank failures. Part and parcel of this tradition within the Bank is the strict adherence to the principle: *pacta sunt servanda*, which has led to the Bank behaving as a first class debtor throughout its existence - even under Communist rule.

The Austro-Hungarian Bank's situation was not altered by the 1918 revolutions - neither by the establishment of republics nor the formation of the Karolyi government in Budapest. Austrian, Czech, Hungarian and Polish representatives all agreed to the Bank continuing to function until 31 December 1919. For their part, Hungarian politicians assumed that the maintenance of the financial community within central and eastern Europe might motivate governments of the successor states, in particular the Czechoslovak government, to co-operate.

The policy of the Hungarian government aimed to dismantle the wartime regime in order to restore the pre-war market economy. Measures were planned which today would be called 'liberalization' (of prices, exchange rates), 'deregulation' (elimination of the vestiges of a war command economy) and 'macroeconomic stabilization' (the gradual re-establishment of equilibria in the real and monetary economies, including the liquidation of the monetary overhang together with steps to eliminate its resurgence involving mainly the recreation of budgetary equilibrium). Consequently, the status and role of the central bank was basically conceived in pre-1914 terms, which meant the re-establishment of its autonomy *vis-à-vis* the budget and, therefore, the ending of the fiduciary note issue.[12]

A majority within the Hungarian government wished to return to the pre-war parity of the crown on the foreign exchanges, although this was opposed by Jeno Varga, a Social Democrat. However, when the successor states introduced their own national currencies, conditions for policy formation changed, especially with the arising amounts of crowns that flooded into Hungary. This influx placed a strong, downward pressure on the currency as well as on interest rates. Consequently, the task of eliminating the monetary overhang became by an order of magnitude more substantial than had been the case in previous stabilization processes. The introduction of measures planned to stem the inflow of crowns, such as stamping bank notes in a certain sequence of holders, was interrupted by the Communist party's coup d'état, leading to their postponement until spring 1920. During the Republic of Councils' few months of existence, there was no central bank and monetary policy in the classical terms, while there were serious ideological discussions over the liquidation, or preservation, of money in general. Due to a shortage of notes, the Council of People's Commissars issued their own to complement those of the Austro-Hungarian Bank, but they were either repudiated, or only reluctantly accepted under duress by the population. After the collapse of the Councils, these 1919 notes were transformed into treasury notes but were debased through the application of a mandatory value.

A peculiar feature of the period 1918 to 1920 is that, although the crown gradually ceased to fulfil the functions of a currency throughout the territory that had comprised the former Monarchy, a common central bank continued to exist as an institution. During the winter of 1919/20, certain Austrian and Hungarian political circles even hoped that it might be possible to maintain a joint central bank.

The peace with Austria, the Treaty of St. Germain, required the immediate liquidation of the Austro-Hungarian Bank and the same provision with an identical text was written into the Treaty of Trianon, the peace treaty concluded later with Hungary. During the liquidation negotiations contradictions among the successor states surfaced. The governments of the new states wanted to establish rapidly autonomous, national central banks and consequently made demands for proportionate shares of the Bank's gold and silver reserves. But they refused to share the burden of the Bank's liabilities, arguing that these had financed a war waged against them. Austrian representatives, supported by some Hungarian delegates, put forward a proposal based upon a strict territorial principle, according to which all properties of the Dual Monarchy and its institutions passed directly to the successor states on whose territory they were physically located. Hence, the Bank's gold and silver reserves would go to Austria and Hungary in a ratio of 80:20. Sándor Popovics was the plenipotentiary commissary of Hungary, having been a former governor of the Austro-Hungarian Bank and the expert for questions regarding the central bank in the Hungarian delegation at the talks leading to the Trianon peace treaty. He maintained that the Austro-Hungarian Bank should be considered as a legal personality under civil law and therefore its property was solely and exclusively owned by its shareholders. Furthermore, the Bank's founding patent stipulated that, in case of liquidation, its shareholders would receive sufficient parts of the gold and silver holdings as compensation.

The peace treaties differentiated between the notes that the Bank had issued before 27 October 1918 and those put into circulation thereafter, while obliging the governments of the successor states to redeem only the former. Both the Austrian and Hungarian delegations argued that it would be impossible to determine, *ex post*, the time of issue of the notes that had subsequently been handed over to their authorities. After a second conference held in February 1922, a compromise was reached. This involved the successor states taking over the commercial assets and liabilities of the Bank with the exception of those consisting of, and denominated in, foreign currencies. The Bank's gold, with other remaining assets, were used to meet the claims of, first, foreign holders of its notes and, thereafter, went to fulfil claims in gold and foreign currencies. The rest of the metallic reserve was distributed among successor states in proportion to the regional volumes of bank notes issued before 27 October 1918. Claims of holders of notes issued after that date were met by Austria and Hungary renouncing 2.5 billion crowns of gold, but this exempted both these countries from meeting all liabilities to the successor states. A small proportion of shareholders' claims was settled through ceding the Bank's real estate outside Vienna (primarily branch offices), and its building in Vienna (at Bankgasse 3) including its equipment and note printing facilities.

This tortuous process reveals how every initial step taken towards the establishment of the National Bank of Hungary, and which brought about the associated Hungarian currency stabilization, was fraught with difficulties. Moreover, these 'reconstruction' measures were peculiar and specific due to the post-war circumstances. Furthermore, developments from 1919, contrary to the wishes of some of those involved, did not lead to a general stabilization and the formation of a unified central bank within the region.

On 26 April 1924 the law establishing the National Bank of Hungary, and which granted the Bank the privilege of note-issuing, came into force. The Bank's first General Assembly was held in the ceremonial hall of the Academy of Sciences on 24 May 1924, and its shares were introduced on the Budapest Stock Exchange on 25 September 1925. That only sixteen months elapsed between these two important stages in the Bank's birth indicates a very creditable beginning in a country that had lost two-thirds of its former area, one third of its former population (but receiving a sizeable inflow of displaced persons from former Hungarian territories), and which had experienced the disruption of its traditional economic ties during a period marked by an astronomic inflation.

The formation of the National Bank of Hungary had been strongly influenced by the Financial Committee of the League of Nations. This had proved to be a positive germinating force and one that largely coincided with Hungarian wishes or desires, although sometimes for the differing reasons. For instance, both the Hungarians involved and League experts had wanted the Bank to be a national institution in terms of its share capital being raised within Hungary. However, whereas the League saw this as a way of deflecting any inflow of foreign capital into solely financing borrowing by the Hungarian state, this motivation was not shared by their Hungarian counterparts.

The Bank's constitution as a joint stock company was the then current norm for the establishment of central banks, being based on the illusion that this constituted a defence against undue government influence, even if its shares were subsequently held by the government. None the less it was a misplaced conception both in the case of the National Bank of Hungary and more generally. In Hungary this was subsequently pointed up by Law 25 of 1938, which subordinated the Bank to the needs of a budget involving the expenditure of an additional 1 billion Pengö (ten per cent of national income), on government investments. This was over and above the regular budget for projects with poor cash flows, mainly rearmament and infrastructure. Although the Bank's founding articles had included the possibility of appeal against government decisions in the administrative law court, it was found that these stipulations provided no defence. The 1938 episode further illustrates that only the exercise of wise self-discipline by both the government and the parliamentary majority constitutes the defence against such practices.

Paradoxically, despite private interests generally wishing to have influence within the Bank, it was the lack of private capital and the market's unwillingness to underwrite - particularly displayed by agrarian capital - which led to the government acquiring a larger portion of the Bank's shares than had been planned. In these circumstances, the government came to hold 39.5 per cent of the Bank's shares, whereas ambitious agrarian groups, which had aimed to obtain 51 per cent, only bought 7.8 per cent. As events rapidly showed, a stake as a founding shareholder was a sound investment because the Bank made significant profits, enabling the declaration of a dividend of 8.6 per cent for 1924.

A dilemma is posed for every central bank by their managements having to attempt to harmonise two valid, but contradictory, prime requirements. On the one hand, there is the preservation of the purchasing power of the currency abroad and domestically and, on the other, assistance for the government's economic policy. A government is justified in having an economic policy conceived as a 'self-correction' of market forces, but it may also constitute a process too long to be endured politically even if it is not an illusion. Unfortunately, such programmes undermine valuable economic assets, primarily, price stability and the propensity to save. In this respect,

Napoleon I was right when he commented in 1806 that the Banque de France 'belongs not only to the shareholders, but to the state, too. As the latter granted it the privilege of note issue, I want the Bank to be satisfactorily in the hands of the Government but not in an exaggerated way.' But it is not easy to map the wise, middle path between 'state-bank' under the thumb of the government and a fully autonomous central bank.

The original statutes of the National Bank of Hungary were an excellent amalgam of the two prime requirements - in terms of the long-established tenets of science, proven by practical experience in the enlightened world, but tempered by the special problems faced by Hungary during the 1920s. An important asset in the Bank's early thinking and approach was the treatment of budgetary reform as the centrepiece of the 1924 stabilization efforts which, in turn, it was able to sell 'lock, stock and barrel' to the political élite. Paragraph 4 of the Law for the Re-establishment of Budgetary Equilibrium stipulated that the government could, without recourse to parliament, undertake every measure necessary to restore balance by either reducing expenditure or raising revenues until this end was achieved. A powerful announcement effect - potent propaganda - aided the very rapid execution of these measures that came to be called 'the cleansing' of the budget. This is a much needed approach when governments might appear to be only paying lip service to this end, possibly resulting in a deficit hanging like a sword of Damocles over the head of a central bank.

Notes

1 In this connection, it is worth mentioning the contribution made by interaction of science and practice in the development of the Austro-Hungarian Bank. During the Banking Conferences of 8-10 March 1892 with Hungarian delegates, and of 8-17 March 1892 with Austrian participants, eminent scholars took an active part, including Karl Menger, one of the founders of the Austrian School of Marginalism. This melding of scholarly and practical opinion has remained a feature of the approach of the National Bank of Hungary.

2 Incidentally, this was equally the case regarding defence expenditure and its financing for about ten years after the Trianon peace treaty - which was not merely a cloak, but a cloak and dagger story.

3 The towns of Pest and Buda were then not yet united.

4 T. Bácskai (ed.), (1994), *A Magyar Nemzeti Bank Története*, I [History of the National Bank of Hungary], I, *Az Osztrák Nemzeti Banktól a Magyar Nemzeti Bankig 1816-1924*, Budapest.

5 Even in the mid-1990s not every country has a central bank. Many small countries share regional central banks; others have monetary boards, like Saudi Arabia, Singapore, and Hongkong; whereas Andorra, the Ivory Coast, the Cayman Islands and Eritrea do without either a central bank or a monetary board.

6 Balint Homan, (1916), *Magyar Penztortenet* [Hungarian Monetary History], Budapest; and idem., (1921), *A magyar kiralysag penzugyei es gazdasagpolitikaja Karoly Robert koraban* [Economic policy of Carlobertus], Budapest.

7 Forrest Capie, Charles Goodhart & Norbert Schnadt, (1994), *The Development of Central Banking*, Cambridge - an excellent monograph prepared for the Bank of England tercentenary in June 1994.

8 An expression coined by the late George Garvy, an eminent and learned Chief Economist of the Federal Reserve Board under Governor Burns, and a scholar of socialist economies.

9 The Bank of England came to be a mainstay in the stabilization process following the Second World War. It is not uninteresting to mention that, in 1982, the Bank of England, the Bundesbank and the Schweizerische Nationalbank guaranteed a BIS loan to Hungary, so helping to maintain international liquidity in the troubled waters of an international credit crisis.

10 And why not any of the 18 central banks analysed in M. Pohl & S. Freitag (eds), (1994) for the European Association for Banking History e.V., *Handbook on the History of European Banks*, Aldershot?

11 György Péteri, (1980), an eminent Swedish historian of Hungarian descent and a co-author of the first volume of *The History of the National Bank of Hungary*, analyses this and other aspects in 'International liquidity and the national economy as a factor in Hungary's

monetary policy 1924-1931', *Acta Historica Academiae Scientiarum Hungaricae*, 26 which has been reprinted in G. Péteri, (1995), *Revolutionary Twenties. Essays on international monetary and financial relations after World War I*, Trondheim.

12 Until the First World War, the currency had largely been issued through rediscounting, with the status of those presenting bills to the Austro-Hungarian Bank in Budapest being rigorously examined through the good offices of principal merchants and industrialists.

CHAPTER TWO

The National Bank of Hungary: from cradle to adulthood whilst striving for independence

György Szapáry

The history of central banking in Hungary is characterized by alternating periods of lost and regained independence on the part of the note-issuing authority, with these being accompanied respectively by high inflation and currency stability.

In 1848, when Hungarians rose against Austrian rule in seeking national independence, their revolutionary demands were laid down in the famous declaration consisting of twelve points, one of which related to a national bank. Those who formulated the declaration were not so much concerned about the independence of the note-issuing institution from the government; rather they wanted to create, as an act of sovereignty, a national central bank independent from the Austrian central bank. Nevertheless, it is perhaps the memory of this famous demand that has inspired successive generations of Hungarian central bankers to stand up for the independence of their institution against government interference. And perhaps it is this same historical background - reinforced by well understood economic self-interests - that motivated governments and parliaments to grant the necessary autonomy to the central bank. However, the National Bank of Hungary, or its predecessor, have several times in their histories had the experience of that autonomy being either curtailed or nullified.

The monetary policies of any central bank are strongly influenced by its economic environment, which, in turn, can only be understood in the context of a country's general political situation. To give an account of the evolution of the National Bank of Hungary's monetary policy, it is necessary to go back as far as the period before the foundation of the Bank. This is because the circumstances of the dissolution of the Austro-Hungarian Dual Monarchy following the First World War had a determining influence on how the Bank was established and what type of monetary policy was pursued from the very outset of its existence. To a certain extent, a glimpse of how the Bank's predecessor - the Austro-Hungarian Bank - operated is also required, since this institution provided a positive legacy comprised of both the personnel and technical infrastructures together with bequeathing the manner in which everyday operations were managed. Since there is a substantial literature dealing with these historical developments,[1] this retrospection will be restricted to matters important only from the perspective of the evolution of monetary policy.

The Austro-Hungarian Bank was established as the successor to the Austrian National Bank (founded in 1816 and therefore one of the oldest European central banks) in the wake of the Compromise between the Habsburg Empire and Hungary of 1867. A monetary and customs union of two autonomous states was created in 1867, with each of those states having their own administrations and budgets but sharing defence and foreign policies. The Bank started to operate as a common Austro-Hungarian central bank in 1878. Thereafter, for nearly four decades, the Bank operated successfully on the basis of an effectively stable gold standard, 'masterly managed' in the view of one banking historian,[2] although the currency was never, *de jure*, on the gold standard.

With its stable policies, the common central bank was able to protect the value of the currency and contributed to the development, modernization and the smooth operation of the banking system of the Dual Monarchy. It supplied the commercial banks and, through them, industry, trade and agriculture with the required liquidity. By its operations the Bank contributed to the convergence of levels of economic development of the various regions comprising the Monarchy. Moreover, the banking system experienced a vigorous growth, of which one outcome was that Budapest gained in importance as a financial centre. The traditions acquired during this period by its staff were to influence strongly the behaviour of the Bank over subsequent decades.

During the years immediately prior to the First World War, the successes of the Austro-Hungarian Bank came to an end, mostly as a consequence of the Balkan Wars. Domestic financial conditions loosened from 1911 as the growth of money supply accelerated, the trade deficit widened and the gold reserves of the central bank fell to 45 per cent of currency circulation in the first half of 1914 from 70 per cent in 1910. The recession, which had affected the Hungarian economy in 1913, eased its grip somewhat in early 1914, but the expected recovery failed to take place even after the central bank had reduced its interest rate. Instead, a sudden rise in the demand for credit and foreign exchange forced the Bank to raise interest rates in repeated steps.[3]

In August 1914, as part of the preparations for war, the Austro-Hungarian government authorized the Bank to ignore the prohibition preventing it from lending to the state, and also suspended gold convertibility. These actions commenced the practice of the central bank assisting state budgetary expenditure through direct or indirect refinancing, which rapidly became an everyday routine and which was to persist until financial stabilization in 1924. It was to be repeated immediately prior to and during the Second World War. As a result from July 1914 to October 1918, currency in circulation rose by about 1,300 per cent and the Austro-Hungarian Bank's gold reserves declined to about 20 per cent of their pre-war level. Thus, when the legal restrictions on the Bank lending to the government were lifted, inflation and payments restrictions followed. Despite the large monetary expansion, there was little wartime depreciation of the Austro-Hungarian crown on the foreign exchanges owing to extensive capital controls and a substantial reduction in trade.[4]

The Saint-Germain-en-Laye and Trianon peace treaties, signed in 1919 and 1920 respectively, determined the political dissolution of the Austro-Hungarian Monarchy. The successor states (Austria, Czechoslovakia, Hungary, Romania, and the State of Serbs, Croats and Slovenes) shared a greatly devalued, hyper-inflating currency - the Austro-Hungarian crown - a collapsed trade and payments system and large external debts. Their governments undertook economic and financial reforms, including currency separation through stamping a national identity upon the earlier common currency - the Austro-Hungarian crown - then circulating within their territories. Since Hungary was the last to implement this measure, its government was confronted by the serious problems arising from the country's absorption of some of the unstamped notes previously held in the other successor states. Garber and Spencer[5] regard this example of individualist currency reforms as currently being particularly instructive, because of its resemblance to recent events in eastern Europe. As then, so now, there has been hardly any harmonization of the currency reforms in successor states of eastern Europe, although economic reasons would have dictated otherwise.

Faced with the task of seeking a viable strategy for rebuilding the economy of a country shrunk to one third of its former size, it was extremely difficult within Hungary even to assess the basic characteristics of necessary financial reform. The mandate of the Austro-Hungarian Bank ended in December, 1919 and a Hungarian Section of the Bank was opened on 2 January 1920 to serve as a temporary central bank for Hungary. This was replaced in August 1921 by the State Note Institute under the control of the Ministry of Finance. The Institute issued its own notes, which replaced stamped Austro-Hungarian notes. The Institute's policy was not characterized by the financial conservatism of the pre-war Austro-Hungarian Bank, but by a lax monetary policy vis-a-vis both the government and the banking sector. During this period, the monetary unit, the *korona* [crown], which had already shrunk to one hundredth of its original value during the war and the revolutions of 1918-19, continued to decline. By June 1924, the crown's exchange rate had fallen to about 0.005 per cent of its pre-war level, but inflation proved to be even more precipitous, reaching double digit monthly rates between 1922 and 1924. Banks were forced to rely on credit from the State Note Institute because of the inflation-induced depreciation of their monetary assets, such as cash, short-term credits, war and post-war state loans, mortgage bonds etc. As a result, the State Note Institute financed the major part of the credit requirements of the economy.

During the mid-1920s, both Austria and Hungary established new and independent central banks as institutional components of stabilization programmes introduced under the auspices of the League of Nations. Each stabilization programme was elaborated and implemented through an agreement with the League of Nations and was supported by an externally raised loan. To obtain foreign financing, the Hungarian government, like that of Austria, had agreed to a detailed financial programme supervised by the League of Nations. The major elements included an easing of Hungary's reparations debt for the duration of the programme, the creation of an independent central bank and agreement on detailed budgetary commitments. Thus, the re-establishment of internal and external balance was to be achieved by the combination of three major elements: the establishment of an independent central bank to guard over monetary stability; the institution of budgetary procedures and practices providing adequate safeguards for a balanced and realistic budgeting; and the availability of external financing. It is worth noting that these very conditions remain prerequisites for stability and balanced growth. Although, in so many respects, the world is very different now to what it was 70 years ago, none the less the laws of financial stability, like those of physics, prevail over time.

The stabilization programme was a success, even if it lasted for only a few years. The National Bank of Hungary started operations on 24 June 1924 and a new currency - the *Pengő* - was introduced in January 1927. The Bank was not permitted to lend to the government unless any such facility had collateral consisting of foreign assets to the same value. The government, forced to raise taxes and cut expenditure to balance the budget, ran surpluses in both 1924/25 and 1925/26 fiscal years. State debt was reduced throughout the period up to 1930, setting the basis for monetary and financial stability.

The world economic depression affected Hungary in a most profound way, upsetting the hard-won stability and growth. By 1933, Hungary's export prices had fallen by almost 60 per cent compared to 1928. The steep decline in world prices of agricultural products was especially detrimental, given Hungary's high dependence on the exports of such goods.

The economic depression and the consequent insolvency of many debtors, aggravated by the foundering of the Austrian Credit-Anstalt in 1931, dealt a severe blow to the largest Hungarian commercial bank, the Magyar Általános Hitelbank [Hungarian General Credit Bank]. As a consequence, the National Bank of Hungary had to pay, as guarantor, the equivalent of more than the total amount of its reserves in gold and foreign exchange with the result that it had to rely on foreign loans, including one from the Bank for International Settlements, to settle these claims. Very quickly, depositors queued at banks to make withdrawals. This sudden run on the banks, exacerbated by the suspension or withdrawal of foreign credits, threatened the whole Hungarian banking system with collapse. To prevent capital flight, foreign exchange controls were introduced while foreign trade was placed under state control. Instead of devaluing the currency, a foreign exchange premium system was implemented to promote exports. As a result of these upheavals, the independence of the central bank suffered its first blow at the end of 1933, when the central bank act was modified so that the government could borrow 100 million pengös from the National Bank of Hungary.

During 1935, a year when Sándor Popovics, the outstanding first governor of the National Bank of Hungary, died, external conditions for the Hungarian economy improved. By 1936, the world economy had virtually recovered from the Great Depression but, unfortunately, this was partly due to the important role played by the world-wide armaments race. In the case of Hungary, the establishment of German influence within the economy dated from as early as 1934. Through successive commercial agreements, large export opportunities were provided for Hungarian agricultural products with, in return, Hungary giving tariff reductions for German products. For a short period, the arising economic recovery resulted in a reduction of the state budget deficit, an improvement in the liquidity position and solvency of debtors, and a significant increase in the National Bank of Hungary's foreign exchange holdings. However, over the longer term, the establishment of these close trade relations, and the financing system that they involved, resulted in Hungary becoming a net lender to Germany, especially when the latter stopped payments during the war.

In 1938, the independence of the central bank suffered a fatal blow. Under the so-called Győr war programme, the government decided to increase investment in defence projects. The funds were provided by the introduction of a property tax and through issuing government bonds. Those obliged to pay the property tax immediately requested corresponding credits from the commercial banks which, in turn, went to the central bank for refinancing. In addition, the banks also approached the central bank for facilities regarding their purchases of government bonds. The National Bank could do no other than satisfy these demands for refinancing because of the manner in which the central bank act was amended. With these developments, the National Bank completely lost its autonomy and, moreover, the stage was set for the subsequent hyper-inflation.

During the war, printing bank notes was the main source of government finance. At the end of 1944, 90 per cent of the refinance portfolio of the National Bank of Hungary consisted of government paper. After the war, in parallel with the payment by Hungary of large war compensation obligations, inflation accelerated to reach a peak in summer 1946, when a 600-fold increase, week to week, in the money supply was recorded.

The first possibility to stabilize the currency came in 1946, when the gold reserves of the National Bank of Hungary, taken to Austria at the end of 1944, were returned by the United States and the payment schedule of war compensation obligations to the Soviet Union was eased. A new currency, the ***Forint***, was introduced on 1 August 1946, providing the condition for reasserting the role of monetary policy, although restrictions on lending were maintained to protect the forint. The exchange rate was set at 11.739 forints to the United States dollar and a limit of 90 million forints was placed on the National Bank's short-term, liquid advances to the government. The money supply was kept on a very tight rein, not only to prevent the re-emergence of any inflationary pressure but also to ensure strict state control over commercial banking. Stabilization was a success and, once again, it was based on the strict limitation of credit provisions made to the government and other sectors of the economy. Stabilization measures were successfully implemented but within an environment of increasing state intervention which eventually led to the establishment of a socialist-type planned economy.

Early in 1948, all financial institutions and those industrial plants which employed more than 100 people were nationalized. The National Bank of Hungary was made responsible for the provision of credits to, and the supervision of the economic management of, all state-owned enterprises, now covering 80 per cent of industry and 50 per cent of trade. This meant an end to the two-tier banking system and the start of the monobank system, a characteristic of centrally-planned economies. Thereafter, the supply of credit became part of the national economic plan and was regulated according to centrally-decided targets for production and prices. Enterprises were obliged to undertake all their financial transactions through their so-called single account kept with the National Bank. In this system, monetary policy lost its traditional regulating role because the extent of production and the prices of goods and services were no longer established by the free operation in the market of the forces of demand and supply, but by central authorities within the framework of economic plans. In summer 1950, controls over foreign exchange were tightened with people forbidden to possess, buy or sell foreign exchange.

Despite all the economic difficulties, the new leadership took a decision which firmly established the policies of Hungary in a very important area: the management of external debt. The National Bank of Hungary decided to meet all its foreign debts and to repatriate those of its shares in foreign possession, while the government tried to reach a negotiated settlement with former foreign owners of companies and landed assets that had been nationalized. This attitude, struck immediately after the war and, thereafter, backed by an impeccable record of debt servicing, has helped to establish world-wide confidence in the National Bank of Hungary and in Hungary.

In its orthodox form based upon the Soviet-type, the command economy existed only for a few years within Hungary. Reforms were attempted as early as 1953, but important steps in this respect were only taken in 1968 with the implementation of a comprehensive package. After 1968, the Hungarian economy underwent substantial changes, with enterprises obtaining more independence and prices approaching world market levels. A train of thought developed regarding the use of instruments arising from a market-based monetary policy but within the concept of a so-called socialist market economy. However, the structure of the banking system and, hence, the role and functioning of monetary policy, remained virtually unchanged until 1987, when the two-tier banking system was re-established. None the less, throughout this period, the National Bank played an important role in furthering reform, pressing for the opening of the economy and stressing the importance of the macro-economic balance. With these objectives in mind, the Bank played a key role in the process that led to Hungary joining the IMF and the World Bank in 1982.

The re-establishment of the two-tier banking system in 1987, the first such step in a former socialist country in central and eastern Europe, has provided the basic condition for monetary policy regaining its traditional, regulating role in market economies. Through divesting the National Bank of Hungary of most of its commercial banking functions (by their hand-over to newly-created commercial banks), this established the nucleus of a banking system which could be influenced by the central bank's monetary policy. However, initially, the other conditions required for monetary policy to play its full role remained absent. This was because a great number of administrative regulations and controls persisted: import, export, price and exchange controls; state subsidies; direct central bank financing of the government budget etc. Nevertheless, liberalization of the economy proceeded - at first gradually but then at a considerably more rapid pace after democratic elections in 1990.

During the mid-1990s only a few prices are still controlled; exports are practically free from restriction; imports are liberalized to the extent of almost 90 per cent; capital inflows are virtually free; and the transfer of investment income is free while current payments are largely liberalized. Further steps to liberalize are being planned in the near future. The most significant restrictions remain in the areas of capital transfers abroad and the convertibility of the forint for individuals.[6]

The financial system has also developed and diversified. In the mid-1990s, there are 42 banks and 255 savings co-operatives in Hungary. All but eleven of the banks are private, of which twenty are foreign-owned or joint ventures. However, four large state-owned banks still dominate the market. New institutions have been created, including the State Bank Supervision Agency, the National Deposit Insurance Fund, the Hungarian Export-Import Bank, the Export Credit Guarantee Agency and stock and commodity exchanges. A very substantial amount of legislation has been drafted and debated, with parliament passing hundreds of laws, to adapt Hungary to the requirements of a private market economy and a democratic political system. For many reasons, privatization has been slower than expected; nevertheless, the private sector accounts for approximately 50 per cent of GDP in the mid-1990s.[7]

On 1 December 1991, a new Central Bank Act and a new banking law came into effect. The Bank's main responsibility, as defined in the Act, is to protect the stability of the internal and external value of the Hungarian currency. In the pursuit of this goal, it has autonomy in the formulation and implementation of monetary policy. The Act stipulates that the Bank must report to parliament, and that the government can not give instructions to the Bank in the area of the implementation of monetary policy. The law also states that the Bank participates in the development of the government's economic programme and, moreover, assists its implementation by the use of its own policy instruments. Thus, the President of the Bank is invited to those sessions of the government which deal with economic policies that have a bearing on the work of the National Bank. The President of the Bank is appointed by the President of the Republic on the basis of a proposal from the Prime Minister, with his tenure being for six years, that is, for a period longer than the political cycle. The highest policy-making body is the Central Bank Council[8], which approves the annual monetary policy guidelines and discusses the use of monetary policy instruments, particularly interest rates and the exchange rate.

Since 1990, the National Bank has developed, and thereby come to rely increasingly on, the use of market instruments in the implementation of its monetary policy. The use of rediscounting and the direct control of credit as the main instruments of monetary control have been replaced by repurchase agreements and the setting of interest rates. Preferential financing by the Bank has been reduced. It is now confined to channelling loans obtained on favourable terms from foreign governments and international development institutions, such as IBRD and EBRD, and to privatization loans. The latter must be used to reduce the government's debt vis-a-vis the central bank and therefore do not add to the monetary base. Direct lending to the government has been discontinued, its place taken by purchases of government securities at market interest rates.

The Central Bank Act of 1991 limits to three per cent of the central government budget's revenue the maximum amount of credit the Bank may extend to the government in any one year. As a transitional arrangement, this amount was set at five per cent for 1993 and four per cent for 1994. This is not an obligation to extend credit to the government, only a limit up to which the Bank may grant credit to the government in any given year. In addition, the Bank may provide short-term liquid advances to the government which shall not exceed a total of two weeks in any one month and two per cent of the central government budget's revenue, but no such liquidity advance shall be outstanding at the end of the year.

In December 1993, Parliament approved a provision in the 1994 budget law which directed the National Bank of Hungary to guarantee the purchase of government paper up to 80 billion forints. This not only exceeded the limit of four per cent of revenue contained in the Central Bank Act for 1994, but it represented an obligation for the National Bank, rather than being a possibility as foreseen in the Act, to grant credit to the government. The National Bank of Hungary protested against this move which it regarded as a serious breach of the independence of the Bank.

There are several factors which constrain the room for manoeuvre of monetary policy in transition economies. As can be seen from the example above, the monetary authorities are under continuous pressure to finance fiscal deficits. The difficulty in reducing budget deficits stems from the shrinking of the tax base as a result of the fall in output (characteristic of all the transition economies at least up to 1993); the burden of growing unemployment benefits; the difficulty in capturing into the tax net the rapidly expanding 'grey' economy; and the tremendous, though understandable, political resistance to rationalizing and trimming the social safety net developed under the socialist system but which weighs heavily on the budget.

Another difficulty in formulating and implementing monetary policy is the uncertainty about developments in the real sector. When an economy has faced such fundamental changes as the collapse of eastern trade; privatization; the elimination of subsidies; and the freeing of foreign trade, developments in the real economy are extremely difficult to predict. Forecasting is complicated by the unpredictability of the behaviour of households and enterprises in the face of the rapidly changing economic and institutional setting, including financial liberalization and the emergence of new instruments and opportunities to save. The experience in Hungary points to large shifts in such behavioural relationships as the financial saving of households or the propensity to import. All these make it difficult to predict the demand for money, complicating the task of judging the appropriateness of the stance of monetary policy.

Distortions in the transmission mechanism of monetary policy represent another complicating factor. These distortions arise in part from the banking structure inherited from the past. For instance, about two-thirds of household deposits are concentrated in one bank, the National Savings Bank, which has resulted in a stickiness, particularly in an upward direction, of the interest rates of this bank in relation to changes in the interest rates directly influenced by the central bank. Because of the concentration of deposits in one bank, other banks which inherited large loan portfolios lack adequate resources and rely heavily on central bank financing. Together with the financing requirements of the government which absorbs a large portion of domestic savings, the unequal resource distribution among banks limits the room for manoeuvre of monetary policy. The inadequacies of the financial intermediation by the banking system are exacerbated by the underdevelopment of the capital markets. Enterprises which are 'crowded out' from bank credit can not turn to the capital market, which increases the bias of restrictive monetary policy against the new private firms lacking a well-established track record. Instead, credit tends to flow to enterprises which enjoy the explicit or indirect guarantee of the government, often being inefficient state undertakings.[9]

The National Bank of Hungary has been adapting and refining its monetary policy instruments in the light of experience. At the same time, it has played an active role in all areas which aim at developing and strengthening the financial system and at improving its functioning. Thus, it has been a leader in strengthening bank supervision and improving the payments system, and participated in the elaboration of the bank re-capitalization scheme, while promoting the restructuring and privatization of banks. As an advisor to the government, it has been calling attention to the dangers of growing fiscal deficits and has been making concrete proposals on how to reduce the budget deficit. It has been closely co-operating with other agencies in the legislative work pertaining to the financial system and in setting up new institutions, such as specialized banks, the deposit insurance agency, and the stock and commodity exchanges.

The lessons to learn from the 70-year-old history of the National Bank of Hungary are the obvious ones: financial stability requires strict restraint on the government's claims on resources, as well as a central bank sufficiently independent to be able to resist the fiscal authority's temptation to use the central bank to finance government spending. However, no central bank can be independent if there is no commitment on the part of the executive and legislative powers to grant it that independence. It is the well-understood interests of the country which must guide governments to ensure and protect the autonomy of the central bank.

Independence implies special responsibilities for a central bank as well. Indeed, autonomy does not mean that the central bank is not accountable. The central bank must be sensitive to the broad economic, political and social environment and must account for its policies to the government, the parliament and the society at large. The monetary authorities must make every effort to explain their policies, otherwise the central bank will come under intense political pressure and lose its independence. Divergence of views between the government and the central bank are sometimes unavoidable, but the better the central bank's policies are understood, the more likely it is that this institution will find political support. Beyond the importance of independence and accountability, a central bank should be non-partisan and have a high level of expertise and professionalism to build and maintain confidence in its analysis and policies.

Notes

1 An excellent guide to the secondary literature is provided by the references to P. M. Garber & M. G. Spencer, (1992), *The dissolution of the Austro-Hungarian Empire: lessons for currency reform*, Working Paper WP/92/66, Washington DC: International Monetary Fund.

2 R. Nötel, (1984), 'Money, banking and industry in interwar Austria and Hungary', *Journal of European Economic History*, 13.2, p.139.

3 T. Bácskai (ed.), (1993), *A Magyar Nemzeti Bank Története*, I. [History of the National Bank of Hungary], Budapest: Közgazdasági és Jogi Könyvkiadó, pp.343-4, 368.

4 Garber & Spencer (1992).

5 Ibid.

6 However, individuals are allowed to hold foreign exchange deposits in Hungary, which can be freely used.

7 For a discussion of the factors that have slowed privatization see G. Szapáry, 'Transition issues as through the experience of Hungary: There is no cookbook to go by', in L. Somogyi (ed.), (1993), *The Political Economy of the Transition Process in Eastern Europe*, Aldershot.

8 The Council is composed of the President and the five Vice-Presidents of the National Bank, together with five outside members appointed by the Head of State for a period of three years.

9 For a further discussion of the difficulties of monetary policy in transition economies see Szapáry, (1993).

CHAPTER THREE

Norman, Strakosch and the development of central banking: from conception to practice, 1919-1924*

P. L. Cottrell

Over the course of the twentieth century, a series of severe shocks has gravely affected Europe's economic, political and social structures. The two world wars had profound economic consequences, whereas the unfolding of events since 1989 has given rise to comparable dislocation. On each occasion - during the early 1920s, the late 1940s and now in the 1990s - reconstruction has proven to be a daunting task,[1] of which one consequence has been that the financial 'expert' has played a role as significant as that of the politician. This contribution will concentrate solely on the reactions to the first of these shocks and will be further confined - to considering the attempts to rebuild eastern Europe over the first half of the 1920s through focusing on the international activities of central bankers, who at that time represented a new cadre of experts. In the aftermath of the war, led by Montagu Norman, they first attempted to define the role of the institutions that they served and then tried to put their ideas into practice in order to rebuild the financial structures of central and eastern Europe.

Central bank co-operation came to the fore during the 1920s,[2] and historians have stressed the importance of the activities of Governor Montagu Norman of the Bank of England and Governor Benjamin Strong of the Federal Reserve Bank of New York. The two first met in 1916 and thereafter they were in regular correspondence and contact. However, the development of Norman's views and policies regarding central banks and their international role was also the result of discourse with others, especially Sir Henry Strakosch. Such was Strakosch's standing that, in February 1921, Norman considered him 'the best authority on the subject [of] the principles which should govern the policy of central banks in any country'. Strakosch had been responsible for the creation of the South African Reserve Bank[3] and, thereafter, his expertise proved invaluable. It came into play generally through his membership of the League of Nations Financial Committee from 1920 while his close personal connection with Norman probably had a greater, particular significance. Strakosch's importance in the post-war development of central banking led him to be one of the shaping influences in the foundation of the Hungarian National Bank and he promoted comparable developments in Bulgaria and Romania.

Neither Norman[4] nor Strong[5] require an introduction, but unfortunately there is no biography of Strakosch. He was described by Norman as of

'Austrian origin; many years in Johannesburg ... full of public spirit, genial, helpful ... and so forth'[6] and these few phrases can be fleshed out to some extent. Strakosch, the second son of a sugar manufacturer, was born on 9 May 1871 at Hohenau, Austria. After attending the Wasa Gymnasium, Vienna and completing his education in England, he began his career in the City of London in 1891, possibly as a foreign exchange dealer. In 1895 Strakosch was commissioned by a group of English bankers to liquidate a syndicate in South Africa and he decided to remain at this then frontier of economic development. Strakosch joined A. Goerz & Co., a mining finance company which was subsequently incorporated in the Transvaal on 29 December 1897 with the backing of English and French capital. On the death of Adolf Goerz, who had been the local representative of the Deutsche Bank, Strakosch became the manager, and then the managing director, of the mining house. He shouldered the difficult task of developing the Modderfontein mine, turning to German finance which only became fully available literally moments before hostilities broke out in 1914. At the same time Strakosch pioneered developments on the 'Far East Rand'. He had taken English nationality in 1907 and, at the outbreak of the First World War, moved his company's head office to London. The mining concern was renamed the Union Corporation and Strakosch served as its chairman from 1924. During the immediate post-war years, Strakosch was thought to be an associate of the London Rothschilds, possibly because of the marketing of South African gold in the City, while certainly he involved Keynes in a number of South African gold mining and banking ventures. Strakosch's involvement with gold-mining finance led to an increasingly academic interest in the supply of this monetary metal and its relationship to the price level. During the 1920s, he became a practising applied monetary economist, which led to his participation not only in the creation of central banks in eastern Europe but also in shaping Indian finances.[7]

Strakosch was a man of affairs, a man of the world and a regular, frequent visitor to Norman's parlour over the first half of the 1920s. The establishment of this personal relationship is difficult to determine, but its post-war foundation would appear to have arisen from discussions over the question of the marketing of South African gold, which ultimately caused the Bank to establish a London refinery.[8] It would seem that Strakosch soon became one of Norman's closest confidants, with his name appearing in the Governor's diary 66 times between 1920 and 1925.[9] Strakosch's ever widening expertise and experience were of considerable assistance to Norman, as the Governor developed his policies for the Bank of England. In the mid-1920s Norman summarized the Bank's efforts as 'the re-establishment of peace in Europe and they [sic] feel that they can help most usefully in the attainment of this end by developing co-operation between themselves [sic] and Central Banks'.[10]

In what follows, Norman's immediate post-war preoccupations are considered in the first section and especially in terms of his growing association with Strong. During the first half of 1921, as a result of initiatives concerned with British 'imperial banks', these came to focus on an exploration of 'central banking', a preoccupation which provoked a seminar by correspondence and which is reviewed in the second section. Having conceptualized the nature of his profession, Norman turned from summer 1921 to the development of central bank co-operation, which is detailed in the third section. This was galvanized by the Genoa conference, but that international forum also led to a false start, and these circumstances are considered in section four. These opening four sections, constituting the first half of this contribution, review events that have previously been considered by both Clay and Sayers with regard to the stand points of Norman and the Bank respectively and, more recently, in rather different terms by Péteri.[11] However, the closer focus of this contribution enables full emphasis to be given to the importance of the 'seminar by correspondence' on the nature of central banks, led by Norman during the first six months of 1921. Furthermore, the Bank's papers also reveal the energy exerted by Norman to establish privately central bank relationships of a personal nature from autumn 1921, prior to the Genoa meeting of Easter 1922 and the arising call for a central bankers' conference.

The roles played by Norman and Strakosch in Hungarian stabilization constitutes the focus of the fifth section, and the subsequent inception of relationships between the Bank of England and the National Bank of Hungary is discussed in the sixth section, especially with regard to how the problem of stand-by facilities was perceived and then initially resolved. The seventh section attempts to bring together the various themes that have been explored by examining the initial development of the central banker as an international 'expert'.

On 1 January 1919 Norman, then Deputy-Governor, began his desk diary for the year by compiling a long list of topics requiring attention. This exercise was out of character, never to be undertaken again. As Clay has commented, most of this extensive itemization comprised internal and technical matters with the result that policy considerations came last.[12] However, their position on the page may not fully reflect the place that they already occupied in Norman's thinking. Yet, neither central banking co-operation nor the relief of central and eastern Europe featured in this agenda. Indeed, Europe's post-war difficulties seem to have had little importance for Norman during 1919. The Deputy Governor appears to have considered them only once, at a lunch, and possibly an uncongenial meeting, with F. A. Vanderlip of the First National City Bank of New York, when there was a discussion concerned with meeting the needs and wants of the continent's prostrate population.[13] The interchange had no immediate outcome and Norman, and the Bank, were not to become directly involved in eastern European affairs until April 1920, when a proposal for the 'Francisation' of the Österreichische Länderbank was first aired in the Governor's parlour.[14] This very particular interest in eastern Europe then widened from December

1920, initially through Strakosch seeking Norman's advice in the selection of an organizer for the ter Meulen credits scheme, a product of the Brussels Conference.[15]

Far more important during 1919 were Norman's meetings with Strong as the American central banker journeyed to, and from, Paris and Brussels.[16] Their mutual concern was the speculative and inflationary excesses, evident within Britain and the United States, of the post-war stockpiling boom. From mid-1919, the Bank of England had exerted pressure upon the British government for higher interest rates[17] and Strong offered friendly trans-Atlantic assistance to defeat inflation, while warning the British Chancellor of the 'historic' dangers if no action was taken.[18] The Bank and the 'Fed' had co-operated since the last years of the war but the two institutions now embarked upon peacetime collaboration - an entirely new venture. In this Norman and Strong only confronted inflation on the continent of Europe from mid-1921, after they had determined the characteristics and functions of a central bank and conjured with the question of the international mission of central banks. However, even by early 1921 Norman felt able to write: 'We are trying to work closely and for the common good with the Federal Reserve Bank of New York'.[19]

Central bank co-operation took a further step forward, following the foundation of the South African Reserve Bank. This institution was essentially Strakosch's creation, but he turned to Norman when he sought to appoint its first Governor during autumn 1920.[20] It was the first of many such requests that Norman was to receive and all proved difficult to meet. In the case of the Union, the Bank of England's Chief Accountant, W. H. Clegg, was eventually appointed and he had clearly been considered of the right calibre from the outset since Strakosch had thought of him as a potential member of the formal selection Board. Clegg's release from London required the consent of the Committee of Treasury, composed of senior Bank directors, before whom Norman made great play of the importance of both the new South African central bank and the post that he hoped they would allow Clegg to fill.[21] With Clegg's departure for South Africa and the consequent arising flow of correspondence between the Union and London, Norman began to give considerable thought to what central banking implied.

It is difficult to establish who coined the term 'central bank' in its modern sense. It was not used at the Brussels Conference[22] where, instead, an older description, 'national banks of issue', was employed. However, during winter 1920/1 Norman and Strakosch wrote regularly of a 'central bank' without seeing any need for elaborating the precise meaning of the term. This correspondence also shows that Norman was giving a great deal of thought to the whole question of the role and place of a central bank, with the Governor maintaining that it was 'of the utmost importance that other Central Banks which are being or may be created should be started on the lines (whatever they may be) which we may agree to be sound'. The Brussels deliberations appear not to have caused this concern, but rather South African and other 'Empire' developments, particularly J. F. Darling's proposals for a 'consolidation of Imperial Banking'.[23] Norman found that much ground work was required as 'It seems to be a subject on which there is no text book'. This gap on the bookshelves proved to be a recurring problem, with Clegg still searching for such a manual four years later. Advice from the Bank of England referred Clegg to the material collected by the pre-war American National Monetary Commission, which had paved the way for Federal Reserve System, and Connant's *History of Modern Banks of Issue*. However, J. A. C. Osborne, Assistant Chief Cashier, writing in Norman's stead, was only able to acknowledge the continuing difficulty before passing the problem back to Clegg for resolution: 'It is quite time that a good book was written on Central Banks, but what is still more required is a good book on Central Banking, and its possible future development. It is a pity you have not time to write it.'[24]

The need to explore the issue thoroughly during early 1921 was highlighted in Norman's considerations of what might occur in Australia and in India.[25] None the less, he had 'all Central Banks equally in mind, e.g. the Federal Reserve Bank of New York and the South African Reserve Bank quite as much as the Imperial Bank of India'. This caused the Governor to draft a paper: 'Central Banks', which he referred to as an 'Epitome' (one of Norman's favourite words for such pieces). The paper was to go through a number of versions [see Appendix[26]] as a result of Norman firing off letters, backed by copies of his own thoughts, initially to Clegg,[27] and then to Strakosch,[28] followed by Strong[29] and Sir Bernard Hunter, the London manager of the Imperial Bank of India.[30] The origins of this seminar by correspondence on the nature of central banking may have been twofold - aspects of the proposed policies of the South African Reserve Bank and the Imperial Bank of India - yet initially arose from a common question: should a central bank have an overseas branch?

Strakosch maintained that a central bank should not have a 'foreign' branch and therefore opposed clauses of his 'own' 1920 South African Currency and Banking Act which had arisen out of his *South African currency and exchange problem*. These sections of the Act permitted the Reserve Bank to have offices abroad through a general power, given to meet South African Nationalist sentiment, although their drafters had intended that there would only be, at most, a London branch. Strakosch considered that the Reserve Bank solely required 'close and intimate connections with the Bank of England', but was forced to acknowledge that a London branch could discharge some useful functions. These were, first, the facilitation of South African government transactions in the imperial metropolis and, second, the provision of a foreign exchange service in order to temper the 'rapacity of Commercial Banks'.[31] Norman was more concerned about the development of the Imperial Bank of India, as 'to my disgust I find that they are bent on starting a branch in London'. Despite this repugnance, the

Governor sought a compromise in overseas agencies, yet realized that 'my distinction between branch and agency [might be] too subtle'. Indeed it was because, in his 'Epitome', Norman clearly wanted an overseas agency to be in practice 'the Central Bank of the other country', which meant of course the Bank of England.

Norman and Strakosch might have sought only direct central bank relationships but, at the close of 1921, other problems caused the Governor to give greater credence to the idea that at least 'Empire' central banks should have London branches. Norman considered Imperial borrowing on the London market to be in 'a muddled state of things', due in part to the lack of 'unbiased advice from an international standpoint'. One solution might come through policy questions being resolved by 'a real and exclusive understanding between the Bank of England and branches of Central Banks or Agents'.[32] However, branches or agencies raised further thorny, and wider, questions since 'Mercifully we have many among us in whom self-interest is entirely dominated by public-spirit but can such arrangements be made as will ensure that they alone shall form the Local Committee [of a branch or agency]?' All in all, Norman concluded that central banking required 'the building of a tradition'.[33]

Particular developments within the British Empire led to more general considerations and Norman's original 'Epitome' was expanded by his correspondents' commentaries which, in turn, led to the circulation of revised drafts. In these the Governor concluded that some of the central banking functions that Strong had inserted arose from the differing sizes of countries.[34] Similarly, he recognized that a central bank could not be 'really free to manage affairs from a purely financial standpoint ... so long as a Government has directly or indirectly a large floating debt'.[35] In all their deliberations over central banking, Strakosch and Norman took somewhat different approaches. Strakosch had time for theory and indeed contributed to the development of applied monetary economics. He tried to attract Norman to its realms, with one attempt involving the presentation of Cassel's devaluation theories over two sessions. The Governor, who had a more practical bent, may have taken theory from Strakosch on sufferance but once, after a discussion with Hawtrey, the Treasury's only economist, he noted: 'combating his memo of 5th on lower Bank Rate: he is all theory'.[36]

The culmination of five months of refinement, through discussion and correspondence, came when Strakosch' presented 'Central Banking' to the Tuesday Club. This was an informal gathering of 'ten or twelve lights from the Treasury and City ... all young', with the Club having been established, as far as the Governor was concerned, for 'blowing off steam'. However, Norman, who did not regard central banking as 'steam', attended the meeting that Strakosch addressed and took representatives from Canada and Australia along with him in order to spread the gospel of central banking at least within the Empire.[37] The Governor had been much taken by Strakosch's draft, calling it 'admirable', and encouraged its publication for wider dissemination 'with the addition of as much ginger as you like'.[38]

Moreover, by the time of Strakosch's talk, Norman was clearly thinking in terms of central bankers as an international professional caste, who should play, as well as work, together.[39]

From mid-1921 Norman, with his conception of central banking now crystallized, embarked upon an outright programme of developing central banks throughout the world economy. This was coupled with central bank co-operation, such concerted action to be deployed in the Governor's approach not only to aid technical operations but also to reconstruct the European economy. As a result, Norman's agenda involved both particular schemes for furthering the development of central banking and the establishment of a general understanding amongst existing central banks. In this, the Governor capitalized upon fortuitous circumstances, such as those requests which led to the appointment of British financial advisers, although some of these particular initiatives proved to be false starts. This was the case, for example, with his attempt to establish a Peruvian central bank, when initially he thought that he had secured the 'latest convert to central banking'.[40] Norman's more general approach to fostering central bank co-operation began as a result of conversations during July 1921 with Jay, Chairman of the Board of the Federal Reserve Bank of New York. The Governor later commented to Strong that I 'spent a couple of hours in discussing many questions which pertain to the sphere of central banks. I need not say that it took less than no time for him to become one of us'.[41] The talks with Jay occurred immediately prior to Norman crossing the Atlantic to meet Strong and other American bankers.

The purpose of Norman's summer visit of 1921 to the United States was heralded to his American colleague by a 'Suggested List of Questions for Discussion'. Foremost were European economic and financial problems, beginning with Austrian difficulties, with which Norman had been increasingly involved since May. The relationship of the items showed what was to be Norman's pre-occupation throughout the first half of the 1920s, and this was clearly spelt out in the second head for discussion:

> The need for financial rehabilitation. How to be divorced from politics. The League as a pivot for this purpose or Alternatively An International Commission or Consortium to comprise the Allied and Associated Powers and the Neutrals and Germany.

Central banking appeared as only the fifth and last item and, furthermore, still as an implicit question: 'what basis of co-operation'. Norman had grave doubts whether this was possible, privately noting: 'Bank of France hopeless; Reichsbank not forthcoming: Vissering dominant in the Netherlands - cranky'. Central banking may have been placed last, but the list's structure was indicative of how Norman now conceived the mission of central banks. Central bank co-operation was to cut through what Norman increasingly regarded as Europe's Gordian Knot,[42] which had been ravelled by political interference and enmity, so complicating and tainting the continent's overwhelming economic and financial problems: post-war reconstruction, reparations and inter-Allied debts. In the Governor's view, these fundamental issues could only be resolved by the efforts of the appropriate experts and technocrats, undertaken in an apolitical approach.[43] Norman subsequently summarized the results of this American visit in the following terms:

> We tried to come to an understanding with the Americans which was later to be extended to other Central Banks that all should work so far as possible in general agreement and should co-operate especially with the object of the rehabilitation of those parts of Europe which have suffered most during the War.[44]

The seminar by correspondence leading to his conversations in the United States resulted in the Governor putting a definite programme for action in place. After his American tour, Norman commenced a series of visits to his European peers to explore whether some consensus could be established. In spite of his personal appraisal of the Dutch central banker,[45] Norman began with Vissering, on whom he called with Jay. It proved to be a meeting of like minds; indeed, Vissering had been making comparable efforts ever since autumn 1919.[46]

> Vissering realises as we do that finance and economics are at present moment too much in the hands of politicians for us central bankers to take any overt action, but I think the time may come when the boot will be on the other leg and when the central banks will openly have to assist one another and so the community at large, and it is a future aim that we are now try to make a beginning.[47]

Through his discussions with first the Americans, then Vissering and thereafter with others, Norman sought general agreement on three issues. The first was to gain, as far as possible, 'an understanding as to the general financial policy of central banks', which was to be matched by 'co-operation on international and economic lines among central banks'. If this ground could be gained, then Norman's August 1921 agenda with Strong came into play, since he saw the first major objective to be 'an eventual consortium of central banks (under the lead of the Federal Reserve Bank) for the rehabilitation of Austria and Eastern Europe on purely economic lines'.[48] However, over the next three months, during which the League's first scheme for Austria immediately encountered substantial difficulties, central bank co-operation came to replace, in the Governor's visualization, both the League of Nations or its alternative - an International Commission or Consortium - as the mechanism for tackling Europe's financial reconstruction. Thirdly and of equal importance, Norman placed stress on day-to-day co-operation and policy co-ordination, commenting to Vissering in November 1921 that:

> you will have noticed that following on the policy which Mr Jay and I discussed with you, the New York Discount Rate was reduced to 4½ per cent last Wednesday and our rate to 5 per cent on the following day.[49]

In all this Norman thought that his growing 'fold'[50] of central bank peers should be 'in constant contact' but soon found Vissering to be an exasperating correspondent.[51]

Norman's attempt to bring European central bankers together during autumn 1921 developed in various and, sometimes unforeseen, ways. It was assisted by a chance meeting in London with Lepreux, Vice-Governor of the National Bank of Belgium.[52] Norman welcomed this opportunity and was pleased with its outcome but, none the less, recognized the difficult position of his Belgian colleague's institution. He remarked a little later to Strong:

> I am not sure how far the National Bank of Belgium would go when it came to standing up and making a commitment; and as regards general European questions they are necessarily tied up with France.[53]

Vissering proved his worth by providing a connection with the Reichsbank. The Dutch central banker's conversations with Havenstein and Kauffmann[54] were followed up rapidly through Tiarks, of the Bank and Schroders, who met informally Reichsbank representatives in Hamburg. Somewhat to Norman's surprise, this brought Havenstein and Kauffmann quickly to London, where they were almost totally ensconced within the Bank of England. The Governor found that his two German colleagues 'wanted above all things some help and some advice and indeed some consolation from your Bank [Federal Reserve Bank of New York] and from ours'. Norman lost no time in capitalizing upon the occasion, stating to Strong that: 'We are going to take over most of the Reichsbank's London business and do the very best for them that we can in the way one Central Bank should I think co-operate with another'.[55]

In these conversations with Havenstein, Norman gained one of his now cherished objectives - 'exclusiveness' - which was to become more public four months hence with the Genoa conference. Exclusiveness was a reformation of what had been previously termed 'matrimony' within the Bank of England. As far as Norman was concerned, it was an essential principle that central banks only dealt with one another and therefore only held accounts with one another. Indeed, when the Imperial Bank of India had proposed opening a London branch, Norman had been 'disgusted' because he thought that central banks, even if only nascent, should solely hold balances with one another. Lepreux had accepted Norman's idea 'although for years he has done business in London with several other concerns'. The Governor also raised the principle with Havenstein and gained acceptance through Reichsbank agreeing to make its other London accounts progressively dormant. Either Vissering had proven to be more obdurate, or Norman had found that his conversations had not provided an opportune moment, since he summarized the situation in November 1921 for Strong as:

> Beyond the general statement that the relations of central banks should be exclusive I have not had the occasion to refer to this subject with [Vissering]. He did not ask us to open an account for him ... I know he has accounts elsewhere in London ... and I did not try to induce him to bring his business to us.[56]

Within two years, as the gold exchange standard emerged, central bank balances took on a greater importance in the view of the Bank of England:

> Free balances on an adequate scale are needed partly in connection with the reconstruction of Europe. Gold centres are required, London being one, and international arrangements should be based largely on the balances of Central Banks held here. It has been suggested by an eminent authority that the free balance kept in London by a Central Bank should be not less than 25 per cent of its funds in this country - cash, short loans, bills & c. - which should be held and managed on its behalf by the Bank of England.[57]

In the case of Austrian reconstruction, behind which Norman had put his considerable energies since spring 1921, the Governor had continually stressed that 'neutral' participation in any League of Nation's scheme was absolutely essential to meet and defuse what he considered to be the political objectives of the continental members of the Entente. Consequently Norman placed great store upon bringing 'neutral' central banks within his 'fold'. Vissering was Norman's emissary to Switzerland, but this approach was initially disappointing as Burckhardt of the Swiss National Bank was only prepared to pledge individual co-operation rather than the full participation of his institution. The Governor thought that this outcome was 'somewhat unsatisfactory', but made no complaint to Vissering, only noting that 'there we must let the question be for the present'.[58] Soundings through others led Norman to conclude that Scandinavian central banks, and especially the Riksbank, would equally be unresponsive.[59] In all this, Norman saw Strong's lead as being important, writing to his American colleague:

> I have put Swiss and Swedish Banks in the same category ... but if one opportunity occurs I should certainly favour our linking up with Copenhagen and Christiania [Oslo], and with your permission I will

take the first chance of trying to do so.[60]

None the less, Norman continually kept an eye on northern European developments, obtaining in November 1921 through Palmstierna, the Swedish Minister in London, a copy of a resolution recently passed by the central banking institutions of the three Scandinavian countries.[61] Norman's perseverance with the 'neutrals' ultimately bore fruit, first shown by Schnyder, Vice-President of the National Bank of Switzerland, coming to London during March 1922 to discuss central banking and gold in preparation for the Genoa conference.[62]

In all his efforts during autumn 1921, Norman seized upon every opportunity that presented itself. He obtained a connection with the Bank of Japan through Strong and then prepared the ground for his meeting with Nakane by utilising a visit to the Bank of England of a Japanese Businessmen's Mission. '[W]hen failing any other matters of interest I gave them a dissertation upon central banking'.[63] Nakane was followed by Fukai in February 1922, who again brought a letter of introduction from Strong. Norman found the Japanese bank official very friendly, discussed central banking and finally sent him on his way with a copy of the 'Epitome'. Two months later, all three again discussed central banking and this time the representatives of the Bank of Japan left with an introduction to Havenstein.[64] By late 1921 entry to the 'fold' had almost become formalized, with the National Bank of Romania receiving a 'letter of invitation' from Norman. Here the Governor, having previously heard 'a very good account of this bank's independence and management', used the occasion of the National Bank of Romania gaining a sizeable balance with the Bank of England through the transfer of a Romanian government war account.[65] Norman's increasingly global perspective did not result in a neglect of central banking within the British Empire - the origins of his concerns with the subject in early 1921. A conversation with Hornsby of the National Bank of Egypt in mid-December 1921, which led to 'agreement as to the policy which should be followed by central banks in various countries', was quickly followed up by Norman sending copies of his 'Epitome' and his plan for an understanding between central banks.[66]

Since Versailles, Vissering had been seeking out ways to establish a forum of bankers and men of affairs to assist European reconstruction. In December 1921, as Norman's fold of central banks expanded, Vissering called for the group to take action. However, Norman thought that the time was still not yet ripe and, furthermore, saw no opportunity for at least a further six to eight months. In his view three problems had to be resolved: first, naval disarmament at the Washington conference; second, how or whether the second German reparation payment would be made; and third, the question of inter-Allied debts. Norman was not putting forward idle excuses, as one of his colleagues maintained that:

The times here are strenuous and the day hardly long enough to deal

> with the conundrums that arise both in and out of the Bank, and one looks forward to the time when such questions as German reparations and Inter-Allied Debts may become solvable and the world's trade gets going again.[67]

Apart from these particular issues, in the Governor's view there were also some general contextual difficulties. He summarized these as, first, 'a shortage of fixed capital both in Europe and in America' and, second, the 'unwillingness of Americans to lend to Europe'. Accordingly, he concluded that: 'There is therefore nothing for us to do but to wait until progress shall have been made'. Norman had been clearly conscious of central bankers' impotence since October, but he was 'anxious that an understanding shall be reached between all Central Banks against the time when politics may come to give way to economics and finance'.[68] Central bankers could only prepare; their time had still to come and, while waiting for that moment, Norman was intent on keeping his powder dry. After an interview with Strakosch and Schuster, Norman rather acidly noted in his diary: 'dreams of credits for all sorts of countries'.[69] In all this, and possibly spurred by Vissering's impatience, Norman drew up and circulated a 'confidential Memorandum [which] epitomises the present economic needs of the World'. This was backed by the latest news of developments, such as the circulation of a letter from Havenstein which dealt with reparation payments for January and February 1922.[70]

Central banking came publicly to the fore with the Genoa conference[71] and part of the Bank of England's preparations consisted of a long discussion between Norman and Strakosch in late March 1922.[72] Moreover, the conference's Financial Commission brought together many of those already within Norman's fold as well as state officials and bankers well integrated within the Governor's circle of acquaintances.[73] Norman did not attend[74] and during the conference's later stages was in any case making preparations for a further 'private and very confidential visit' to America, possibly to deal with one of the indicated outcomes of the Genoa meeting. Trotter, the Deputy-Governor, explained the situation fully to Clegg:

> We have been and are very full of Genoa... The Bank of England are to be asked to summon a meeting of 'Central Banks' to discuss the question of co-operation between such banks and the advisability of convening a further Conference to discuss certain proposals for the economic reconstruction of the world in general. It is suggested that the later Conference should be held in Washington but it is felt that no useful purpose would be served in summoning this further Conference until the question of inter-allied indebtedness caused by the War (including of course reparations) has been definitely settled once and for all.[75]

Central bankers in London still felt that the time for action had not yet arrived and Norman soon began to make it plain that the arising post-Genoa meeting had neither been sought, nor desired, by the Bank of England.[76] Anything approaching a public convocation was not Norman's way; he preferred discussion within small groups, preferably unknown to the Press, and contact maintained by a continuous stream of bi-lateral correspondence. This allowed privacy, which in turn allowed confidence in what was being said as no public positions had to be maintained. Typical of Norman's approach is his summary of a meeting with Hautain, the Governor of the National Bank of Belgium: 'general friendly talk, agreed all in confidence as between Central Bankers'.[77] However, Norman's hand had been forced in spring 1922 and, with the momentum he had given to central co-operation since mid-1921, he was prepared to undertake the task that had been presented to him.

The difficulties of holding a meeting of the whole 'fold' soon became apparent. Initially it had been thought in Threadneedle Street that it would take place in mid-June 1922, but, in a matter of days, Norman decided that it would not be feasible before September. The proposed agenda for the meeting was quickly 'whittled down by the Federal Reserve Board to suit American susceptibilities'[78] and Vissering, for one, accepted these changes because, 'while he would have liked more ginger [he] considers attendance of an American Representative to be of paramount importance'.[79] Vissering spent nearly four hours with Norman on 13 June going over the draft agenda for the proposed conference and left the Bank of England to compile a list of banks to be invited. Norman had prepared himself for this long session with the Dutch central banker by previously going over the ground with Strakosch.[80] The second part of the agenda was settled in terms of discussing the Genoa report, but that had always been the conference's task. Norman turned to his new international colleagues - Fukai and Nakane - in order to elicit the views of the Bank of Japan with regard to the draft agenda.[81] This went back and forth, although in June 1922 Norman still had not had an opportunity to obtain the comments of the Federal Reserve Board. He explained to Clegg his conception of his task and the difficulties involved:

> My idea [is to] obtain agreement to [the] Agenda by the principal Central and Reserve Banks - the United States, Sweden, Holland, Germany, India, South Africa and perhaps one or two others before issuing invitations ... [The] Americans may be kept away by domestic politics, by fear of becoming embroiled in European quarrels or troubles and by their legal disabilities for making commitment with overseas banks. The Agenda would not perhaps prevent informal discussion on other subjects, and it is really by *informal* discussion between individuals that co-operation can best be brought about and stability tempted back into our Economic

> World: that is to say, when inter-state Debts and Reparations shall have been dealt with.[82]

Hopes for substantial Swedish involvement were dashed when Moll, Governor of the Riksbank, met Norman in London during early June 1922. The Swedish central banker, who earlier in the year had made it plain in correspondence that he saw the restoration of the gold standard in Europe coming about through a chain reaction initiated by Britain's return, now entered his caveats over Genoa. He doubted whether the gold centres of the gold exchange standard would bring about an economy in the monetary use of that metal, while indicating that the Riksbank would keep its holdings in its own vaults rather than in London. Equally, Moll made it clear that Sweden's ability to participate in reconstruction loans for central and eastern Europe was 'extremely limited'.[83] In all this, with Sweden's monetary experience of the First World War, Moll was concerned about domestic, national interests which he regarded as paramount and, thus, above international, uniform, solutions. Scandinavia had learned other historical lessons too, since 'conventions ... like the Scandinavian currency-convention, break to pieces, when they are most needed'.[84] Both Moll and Norman had the benefit of substantial pre-war experience and both wished to recreate the '1914 world' of fixed currencies, if only because their respective national economies were highly dependent upon foreign trade. Yet Moll had developed a different approach through seeing, on the one hand, post-war Europe's problems stemming from national currencies and, on the other, the world's difficulties caused by a potential rivalry between sterling and the dollar due to the precocious wartime rise of New York. The route forward for the Swedish central banker was simple; Britain should take the lead in Europe in restoring the gold standard and 'other countries will undoubtedly follow as soon as possible'.[85] All in all, Moll feared how American bankers would behave, doubted their international experience and saw United States monetary policy as being conducted in domestic, as opposed to international, interests. In these circumstances, Moll considered the restoration of a free gold market in London as the most desirable step, providing Sweden with a shield from external inflationary pressures, especially from New York, or, as a second best solution, the early, concerted return of the European 'neutrals' to gold, a route which Swedish officials had attempted to take since December 1921.[86]

September 1922 came and went and, by autumn, it appeared that the proposed conference of central banks would not take place before the year was out. Indeed, as the months passed, it became increasingly clear that the conference would have to be postponed indefinitely. Trotter explained the reasons in terms of the increasingly adverse German situation, with the 'reparation question still entirely unresolved ... and the mark goes from bad to worse'. Furthermore, a surprise British General Election had complicated matters. Norman and the Chancellor had been on the point of going to America to deal with the question of British war indebtedness, but Trotter remained optimistic: 'I still hope a mission will go to America shortly as one feels that with the funding question out of the way America may be prepared to take a more intelligent interest in the European situation'.[87] By mid-1923 this optimism was clearly misplaced and Norman, for one, was becoming ever increasingly pessimistic:

> In some European countries a growing sentiment of nationality has increased the difficulties of financial or any other co-operation, in the United States, great prosperity and the preparations for a Presidential election have concentrated attention upon their own affairs, and we could not at present hope that a representative (among others of the United States) would receive from his countrymen the support which would be necessary to ensure the usefulness and success of his presence at a Meeting.[88]

The central bankers' conference, which Norman had never sought, withered like a leaf on the vine due to the cold winds generated by the Ruhr occupation. Norman had always recognized that the problems of inter-Allied indebtedness and reparations constituted almost insurmountable obstacles in the way of the world's central banks openly and fully co-operating in order to resolve Europe's post-war problems. The only immediate follow up to Genoa was the Currency Committee of the Imperial Conference, that met in London during October and November 1923, and which called for the creation of central banks and 'mutual co-operation as recommended by the Genoa Conference'.[89]

It is remarkable that Norman was able to succeed in developing bi-lateral international central bank co-operation during the mid-1920s. This was of many kinds, across a broad spectrum, from the interchange of staff,[90] through attempts to concert medium-term policy, to securing the required financial resources for the reconstruction of central and eastern Europe. In facilitating European reconstruction, Norman worked with the League of Nations and especially its Financial Committee of which Strakosch was a member. The Governor had been invited to occupy this unofficial and private role in 1921, when League plans for Austria were first considered. Norman redoubled his efforts from autumn 1922, once a fresh League plan had secured in the Geneva protocols an internationally agreed political foundation for Austrian reconstruction.[91] Inevitably the process of European reconstruction and stabilization became piecemeal and in hindsight Norman saw its origins lying in the 1922 Czechoslovak loan.[92] Subsequent Austrian developments, under League auspices, from autumn 1922 came to provide a precedent and, more practically, a set of procedures, although at times their execution proved to be fraught with difficulties. Through Norman, the Austrian League stabilization loan gained American support and led to the creation of an independent central bank in Vienna.[93] Although difficult to accomplish, Austrian reconstruction was carried out, following the flotation of a stabilization loan across Europe's capital markets, and in spite of the tensions generated by the Ruhr occupation. The success of the Austrian stabilization loan led to other eastern European governments seeking comparable assistance and a similar League scheme designed to bring about Hungarian currency stabilization began to be aired during early 1923.[94]

Norman became aware of the intentions of the Hungarian government during April 1923 as a result of the necessary prior application to the Reparation Commission for the release of liens.[95] This was to enable the Hungarian government to have sufficient securities to constitute the collateral for an international loan and followed the procedure finally adopted for Austria. The Governor learnt of these developments from press reports, but had already been alerted a month previously through the attempts in London of Sir William Goode, the former head of the Austrian Section of the Reparation Commission, to raise credits for Hungary. These efforts may well have arisen from the failure of Hungarian bankers to raise a loan in Switzerland, while the lack of response in both Zürich and London led Goode to advise the Hungarian government that the only solution lay in an approach to the Reparation Commission. This received unofficial support from the British Foreign Office, which suggested to the French and Italian governments that Hungarian reparations should be postponed and liens released.[96]

Norman had already anticipated the Hungarian application, seeing it as the next step along the road after Austrian stabilization and 'then [thereafter] perhaps the Balkan Countries'. Here he had a politico-economic objective, explaining to Strong that 'Only by thus making the various parts economically sound and independent shall we reach what I believe to be the ultimate solution for Eastern Europe viz an Economic Federation to include half a dozen countries on or near the Danube free of customs barriers &c.'[97] The Governor promptly wrote to Bradbury at the Reparation Commission, giving his full support to the Hungarian government's initiative and stressing the urgency of the situation. Norman envisaged a replication of the Austrian process, beginning with a release of liens, following which 'we will then try to get the question taken up by the League of Nations or through some other channel'.[98] Even before the Reparation Commission had reached a decision, the Governor saw Count István Bethlen and de Kallay, the Hungarian Finance Minster.[99] These emissaries made a good impression upon Norman, especially as they had 'promised to submit to foreign control and to put all sorts of economies into effect'.[100] The Hungarian mission also met Curzon, who had been briefed by Niemeyer of the Treasury that the only route forward was a League scheme, but who none the less indicated that, even if this was agreed at Geneva, the financial markets would not necessarily support the arising stabilization loan.[101]

The Austrian scheme had first got under way in spring 1921 but it took until May 1923 for the first tranche of the stabilization loan to be issued and thus had revealed that progress could be retarded by political complications.

The Hungarian scheme, not yet a full proposal, was similarly stymied through the Reparation Commission requiring that the details of any loan be submitted to it in the first instance and, furthermore, that they 'must include the allocation of a definite part of any loans raised to reparation'.[102] Bradbury, the British member, informed his colleagues on the Commission that this decision would mean that no loan could be raised in London. Moreover, Norman was incensed by both the attitude taken by some members of the Reparation Commission and the decision that they had reached.

Initially the Governor maintained that the French member of the Commission, who had held the casting vote, had 'virtually turned down' the Hungarian application. Then he thought that he had discovered that 'the French seem to have been in league with the Little Entente and the Little Entente seem to have been poked forward by the Czechs'. If this was the case, then Norman realized that he had means to bring pressure to bear. He promptly wrote to Gaspard Farrer of Barings, the merchant bank which had been responsible for the 1922 Czechoslovak loan in London, exclaiming:

> I do not think this is the way the Czechs ought to behave. How does Mr Pospisil explain it and what consideration does he expect to receive in London for helping to shut the door in the face of his neighbour.
> Doesn't it all mean more trouble and unnecessary trouble.[103]

This angry protest was followed by a more measured statement to Barings of the Governor's ire, which was all the more important since Norman was aware that the Czechoslovak government was anxious to issue in London a further tranche of the 1922 loan. Moreover, the Governor widened his campaign of exerting financial pressure to affect all the countries that he considered responsible for effectively blocking the still nascent Hungarian scheme. This involved informing John Noble, and Helmut Wagg, a London merchant banker, that Romania 'should have no money before Hungary as they opposed Release of Latter's Reparation Liens in Paris'.[104]

Norman ensured that his displeasure was known beyond the City by sending letters explaining his reasoning for barring further Czechoslovak issues on the London market to Niemeyer at the Treasury and Eyre Crowe at the Foreign Office. He maintained to Niemeyer, who was also a member of the League's Financial Committee, that:

> In view ... of the attitude of the Czechoslovaks having prevented the release recently requested by Hungary, I have informed Messrs Barings that until the decision of the Reparation Committee shall have been altered and an arrangement for the economic rehabilitation of Hungary shall thus have been made possible, I should strongly advise His Majesty's Government not to facilitate a further issue of the Czechoslovakian loan.

> I know you would agree that this advice is in the interest of Europe as well as of this country.[105]

Norman was well aware that his action would affect British state finances since proceeds from the second tranche of the 1922 Czechoslovak loan were earmarked to pay debts owing to the United Kingdom. However, Niemeyer shared the Governor's view, while earlier, at the beginning of the Hungarian initiative, he had advised the British government that Hungarian reparations should be fixed at zero. Norman was also conscious of the narrow path he was trying to tread between finance and politics, as his commentary to the Foreign Office reveals:

> We are determined to prevent both the Czechoslovaks and the Roumanians from raising money in London until the position of Hungary has been secured. This is a financial rather than a political question, but I do not hesitate to ask for your support in the line we have taken ... and intend to take ... in the interests of Eastern Europe.[106]

Norman need not have been worried about the impact his actions might have had in Whitehall as both the Foreign Office and the Treasury concurred with his decision.

The Governor maintained this position throughout July 1923, speaking out to those who might have an interest when they visited him in his parlour. In this way Young and Spencer Smith of the Anglo-Austrian Bank were directly informed, as were Gardener, an American banker, the Romanians Bratianu and Ormulu, and Beneš together with Masaryk's son.[107] It would appear that Norman's objections arose solely from the imposition of reparations, which he had regarded as the major obstacle to general European reconstruction since at least 1921. From a banker's perspective, the maintenance of Hungarian reparation charges also reduced the security available for loan and, equally, would be a burden during the reconstruction period. However in all this, Norman was not a supporter of the Hungarian government and considered the Hungarian scheme to be a curate's egg. The good part was its reconstruction element, the bad was twofold - not only the continuance of the Treaty charges but also that it was being undertaken on behalf of what Norman regarded as an autocratic government lacking democratic support.[108]

The Governor's attitude may have had some bearing upon the Sinia meeting of the Little Entente held during July 1923, of which one outcome was a more amenable attitude to the Hungarian application. This led to the matter being considered by the League Assembly in September, a year after the Austrian problem had been similarly resolved. As a result, the Reparation Commission agreed to let preparations begin, which commenced with a visit of a League representative to Budapest in November. Norman was supportive to the extent of being concerned that nothing should complicate the possible financial outcome of this process. Therefore, for instance, he informed the British Treasury in October that it would be inadvisable for there to be any official connection with a projected Land Mortgage Company of Hungary and maintained that no steps should be taken with respect to this venture before a stabilization loan was raised for Hungary.[109]

Strakosch, Niemeyer and other members of the League's Financial Committee[110] heard the report of the League mission to Budapest at a meeting in London held between 20 and 28 November. A large Hungarian delegation was also present in the British capital and played an informal role in drawing up a scheme of reconstruction. Yet the arising draft still left open 'what limit upon reparation payments was necessary if the raising of the loan or the execution of the scheme was not to be rendered impracticable by too heavy a burden upon the Hungarian budget and currency'.[111] During these London discussions, Norman was sounded out by a range of interested parties. Before the Financial Committee had convened, Kindersley, of Lazard Brothers and a Bank director, tried to explore with the Governor the possibility of Hungary raising finance domestically, but received a retort, which Norman subsequently noted in his diary as 'I say it may not be against our Rules but is unnecessary so wrong in principle being internal and not External'.[112] As the Financial Committee's formal deliberations opened, Norman commented to Janssens, the Belgian representative, that he had 'hope'.[113] This may have been due to an appraisal that Wagg and his partner Palache had made during two weeks in Hungary, in which they had concluded that Hungary could overcome its problems from its own resources, although they estimated that this would take at least four to five years. However, in their view Hungarian 'sentiment needs a Loan and sympathy from the West to ensure internal control and good neighbourly relations'. Wagg may have gone to Hungary to assess whether his banking house should try and become the issuer for any arising League loan. Other bankers, like J. Nathan, the London representative of the Banca d'Italia, had different reasons for approaching the Governor. He, too, was anticipating the outcome of the Financial Committee's considerations and, for reasons associated with Italian foreign policy, wanted to ensure that the League Commissioner-General for Hungary would be an Italian. A comparable point had repeatedly occurred in the development of the prior Austrian scheme and this had been much to its detriment. Consequently, Nathan could not have been surprised by the Governor's insistence that the Hungarian 'controller' 'should not come from any interested country but from a Neutral and only so can money perhaps be raised'.[114]

During the course of the Financial Committee's London meeting, Norman saw the Hungarian delegation and members of the League's secretariat - Salter and Avenol.[115] The day after the Committee had concluded its business, the Governor spent some time with de Kallay, the Hungarian Minister of Finance, and Sir William Goode, who had become a financial adviser to the Hungarian government. They showed Norman the

League plan but probably only in a draft form. In response, Norman asked that 'as soon as the Commissioner General and the plan have been fully adopted, send a competent Delegation here, privately and then elsewhere - I will direct them to proper Bankers'.[116] As a result, all seemed well since Norman had apparently given the Hungarian scheme his blessing. The project went forward to the League's Council meeting of 10 to 20 December held in Paris, where a Hungarian sub-committee was established, again following the Austrian precedent.[117]

Before the League's Council meeting opened, Norman had changed his mind and, following a discussion with Bradbury of the Reparation Commission,[118] he explained this to Niemeyer, the British representative on the Financial Committee. He did so in a letter that the Governor was subsequently to show repeatedly to others.

> Ever since the Hungarians went away, I have been considering the prospects, such as they are, of the eventual issue of an International Loan. Even assuming that there are no political troubles in this country and that all goes well in connection with the League and the Reparation Commission, a Hungarian Loan can not be at all an easy operation for it will lack the guarantees which were provided in the case of Austria who was, moreover in some ways less unfavourably situated than Hungary both geographically as well as politically.
> There are, however, certain points which we must bear in mind from the outset, e.g. -
> (1) The control (probably two separate controls) should be adequate in time and scope.
> (2) Proper and mutual territorial guarantees should be provided.
> (3) Whatever surplus can possibly be obtained in any year should be devoted solely to accelerating the repayment of the loan.
> (4) No payments under relief or reparation liens should be made so long as any part of the Loan is outstanding.
> On the other hand, the Hungarians, if they succeed in negotiating a Loan, might retain an option of repayment in ten or 15 years and after such repayment the services of any Relief or Reparation lien might begin.
> I mention these points because they seem to constitute, so to speak, conditions precedent to any progress towards an international loan. There are other points which are likely to cause trouble later on in one or other of the potential lending countries.[119]

In May 1923 Norman had displayed his repugnance towards reparations being maintained during the course of Hungarian reconstruction by acting forcefully albeit only in his own personal capacity. He now judged that the situation required him to have the backing of the Bank of England's Committee of Treasury, which was composed of the most senior directors and acted as the Governor's sounding board. Norman addressed them on 9

January 1924 and explained that, since charges under the Treaty of Trianon were not going to be raised, the Bank 'could not support or approve the [League] scheme'[120] for Hungary which had now been published. So armed, Norman wrote again to Niemeyer explaining that he had consulted his colleagues within the Bank and he went on to elaborate his view that 'In the present situation ... no expectation of a Loan should be held out to the Hungarians'. The Governor based this decision on both general and particular factors. He argued that conditions were unfavourable in Britain, the United States and Europe, but then returned to the bone that had stuck in his throat since May 1923, namely that the 'provision for Reparation payments ... creates a difficulty which, in principle, I consider to be insurmountable'. The position of Hungary contrasted sharply with that of Austria, in that reparations had ultimately been suspended for the stabilization loan raised for the Alpine republic and, furthermore, that the Austrian stabilization loan had been internationally guaranteed. In the case of Hungary, reparation charges were to be maintained, while there were no guarantees for the projected loan.[121] This letter joined that of 7 December to form a corpus of material that Norman showed to all concerned. In making his views known the Governor also emphasized that he did not want the Hungarian scheme, as it presently stood, to become case law because 'There is also the fundamental question of the status of reparation payments as matter of principle and precedence'.[122]

Norman lost no time in ensuring that the City was aware of his attitude towards the proposed Hungarian League loan. He wrote to Baron Schröder almost immediately after his second letter to Niemeyer and then went personally over the ground with the London merchant banker both in general and particular terms to make it clear that his objection embraced 'any Reconstruction Loan which provides or permits Reparation payments'.[123] The same trenchant view was despatched to Kindersley of Lazards and, through E. C. Grenfell, to J. P. Morgan & Co. New York, which had undertaken the Austrian stabilization loan in the United States at the Governor's prompting.[124] With Rothschilds, Norman saw Anthony on 11 January and both Anthony and Lionel on 16 January and, in these conversations with the most likely London issuers of a Hungarian loan, the Governor was initially very discrete but ultimately put his letters to Niemeyer on the table. It would appear that Anthony de Rothschild was not surprised by Norman's views. He, too, had seen great difficulties in the scheme, while his discussions with Otto Kahn of Kuhn Loeb & Co. New York, who might have handled an American tranche, had similarly reached a negative outcome. The Governor noted privately with implicit satisfaction, 'They are quite solid'.[125] Norman rounded off his tour of the City by meeting Eric Hambro which brought a further merchant banker into the Governor's opposition party.[126]

It would appear that Salter of the League had been kept in total ignorance of Norman's change of mind, having not got wind of it from either Bradbury or Niemeyer. This League official arrived in the Bank to inquire 'as to the prospects of a loan for Hungary' on 11 January 1924. Norman showed him the two letters to Niemeyer which caused a startling reaction, with the Governor noting subsequently:

> [Salter] seems surprised ... indeed aghast a blow for the League and may upset the Hungarian Government ... He goes to take counsel with Cecil [Lubbock] on my declaring our view is considered and now unalterable at present.[127]

Norman made sure that there was to be no misunderstanding by sending to Salter, somewhat unusually, his note of their conversation, which also was circulated to Revelstoke of Barings, E. C. Grenfell of Morgan Grenfell and F. C. Tiarks of Schroders.[128]

Salter's astonishment on 11 January led to the Governor receiving on 23 January two further delegations which sought to change his mind. He may have been forewarned as Cecil Lubbock, his new Deputy Governor and who was possibly inclined to compromise on the matter, was present in the parlour for both interviews. Strakosch pleaded with Norman, and this may not have been his first supplication, but in reply was shown the letter to Niemeyer of 10 January whilst the Governor repeated that he was opposed. Strakosch may been trying to prepare the ground for the second delegation, comprising Bethlen, de Kallay and Goode, who had come to apply officially for assistance in raising a loan under the League scheme.[129] This is what they had been asked to do by Norman on 29 November 1923, but the Governor was now no longer prepared to 'direct them to proper Bankers'. Norman reiterated to the Hungarian representatives all that he had written to Niemeyer by stressing the adverse general financial conditions on Western markets as well as his insistence that Hungarian reparation charges must first be suspended before anything could be accomplished. Bethlen inquired whether a short-term loan might be provided, but Norman saw no hope for this temporary measure since in his view it could only succeed if it was to be clearly funded by the issue of a long-term loan.[130]

Norman carried his campaign to the utmost ends. When G. Strutt obtained an interview with the Governor on 31 March to seek a donation to the League of Nations Union, he obtained a response which Norman later noted as 'I say very unlikely especially in view of League's policy over Loan for Hungary (Repns and Reconstruction) to say nothing of Saar Valley'. Either Strutt was persistent or Norman wanted to ensure that his view had been fully received, because very shortly afterwards the two had a further meeting, when the Governor once more explained his objections to the League's Hungarian scheme 'owing to the provision for payment of Treaty charges'.[131]

Norman's closure of the London capital market to a Hungarian reconstruction loan failed to prevent the inception of the League scheme. It was accepted by the Reparation Commission on 21 February 1924 and the necessary protocols were signed at the League Council held in Geneva between 10 and 15 March 1924 with, simultaneously, the Council accepting full responsibility for the execution of the scheme. It went into effect immediately as, while the Council meeting deliberated, a League delegation, headed by Strakosch, was busy in Budapest establishing the bases for fiscal reform and the creation of a central bank.[132] Norman kept abreast of these developments and also reported critically upon them to his Committee of Treasury, commenting that the League's Financial Committee were 'relying apparently on obtaining later an external loan in London'.[133] On 1 April Strakosch attempted to discuss the success of the Financial Committee's Hungarian visitation with Norman. It would seem that Strakosch received a frosty reception, as the Governor informed his Committee of Treasury the following day of the protest that he had delivered to the League representative over Hungary still being subject to Treaty charges.[134]

Within a fortnight Norman's mood began to change, although the underlying reason for this was not to become evident until some weeks later. By mid-April 1924 Norman was prepared to discuss with Strakosch suitable candidates for the post of Adviser to the proposed new Hungarian central bank[135] and in early May the Governor had two discussions concerning Hungary, one with Strakosch and one with Lubbock his Deputy.[136] Norman alerted the Committee of Treasury to his total change of approach on 7 May 1924, explaining that he expected that the Bank of England would receive a request from the British government asking for every assistance to be given to a London issue of a Hungarian loan. Probably Norman had already seen the Chancellor, but no letter was sent from 11 Downing Street to the Bank until 7 May.[137] In this, Snowden talked in generalities by alluding to the Dawes Report and the new prospect that this opened up for Europe. It was sufficient for Norman, who none the less maintained his underlying attitude to the affair, for instance commenting to Vissering that:

> The British government now deem it politically expedient to proceed with the Scheme, and, although on the question of principle my views regarding the proposed foreign Loan, looked at solely from the economic aspect, remain unchanged, I shall nevertheless, in view of this decision, now give it *every support* in my power.[138]

Despite his own programme and his now long-standing objections to politicians meddling in the worlds of finance and economics, Norman saw himself and his Bank as servants of the British government, who were there to do its bidding. So complete was Norman's public change of mind that on 14 May he made no objection to Pospisil and Novak over Barings issuing the second tranche of the Czechoslovak loan in London. However his eleven month campaign had some pleasing, if fortuitous, results, because Pospisil undertook to urge the rapid creation of a Czechoslovak central bank, which would also ensure the abandonment of foreign exchange control in Prague,[139] steps which Norman had desired for at least a month.

Even before Norman had formally consulted his senior colleagues, let alone received Snowden's letter, he had set the wheels in motion to secure the successful issue of the Hungarian loan. On 6 May, he saw Anthony de Rothschild and established that the London Rothschilds would be 'glad to handle the Hungarian Loan, if at all possible'.[140] Over the next two days he busied himself with Strakosch by first considering the League's Hungarian scheme in general and then the international loan on which it was premised.[141] Having made his preparations, Norman now replied to Snowden, through Niemeyer, informing the Treasury that a Hungarian loan delegation should call first on Rothschilds in London and then go to J. P. Morgan & Co. in New York.

The Governor had learnt from bitter experience with Austrian reconstruction that inquiries regarding a loan issue could be mishandled as a result of being conducted simultaneously by various emissaries despatched by the prospective borrower. To overcome the problems that this had caused, Norman had established the mechanism of a small delegation which would have sole powers to undertake necessary negotiations on all Western capital markets. In the case of Hungary, this was convened in the Governor's parlour on 12 May and consisted of Teleszky and Jakob, on the part of the Hungarian government, and Pierre Bark, to whom Norman had entrusted much of the Bank's business in eastern and central Europe since late 1921, resulting in him playing a comparable role in the case of the Austrian loan delegation. With the party assembled and after a preliminary discussion 'on General Lines', Norman arranged that they should see Rothschilds.[142] Furthermore, the Governor asked Sir William Leese of the Bank's solicitors, Freshfields, to guide both the delegation and Rothschilds, Leese having been the adviser for the Austrian loan.[143] All in all, over the course of a week, Norman had used nearly all of his considerable influence to meet the request made of him by the British government.

Norman had always been doubtful about the market's reaction to a Hungarian loan, indeed the Austrian loan, which had better security both politically and financially, had nearly miscarried at the beginning of 1923. His worst fears were confirmed by Rothschilds' first soundings which indicated that London would only take a quarter - £3 million out of £12 million. Norman turned to Baron Schröder to see what could be done in Vienna,[144] but after five days which only confirmed the most pessimistic prospects, Norman was forced to reconsider the matter with those concerned in London. Initially he turned to Strakosch, then to Snowden the Chancellor, then back to senior League members - Niemeyer, Salter and Strakosch - and lastly, accompanied by Lubbock, went into a huddle with Strakosch.[145] Having taken the widest possible soundings, Norman addressed the Committee of Treasury to present the formula that had emerged - that the Bank of England, if requested by His Majesty's Government, would subscribe £4 million to the Hungarian loan and furthermore, if necessary, make advances.[146]

The Governor spent an hour the next day looking at the necessity of an advance from the Bank to Hungary, before once more seeing Snowden,[147] an interview which produced the letter that Norman required. It was a further appeal to the Bank for help, arising from the Hungarian loan delegation only having been able to obtain a £4 million tranche in London and £4 million on other European markets. There had been no positive response in the United States, which Norman later attributed to the Presidential election,[148] and consequently the scheme was endangered. It was argued in Snowden's letter that the provision of the remaining £4 million was 'critical' and required 'without delay', and the Chancellor now looked to the Bank.[149] In practice the Bank was making good the amount that it had been hoped could be raised in America.

The draft conditions for the Bank of England to make an advance of £4 million to the still nascent National Bank of Hungary[150] were agreed between Norman, Lubbock, Harvey and Strakosch. This proposal was then further developed and finalized through subsequent meetings also involving President A. Popovics for the National Bank of Hungary, Leese and de Bordes of the League.[151] The result was that the Bank would advance up to £4 million, to be placed under the control of the League's Commissioner-General, Jeremiah Smith, who had taken up his post on 1 May. The advance was to run until mid-1927, be secured on six-months Hungarian Treasury bills which were to be exchangeable with issued bonds of the long-term stabilization loan, and was to bear a rate of interest of one per cent over Bank Rate with a minimum of five per cent. Further security was provided through the requirement that the proceeds of the London tranche of the long-term loan were paid into the Bank of England.[152]

The conditions for the advance were also used to frame the nature of stabilization as they required that the Hungarian government paid over all foreign valuta to the National Bank of Hungary.[153] Moreover, the terms went further. The Hungarian currency was to be stabilized against the pound sterling, with the latter being the numera, whereas the Austrian crown had been stabilized against the dollar. As might be expected, the National Bank of Hungary was required to undertake all its London business exclusively with the Bank of England. Furthermore, while the advance remained outstanding, the Bank of England could recommend a rise in the National Bank of Hungary's discount rate.[154] Subsequently, Siepmann, the National Bank of Hungary's first foreign adviser, thought that Norman's requirements were 'tough'. The Governor did not demur, but pointed to the Bank of England having had to assume at least a third of the long-term stabilization loan.[155]

The advance provided an uncertain bridge and exposed the Bank of England, should the long-term loan not be successful. Norman may have been irked when Nathan called on 31 May to inquire, as the Governor put it, 'rather peevishly' about Hungary. The Banca d'Italia's representative was seeking answers to two questions: why had nothing been settled in London; and why was there no American tranche of the loan?[156] Actually, with the details of the advance to the Hungarian National Bank nearly settled, Norman was turning to his international circle of central bankers in order to drum up subscriptions for the Hungarian loan, especially from, in his view, all important, 'neutral' financial centres. After mentioning the matter to Wallenberg, who had been a member of the March League delegation to Budapest, the Governor made a personal appeal to Moll of the Riksbank, stressing the necessity of a 'substantial Swedish tranche' and the need to have 'definite promises by the end of the week'.[157] Rothschilds' pessimistic prognostications were confirmed in the case of the Netherlands by ter Meulen, especially if the Amsterdam tranche was issued in guilders. Consequently, Norman asked Vissering whether ter Meulen represented the general view of Dutch bankers, and he followed this up by inquiring if the Dutch central banker could take some steps.[158] Despite these attempts, by 12 June, when the Rothschilds called on Norman to discuss the Hungarian loan statements that were to be made by the negotiating delegation to the League, all that the Governor could rely on was the provisional arrangements for placing an Italian tranche, for which he thanked Stringher.[159]

Even with Norman's considerable position within international finance, the Hungarian loan proved to be a troublesome affair. As had been signalled to Norman by ter Meulen, the first difficulty arose over the Dutch tranche caused by bankers in the Netherlands expecting to issue bonds denominated in sterling. This ran against Norman's careful control of the export of sterling, caused the Governor to object to such procedures in Amsterdam and which, in turn, led to the Dutch portion being initially cancelled.[160] On 18 June the loan delegation reported that only £4 million would be taken on continental European markets if 'expectations all realized',[161] which caused Norman to redouble his efforts. Following the advice of Nathan, he wrote to Bianchini, who had been a member of the League delegation to Budapest, to secure firmly the Italian portion[162] and then the Governor turned his attention to the difficult matter of the Paris market. It is clear that, even at this late stage, no approaches had been made in Paris and Norman wrote to his peer, Robineau, at the Banque de France, asking for his support and assistance.[163] Although no Parisian tranche was subsequently issued, this was due to a lack of funds and interest among French banks, rather than officially inspired obstruction.[164]

In Norman's perspective an American financial stake was equally important as 'neutral' participations in the loan. This would mark further American involvement in curing Europe's ills, would act perhaps as a further moderating control rod in European politics and, equally, would relieve the strain on Europe's capital markets and foreign exchanges. However, neither Rothschilds' connection with Kuhn, Loeb & Co. nor Norman's very close personal relationship with J. P. Morgan & Co. had been sufficient to bring American bankers behind the Hungarian loan so causing the Bank of England to take their place. A further and last chance of an American placement arose when Gordon Leith, on behalf of Speyers, began to indicate an interest, which emerged as a tranche amounting initially to £5 million.[165] However, Speyers wanted to gain two options as a result of this participation and their nature only became evident on 28 June, a week after

Leith's first approach. Speyers' main aim was to have all future Hungarian state business in New York 'on equal terms', a requirement to be written into their loan contract. This condition proved to be too much so that the loan delegation terminated the negotiations. The Bank of England came in immediately to take up £7.5 million, which had been the amount of Speyers' final option. Bark and Telesky signed the loan contract with Rothschilds, while Rothschilds for their part announced that the Hungarian loan had been underwritten.[166] Telesky left for Budapest on 2 July and, according to Norman, the Hungarian representative was 'well satisfied with arrangements for [the] loan here and abroad'.[167]

The National Bank of Hungary formally began operations on 24 June 1924. The advance that it had subsumed from the Royal Hungarian State Note Institution meant that it was closely tied to the Bank of England, just as the Hungarian crown was related to the pound sterling. A further link came with Siepmann, who was appointed as the Bank's foreign adviser in July. However, previously Norman had made strenuous efforts to search amongst the 'neutrals' and the United States for a suitable person from the moment when he had been first consulted by Strakosch over filling this post.[168] By 4 June the Governor and Strakosch had compiled a list of eight recommendations, three of whom were American bankers. However impediments were detected amongst those who had been suggested; for instance, one had a 'militant' character and was 'unused to methods of diplomacy', while another was considered to have 'not much banking practice'.[169] Consequently Siepmann was appointed, but it must be stressed that an Englishman had never been Norman's first choice. He had the necessary attributes but nevertheless was not totally qualified for assisting the new central bank. After an education at Rugby and Oxford, Siepmann had worked in the British Treasury between 1912 until 1915, and then had served in the British Army as a Captain in the Royal Horse Artillery. During 1919 he had been part of the British Treasury delegation at the Versailles peace conference while, immediately prior to taking up his appointment in Budapest, he was with the Government of India as the Assistant to the Finance Member of the Viceroy's Council.[170] Somewhat like Strakosch, Siepmann during the early 1920s was essentially a currency expert, but he quickly came to share Norman's broadest objectives:

> The doctrine which I seem to have learned from you and which whether that is so or not, I do profoundly believe, is that to a great extent it may and should prove possible to substitute other means for the traditional and political means of associating nations. One part of the new methods is to work for the association of Central Banks. But I feel that this - though it is a task which may well provide whole time occupation for more people than are at present engaged in it - needs to be supplemented by some sort of spiritual association (I use

> this offensive phrase for want of a better contrast to 'material' or 'financial'). In India I came to the same conclusion. The personal 'gulf' was only one part an immense national gulf.[171]

In the midst of the international conference considering the Dawes report, Siepmann came to London to have two long discussions with Norman. The new adviser was clearly concerned about his responsibilities, having already informed the Governor that he was 'afraid of this job on the banking side'. Consequently he looked to Norman 'in matters both of policy and of detail ... and generally ... at any rate for the first six months or so to be my mentor'.[172] This was to create an irony for, although Norman was a great believer in maintaining regular contact, largely by correspondence, he soon came to find the almost incessant flow of Siepmann's very lengthy letters too much to bear.[173]

In summer 1924 Norman promised close and intimate co-operation with the new National Bank, suggesting that this could begin by exchanging personnel, including the despatch to Budapest of a specialist in central banking who might stay for some months. At the same time Siepmann felt that there might be an implicit challenge as 'The Governor regards the National Bank as one member of an association of Central Banks from which he expects great things'.[174] Almost inevitably Siepmann approached his task initially from a perspective gained from his recent stay in India, indeed he found Hungary as bewildering as the sub-continent. He was anxious to increase his Bank's earning power and therefore saw no use for its gold holdings, which he admitted to be perhaps an extreme personal view, while similarly he wanted to deploy profitably its London sterling balance.[175] These objectives soon received rebuffs from London. Lubbock reminded Siepmann that gold had an important psychological function, especially after the trauma of inflation and hyper-inflation. It was needed to create and maintain confidence and the Deputy Governor saw no reason why gold cover for the Hungarian currency should not rise from its current level of 13 per cent to 25-30 per cent. Furthermore, the Bank of England official argued that gold would play an even greater role once Hungarian bank notes became convertible and a free gold market was restored. London agreed to the National Bank lending its sterling, over and above that required for the note reserve, but only to provide assistance to Hungarian nationals, rather than foreign banks, even if such institutions might be offering high rates of interest. Here, Siepmann was reminded by Lubbock of the founding articles of the National Bank and also of Norman's own stricture that a central bank should not lend outside of its own country.

Heresy on Siepmann's part was mixed with the new orthodoxy as he took steps to draw the National Bank together with its local peers - the Bankamt at Prague, the Romanian National Bank and the Serbian National Bank. However, he had little of a foundation on which to erect a structure of regional relationships as the only central bank account that the National Bank held was that of the Austrian National Bank, largely used for exchange dealings. This sole central bank account was further complicated by the practice of Austrian nationals having considerable balances with Budapest private banks, which in turn were lent out locally on a short-term basis at high interest. The National Bank of Hungary also had a 'Serbian' account but this essentially operated as a 'clearing', used to balance disbursements for refugees against revenues arising from railway rolling stock repairs in Hungary. Finally there was a Norwegian account, yet this was a special case, having arisen from the crisis experienced by Norwegian banks in spring 1923.[176]

A consideration of the initial operations of the National Bank arose with the visit of President Popovics to London in early October 1924. Popovics had a long discussion with Norman, Strakosch and Lubbock in which the central concern was the consequences of seasonal variations in the adverse Hungarian trade balance and, especially, the likely worsening trade deficit over the first half of 1925. However, this particular Hungarian problem soon came to be recognized as having wider ramifications. It led to a long debate in London and elsewhere over the course of autumn 1924 as to how stand-by facilities could be provided for the new central banks of central and eastern Europe.

Hungary's particular, anticipated problems constituted the agenda of the London meetings of October 1924. Various aspects were explored, beginning with the impact of the relaxation of controls over foreign exchange dealings. The National Bank considered that the Hungarian crown had been effectively stabilized against the pound sterling but, none the less, the Bank had been amassing a hidden reserve of foreign exchange to meet anticipated demands from the close of the year. The Bank had also experienced a seasonal increase in discounting, augmented by it 'still [being] the cheapest source of credit'. Despite Strakosch, who Norman had once called 'a visionary arbitrageur',[177] pointing out that 'large gains ... could be realized ... where the margin between the Bank Rate and Market Rate was so considerable (about 12 points)', Popovics, like his directors, felt that a further rise in the National Bank's rate 'would be ineffective or inadvisable and penalize agriculture'. However, it was recognized that a rise in discounts, even if controlled qualitatively, would lead to an increase in the note circulation which would have direct consequences for the Bank's currency reserve. In Popovics's view, the real necessity was to encourage the inflow of foreign capital, both short- and long-term, in order to assist Hungarian agriculture and to prevent the National Bank's reserve ratio falling. He thought that there was a possibility of the ratio declining from 62 to perhaps 44 per cent, which 'While in normal times this would not give alarm, during the next year or two it is feared a bad effect would be produced'. The Hungarian banker considered that local savings had been absorbed by subscriptions to the capital of the National Bank and the stabilization loan, whereas current inflows of short-term capital 'increases the anxiety which may be felt for the maintenance of a stable currency, with all its psychological economic consequences'. Here, Popovics stressed that

Hungary's economic development had historically involved the import of long-term funds and saw stabilization as the means to encourage its recurrence.[178]

Norman was prepared to provide the National Bank with an advance, but Strakosch went further by casting the issue in terms of 'the whole question of co-operation between central banks' and maintaining that 'it was reasonable that the banks whose period of strain was say in the Autumn should assist others whose period of strain was in the Spring'. The unresolved conundrum proved to be the necessary collateral securities for seasonal advances, which all at the London meeting agreed were required.[179]

Strakosch articulated his reactions to the London meeting for the benefit of Siepmann in Budapest. He saw no reason why there should not be fluctuations in a foreign currency reserve since seasonal movements in the balance of trade could be explained to the public in terms of being a natural phenomenon. The lean time of the year, spring in the case of Hungary, would produce a fall in the reserve, whereas the autumn harvest and consequent exports would generate a rise. Strakosch continued to favour a further rise in the National Bank's Bank rate, as opposed to the application of credit restriction, to prevent currency outflows. However, he maintained that there was a considerable case for central banks making temporary advances to one another,[180] calling them 'facilities', but, despite his considerable experience, could not put forward what might constitute the necessary required collateral. Neither gold, which would have to be publicly disclosed, nor domestic bills, which were contrary to the custom of the Bank of England, could serve. All that Strakosch initially could suggest, now that the German reparation problem had been resolved, was a central bank conference to develop mutual assistance, probably in the form of bill finance.

The reason for a conference arose from Strakosch perceiving that the 'League's central banks' - Austria, Danzig and Hungary - faced comparable problems. The collapse of the Vienna Börse during spring 1924 with the 'franc crisis', had led ultimately to the League Commissioner-General for Austria releasing 21 million gold Austrian crowns from the proceeds of the Austrian stabilization loan. Zimmerman had placed this sum at the disposal of the Austrian National Bank, although this action incurred Norman's wrath, since the Governor regarded it as help to speculators. Moreover, Popovics's October 1924 request to Norman had but followed in the wake of a similar approach from the President of the Bank of Danzig for a stand-by credit.[181] However, thinking in Budapest had gone further than Strakosch's suggested conference to seeing a solution lying in 'a new organism', which would act as an intermediary between central banks. Popovics envisaged it in the form of a 'Federal Reserve Board of Europe', which would have a small staff who would manage a fund contributed by member banks out of their reserves. If this was a step too far, and a conception that took no account of institutional and political impediments, then the way forward was a conference. However, it was felt in Budapest that this forum would have to consider a developed solution - 'worked out in detail and reduced to black and white by those chiefly interested in the idea'.[182] Siepmann backed Popovics's approach by explaining that:

> Every one of us weaker members would be afraid of a super-bank which might tell us, for example, that the way to get out of our difficulties was to raise our rate instead of relying on outside assistance, or which might make the grant of indispensable assistance conditional upon our accepting terms - possibly even irrelevant terms - that we should never have accepted but for the fact that we had our backs to the wall.

Norman's reaction to his pupil's argument is not available, but the Governor might have been able to read into Siepmann's reasoning much that could have caused him disquiet, if only in terms of the relationship between the Bank of England and the National Bank of Hungary. However, Siepmann's support for Popovics was not total, as he did not accept the conviction that the new body would also restrict currency speculation. Rather the adviser maintained this desired effect would only come about once 'comparative currency and moreover natural, self-supporting stability' had been reached, by when the 'new organism' would inevitably be redundant in this aspect of its functions.

Strakosch took the matter to the Financial Committee of the League, where it was quietly and privately discussed. It was treated as an informal approach from the Bank of England to which the League responded by exploring the elasticity within the statutes of the new central banks. In coming to its initial conclusions, the Committee followed Strakosch by wishing to encourage co-operation in the 'Genoa spirit'. The Committee maintained that there was no undue risk in advances to central banks secured on domestic bills where the local currency was stabilized against either the pound sterling or gold. Furthermore, the conclusion was reached that 'League central banks' had the power to borrow abroad and lend against collateral comprised of domestic bills. The only reservation was that the exercise of these powers in the cases of Austria and Hungary would require the prior approval of the respective foreign financial adviser to the central bank.[183] A further draft of the League's reply was considered in late November when Siepmann came to London and saw Norman and Strakosch. Additional refinements were made with regard to the vexed question of proper security and the extent of the margin a lender should enjoy.[184] Ultimately the problem was circumvented by the Bank of England opening accounts with the National Bank of Austria and the National Bank of Hungary. These had two functions: one was to 'serve as a symbol of the permanent and exclusive relations already so happily established between our institutions', while the other was to constitute a conduit by which to 'provide necessary facilities'.

The rest of Siepmann's nine days in London during November 1924 were mostly spent within the Bank dealing with current problems, although he also looked ahead to likely future developments and their consequences. Detailed points regarding the provision of 'facilities' took up much time, but there were also issues regarding the position of the Hungarian crown once sterling had been restored to the gold standard. Siepmann had an eye on the Budapest-Vienna exchanges, but Norman was nonplussed over this point, accepting that there could be minor variations in exchange rates, while expecting 'when sterling approached parity there would be considerable speculation causing sharp fluctuations in the rate'.[185] Norman supported Siepmann's idea for establishing a small Intelligence Department within the National Bank and undertook to include the financial adviser on the mailing list for Bank of England's monthly statistical report and Norman's own weekly letter which covered 'the course of Stock exchange prices, Commodity prices, Money, Forthcoming Issues, etc.'.

At the conclusion of this intensive period of discussions, Norman wrote to Popovics, stating:

> It has been a great pleasure to welcome Mr. Siepmann and to have an opportunity of hearing at first hand from him an account of the various problems by which you are confronted from time to time in your efforts to secure the re-establishment of a sound financial position in Hungary. Such personal intercourse affords the only really satisfactory channel through which to gain appreciation of the infinite variety of points which constantly demand your attention - points too numerous and complicated to permit of adequate exposition in correspondence.[186]

By Norman's standards it was a long letter, consisting of more than four pages of text. He took the opportunity to stress another of his basic principles: 'The Bank of England hold it to be a cardinal principle that no central bank should have business relations with the Government of any foreign country'. Norman recorded in his desk diary: 'Siepmann going back to Budapest tomorrow. All queries cleared up so far as he is concerned. ... I warn him as to B[an]k R[ate]'.[187] The Governor's eye was now firmly fixed on the restoration of sterling.

The world of experts, like that of Norman, Strakosch and Siepmann who have been considered here, was cosmopolitan and generally did not acknowledge national boundaries. As with many of their successors, they looked to a world economy, which they wanted to operate smoothly. From their different early careers before 1918, Norman's largely in Anglo-American merchant banking, Strakosch in the finance of South African gold mining and even Siepmann within the British Treasury, they were accustomed to the almost frictionless operation of the global economic system, which seemed to be ensured by free trade, the free movement of capital and labour, and the gold standard. That world, and especially its central and eastern European component, was set awry by the First World War. Post-war chaos within Europe appeared to be made worse by national antipathies which motivated the actions of politicians. 'Central banking', as Norman, Strong, Strakosch and later Siepmann conceived it, seemed to provide a solution to many of Europe's problems and not just the quelling of monetary maelstroms. Here again was an internationalist aspiration which, as Siepmann put it, could bridge many 'gulfs'. However, Norman's vision of international central co-operation never fully became reality, as was shown by his failed attempt to convene a post-Genoa conference. As a result, Norman was forced to make do with second best and arrange financial support for League stabilization schemes as they came about. None the less these efforts have been regarded as constituting the forerunner of the IMF, despite crumbling into dust from May 1931.

Norman always tried to divide the world into realms - political on the one hand, and finance and economics on the other - with the latter being that of central bank experts. However he was conscious that many of Europe's post-war problems could not be readily so compartmentalized, as for instance, when he commented to Strong:

> This question of reparations is not as it should be, and as Mr Keynes assumes it to be, a purely economic question. It is almost entirely a political question over which the French government is forced to tug in one direction and the German government in another.[188]

Indeed, Norman faced an underlying problem that had confronted London merchant bankers since at least the mid-nineteenth century and which took in many guises as, for instance, the question of whether a banker, acting as a government's Financial Agent, should be 'a foreign Chancellor of the Exchequer'.[189] Stabilization plans, such as those drawn up by Strakosch, privately approved by Norman and executed by Siepmann, went further than framing the budget through establishing the institutional structure of an economy. Here, these experts would have argued that they were purging the system of inflationary evils and re-creating stability. However, the potential to apply stabilization ran into European political antipathies, but Norman saw no difficulty in making his opposition known and using what powers were available to him to overcome political impediments. Yet, for all his attempted separation of politics and finance, Norman was prepared, as in the case of the Hungarian stabilization loan, to act in accordance with his own state's policy, even if he privately opposed it. Norman, the greatest of international central bankers, recognized that he was first and foremost a servant of his nation state.

There can be no doubt that Norman, and his cadre of central bankers and financial experts, believed in the mission that they had developed over the second half of 1921. Yet Norman's own immediate cosmopolitan circle in London was not totally altruistic. Rebuilding the pre-1914 world economy meant also re-establishing the global position of the City of London, of the British economy and, above all, of the pound sterling. Attempting to solve the economic and financial problems of central and eastern Europe - the 'distressed countries' - was important in itself and was a noble goal for international bankers and humanitarians, but it also constituted a stepping stone on the way to restoring British monetary and financial stability. As Strakosch put it to Clegg:

> With the German Reparation question in a fair way of settlement and with Austria and Hungary on the high road to financial and economic recovery; in other words, with the most important economic units of central Europe fairly equipped to resume - gradually it is true - their normal measure of production in condition of monetary stability[190]

In such circumstances, the pound sterling could take up its old position in the world economy.

Appendix: Norman's 'Epitome' of Central Banking

CENTRAL BANKS

A Central Bank should not compete with other Banks for general business.

A Central Bank should not take monies at interest on its own account nor accept Bills of Exchange.

A Central Bank should have no Branch outside its own country.

A Central Bank should not engage in a general Exchange business on its own account with any other country.

A Central Bank should be independent but should do all its own Government's business - directly or indirectly - including Gold and Currency.

A Central Bank should be the Banker of all other Banks in its own country and should assist them to develop its business and economic resources.

A Central Bank should protect its own Traders from the rapacity of other banks in its own country.

[*] A Central Bank should act as the settling agent for Clearing House balances arising between the Banks of its own country, and to the widest extent practicable.

[*] A Central Bank should handle domestic collections for its members and so regulate the domestic exchanges.

[*] A Central Bank should have power to examine Banks which come to the Central Bank for credits and assistance.

A Central Bank may have an Agency in another country.

That Agency should either be in its own name or should be the Central Bank of the other country: in the former case it should do all its Banking and all kindred business with the Central Bank of the other country.

And should co-operate in practice and principle with the Central Bank of the other country.

And should receive the most favoured treatment and information from the Central Bank of the other country.

And should do the Banking and kindred business of its Principal's Government in the other country.

March, 1921.

Points marked * were added by Strong to Norman's original compilation of January 1921 [for which see BoE; OV 37/20, Norman to Clegg, 28 Jan. 1921.]

Source: BoE; OV 37/20, Norman to Clegg, 1 Apr. 1921, f.6A

Notes

* I am grateful to the Governor and Company of the Bank of England for permission to use the Bank's archives. The underlying research behind this paper could not have been accomplished without the considerable help and assistance of the staff of the Archives of the Bank of England, especially Henry Gillet, Archivist, and Elizabeth Ogborn, Deputy Archivist. Equally I am grateful for the comments made by participants at the Budapest 1994 conference and further positive critiques from members of both the Monetary History Group (meeting at the University of the West of England, October 1995) and the Economics Seminar of Manchester Metropolitan University, December 1995.

1 This point has been underlined as the text was being finally revised; on 3 October 1996, German unity day, Chancellor Kohl admited that the reconstruction and integration of east Germany had proved to be far more difficult and onerous than had been initially envisaged.

2 The seminal text is S. V. O. Clarke, (1967), *Central bank cooperation, 1924-1931*, New York; see B. Eichengreen, (1992),*Golden Fetters. The gold standard and the Great Depression, 1919-1939*, Oxford, for a critique and reappraisal of the subsequent literature.

3 G. de Kock, (1954), *A history of the South African Reserve Bank 1920-52*, Pretoria.

4 There are two biographies of Norman; that by Sir Henry Clay [*Lord Norman* (London, 1957)] arose from a close, personal relationship, whereas A. Boyle, (London, 1967), *Montagu Norman, a biography* has other and more serious faults and so does not provide an objective assessment.

5 L. V. Chandler, (1967), *Benjamin Strong, central banker*, New York.

6 Federal Reserve Bank of New York, Strong papers, 1116.7, Norman to Strong, 28 Nov. 1927; quoted in R. W. D. Boyce, (1987), *British capitalism at the crossroads 1919-1932. A study in politics, economics, and international relations*, Cambridge, p. 160.

7 E. T. Williams, (1959), *The dictionary of national biography, 1941-1950*, Oxford, pp. 846-7; and P. Gawith, 'Gencor Ltd.', in A. Hast et al. (eds), (1991), *International directory of company histories*, IV, Chicago & London, pp. 90-1.

8 On the refinery see E. Hennessy, (1992), *A domestic history of the Bank of England, 1930-1960*, Cambridge, p. 169, fn † and, more generally, R. Ally, (1994), *Gold and empire: the Bank of England and South Africa's gold producers, 1886-1926*, Johannesburg.

9 See R. S. Sayers, (1976), *The Bank of England 1891-1944*, I, Cambridge, pp. 202-3 & p. 202, fn 2.

10 Bank of England Archives, London [hereafter BoE]; G3 [Governors' letters], Norman to Havenstein, 3 Oct. 1923, explaining the support to

be given to the new central bank in Danzig, being established under the auspices of the League of Nations. In another part of this letter, Norman emphasized 'I have no concern with the political considerations which have given rise to the present situation and have therefore no wish to enquire in this connection as to your views ... I am aware, of course, that the Reichsbank has been established in Danzig'.

11 The first four sections parallel György Péteri's commentary - 'Central bank diplomacy: Montagu Norman and central Europe's monetary reconstruction after World War I', *Contemporary European History*, 1 (1992) and reprinted in G. Péteri, (1995), *Revolutionary Twenties. Essays on international monetary and financial relations after World War I*, Trondheim. I am grateful to Professor Péteri for providing me with a copy of his collected essays which greatly aided the revision of this paper.

12 Clay, (1957), pp. 115-6; BoE; ADM 34/8 [Norman's diary], 'preface'.

13 BoE; ADM 34/8, entry 8 May 1919.
Norman never warmed to Vanderlip and his designs for Europe, as he commented to Strong in November 1921: 'F. Vanderlip is wandering about Europe with thunderings of a new plan [Gold Reserve Bank of the United States of Europe] to settle all European difficulties. I hope the time has already come when he has gone so far as to be able to do a good deal less harm than when he was last similarly engaged!' BoE; G3/177, Norman to Strong, 7 Nov. 1921.
Sir E. M. Harvey, a Bank director, did submit in May 1920, i.e., before the Brussels conference, a scheme for an Austrian Privileged Bank, in effect a new central bank for the new republic. See Public Record Office, London; FO 120 [Papers of the British Legation in Vienna] 962/590/2, 5 May 1920.

14 BoE; ADM 34/9, entry 12 Apr. 1920; P. L. Cottrell, 'Aspects of western equity investment in the banking systems of east central Europe', in A. Teichova & P. L. Cottrell (eds), (1983), *International business and central Europe 1918-1939*, Leicester.

15 BoE; ADM 34/9, entries: 7 & 23 Dec. 1920.
This post proved exceptionally difficult to fill and Drummond Fraser was not appointed as the organiser, *pro tem* for the scheme until spring 1921. With this outcome, Norman commented: 'I think they have taken the best man available but I fear his sight is rather limited to Manchester, where he has passed his life. I guess he ought to begin at the other end, viz, in the distressed countries.' BoE; G3/177, Norman to Strong, 2 Apr. 1921.

16 BoE; ADM 34/8, entries: 24 Jul. 1919; 8 Sep. 1919; & 20 Sep. 1919. Clay, (1957), p. 119.

17 S. W. Howson, (1974), 'The origins of dear money, 1919-20', *Economic History Review*, n.s., 27.

18 Clay, (1957), pp. 120-3.

19 BoE; OV37/20 [Overseas finance - South Africa], Norman to Clegg,

f.4.

20 BoE; ADM 34/9, entries: 19, 21 & 27 Oct. 1920; & 2, 5, 9, & 19 Nov. 1920.

21 Clay, (1957), p. 285; Sayers, (1976), I, p. 203.

22 On the conference generally, see A. Orde, (1990), *British policy and European reconstruction after the First World War,* Cambridge, pp. 105-7; Clay, (1957), pp. 136; Sayers, (1976), I, pp. 153-4.

23 BoE; OV37/20, Norman to Clegg, f.4.

24 BoE; OV37/21, Osborne to Clegg, 28 Aug. 1924, f.53.

25 He also had Canadian concerns - see BoE; ADM 34/10, entry 31 Jan. 1920.

26 Also reprinted in Clay, (1957), pp. 283-4.

27 BoE; OV 37/20, Norman to Clegg, 28 Jan. 1921, f.4.

28 BoE; G3/177 [Governor's letters], Norman to Strakosch, 16 Feb. 1921.

29 BoE; G3/177, Norman to Strong, 17 Feb. 1921.

30 BoE; G3/177, Norman to Hunter, 28 Feb. 1921. Sayers adds Addis, a Bank director, to this list; Sayers, (1976), I, p. 204.

31 BoE; OV 37/20, Sir H. Strakosch, 'A Central Bank should have no branch outside its own country', n.d, but possibly written before 16 Dec. 1920, n.f. but lead paper in the file.

32 BoE; OV 37/20, Norman to Clegg, 17 Dec. 1921.

33 BoE; OV 37/20, Norman to Clegg, 28 Jan. 1921.

34 BoE; G3/177, Norman to Strong, 2 Apr. 1921.

35 BoE; G3/177, Norman to Strong, 3 May 1921.

36 BoE; ADM 34/10, entries 30 Jun., 4 Jul. & 7 Jul. 1921. However, Norman always made a point of graciously acknowledging the copies of books that the Bank received from Hawtrey and others; see BoE; G3/179, Norman to Hawtrey, 6 Feb. 1923, 25 Sep. 1923 [re: *Currency and Credit*]; Norman to Cannan, 21 Nov. 1923 [re: new edition of *Money*].

37 BoE; OV37/22, Norman to Clegg, 31 May 1921; Sayers, (1976), I, p.204.

The Tuesday Club had been started by Oswald Falk as a monthly dining club for the discussion of economics. Its membership during the 1920s was broader and more senior than Norman implied, in spring 1921 consisting of Keynes and other Cambridge economists, Charles Addis (a Bank director), Robert Brand, Reginald McKenna (former Chancellor and chairman of the Midland Bank) and Strakosch for the City, Blackett and Niemeyer of the Treasury together with other public servants such as John Anderson and Josiah Stamp, and the financial journalists A. W. Kiddy and Hartley Withers. Norman was not a member but more than an occasional guest. See R. Skidelsky, (1992), *John Maynard Keynes*, II, *The economist as saviour 1920-1937*, London, pp. 22, 196-7.

38 BoE; G3/177, Norman to Strakosch, 25 May 1921. The two had specifically discussed central banking on 21 February, along with

Benjamin Strong Jnr., and again on 14 April; see ADM 34/10, entries 21 Feb., & 14 Apr. 1921.

39 'Believing that games as well as work are as necessary to Central Bank men as to any others, I send for your entertainment some photographs taken at Easter when two of our Football teams went over to Paris to play against the Bank of France'. BoE; G3/177, Norman to Strong, 27 Apr. 1921.

40 BoE; G3/177, Norman to R. R. Schreiber, Peruvian Chargé d'Affaires in London, 4 Jun.; 21 Jun. 1921; Norman to Erskine, 13 Jun. 1921; Norman to O. E. Niemeyer, Treasury, 10 Oct. 1921. OV37/20, Norman to Clegg, 31 May 1921.

41 BoE; G3/177, Norman to Strong, 13 Jul. 1921.

42 Moll, Governor of the Riksbank, used the phrase 'Gordian Knot' to describe Europe's post-war monetary problems. See Péteri, (1995), p.10.

43 The need for an apolitical approach was shared by a whole group of international bankers and economists in reaction to the Versailles Conference and then the subsequent workings of the Reparation Commission. See Péteri, (1995), pp. 58-9.

44 BoE; OV 37/20, Norman to Clegg, 13 Oct. 1921.

45 Norman continued to regard Vissering as 'cranky'; see BoE; G3/177, Norman to Strong, 7 Nov. 1921.

46 E. Johnson (ed.), (1977), *Collected writings of John Maynard Keynes*, 17, *Activities 1920-22*, London, pp. 128-30, 136, 147, 149-50; and, more generally, *Geschiedenis van de Nederlandsche Bank;* J. de Vries, (1989), *Vifde deel De Nederlandsche Bank van 1914 tot 1948. Visserings tijdvak 1914-1931*, The Hague.

47 BoE; OV 37/20, Norman to Clegg, 13 Oct. 1921.

48 BoE; G3/177, Norman to Lepreux, Vice-Governor, National Bank of Belgium, 22 Oct. 1921.

49 BoE; G3/177, Norman to Vissering, 5 Nov. 1921.

50 'Fold' was Norman's own term during late 1921, see BoE; G3/177, Norman to Strong, 5 Dec. 1921.

51 BoE; G3/177, Norman to Vissering, 28 Nov., 3 Dec. 1921.

52 BoE; G3/177, Norman to Strong, 21 Oct. 1921.

53 BoE; G3/177, Norman to Strong, 16 Nov. 1921.

54 BoE; G3/177, Norman to Vissering, 26 Oct. 1921.

55 BoE; G3/177, Norman to Strong, 28 Oct. 1921.

56 BoE; G3/177, Norman to Strong, 16 Nov. 1921.

57 BoE; OV 37/20, Norman to Clegg, 26 Jul. 1923, f.103. On the gold exchange standard, see also Trotter to Clegg, f.54.

58 BoE; OV 37/22/G3/177, Norman to Vissering, 12 Oct. f.12/5 Nov. 1921.

59 BoE: G3/177, Norman to Strong, 7 Nov. 1921. On the development of the Riksbank's policies, see G. Péteri, (1984), 'The inflation-proof gold standard: the foreign policy of the Riksbankschefen Victor Moll and

the origins of the Swedish ban on gold imports in 1924', *Journal of European Economic History*, 13, and reprinted in Péteri, (1995).
60 BoE; G3/177, Norman to Strong, 16 Nov. 1921.
61 BoE;G3/177, Norman to Palmstierna, 24 Nov. 1921. The resolution, an 'expression of opinion', is discussed by Péteri, (1995), pp. 6-8. Norman did not receive a copy from Moll, the Governor of the Riksbank, until late January 1922; see Péteri, (1995), pp. 9-10.
62 BoE; ADM 34/11, entry 14 Mar. 1922.
63 BoE; G3/177, Norman to Strong, 5 Dec., 29 Dec. 1921.
64 BoE; ADM 34/11, entries 27 Feb., 3 Apr. 1921.
65 BoE; G3/177, Norman to Strong, 5 Dec. 1921.
66 BoE, G3/177, Norman to B. Hornsby, 19 Dec. 1921.
67 BoE; OV 37/20, H. A. Trotter [Deputy-Governor] to Clegg, 1 Dec. 1921, f.25.
68 BoE; OV 37/20, Norman to Clegg, 2 Nov. 1921, f.20.
69 BoE; ADM 34/10, entry 7 Oct. 1921.
70 BoE, G3/177, Norman to Vissering, 28 Nov., 3 Dec. 1921.
71 See Clay, (1957), pp. 136-8; Sayers, (1976), I, pp. 156-60; C. Fink, (1984), *The Genoa conference. European diplomacy, 1921-1922*, Chapel Hill, NC.
72 BoE; ADM 34/10 / 34/11, entries 14 Nov. 1921, 29 Mar. 1922.
73 The Commission was chaired by Sir Robert Horne, the British Chancellor and was composed of Addis and Peacock from the Bank of England, as well as Blackett, Brand, Hawtrey, Strakosch all from Britain, Cassel and Wallenberg from Sweden, Cuno and Melchior representing Germany, Vissering from Holland and Vanderlip from the United States.
74 For the proceedings of the conference see Skidelsky, (1992), II, pp. 106-11.
75 BoE; OV 37/20, Trotter to Clegg, 28 Apr. 1922, f.33; Sayers, (1976), I, pp. 155-62; J. L. Kooker, 'French financial diplomacy: the interwar years', in B. M. Rowland (ed.), (1976), *Balance of power or hegemony: the interwar monetary system*, New York.
76 BoE; OV 37/20, Norman to Clegg, 1 Jun. 1922, f.38.
77 BoE; ADM/13, entry 18 Feb. 1924.
78 BoE; OV 37/20, Norman to Clegg, 1 Jun. 1922, f.38.
79 BoE; ADM 34/11, entry 13 Jun. 1922.
80 An indication of the nature of the agenda can be gained by the draft resolutions, as formulated in London by mid-June 1922. See Péteri, (1995), pp. 64-5.
81 BoE; ADM 34/11, entries 7, 12 Jun., 7 Jul. 1922.
82 BoE; OV 37/20, Norman to Clegg, 22 Jun. 1922, f.47. Norman's emphasis.
83 Péteri, (1995), pp. 13-15.
84 Quoted in Péteri, ibid., p.19.
85 Ibid., p.20.

86 Ibid., p.29.
87 BoE; OV 37/20, Trotter to Clegg, f.54. See also Trotter to Clegg, 11 Jan. 1923, f.56.
88 BoE; G3/179, Norman to Fukai, 22 May 1923.
89 Sayers, (1976), I, p. 204.
90 For example, J. A. C. Osborne, Assistant Chief Cashier, and E. N. Dalton of the Chief Cashier's Department, Bank of England, visited the Federal Reserve Bank of New York during early spring 1923. See BoE; G3/179, Trotter to Jay, 14 Mar. 1923.
91 BoE; OV28/62, F. W. R. Laverack, 'Outline of the general scheme for the rehabilitation of Austria with special reference to the part played by the Bank of England (Apr. 1927); Clay, (1957), pp. 179-90; N. Pietri, (1970), *La Société des Nations et la reconstruction financiere de l'Autriche 1921-1926*, Geneva; Sayers, (1976), I, pp. 163-71; Orde, (1990), pp. 123-9.
92 See A. Orde, (1991), 'Baring Brothers, the Bank of England, the British government and the Czechoslovak state loan of 1922', *English Historical Review*, 106 and Péteri, (1995), pp. 68-9.
93 H. Kernbauer, (1988), *Das Österreichische Noteninstitut*, 3.1, *1923 bis 1938, Währungspolitik in der Zwischenkriegszeit*, Vienna.
94 See M. Mitzakis, (1925), *Le relèvement financier de la Hongrie et la Société des Nations*, Paris; League of Nations, (1926), *The financial reconstruction of Hungary. General survey and principal documents*, Geneva.
Hungarian inflation during the first half of the 1920s is treated by G. Ránki, 'Inflation in Hungary', in N. Schmukler & E. Marcus (eds), (1983), *Inflation through the ages: economic, social, pyschological and historical aspects*, New York; E. A. Borross, 'The role of the state issuing bank in the course of inflation in Hungary between 1918 and 1924', in G. Feldman et al., (1984), *The experience of inflation: international and comparative studies*, Berlin; Á. Pogány, (1987/8), 'Két Szempont a Magyarországi infláció vizgálatához (1914-1924)', *Történelmi Szemle*; P. L. Siklos, 'Interpreting a change in monetary policy regimes: a reappraisal of the first Hungarian hyperinflation and stabilisation, 1921-28', in M. D. Bordo & F. Capie, (1994), *Monetary regimes in transition*, Cambridge.
95 The various roles of Britain, and of the Bank of England, in Hungarian stabilisation have already been treated by Clay, *Norman*, pp.190-2; Sayers, *Bank*, 1, pp. 171-3; Orde, (1990), pp. 266-74; G. Péteri, (1984), 'Tying up a loose end. British foreign economic strategy in 1924. The Hungarian stabilization', *Acta Historica*, 30; idem., (1985), '"Montagu Norman és a Magyar szanallási mü." Az 1924- ós Magyar pénzügyi stabilizaciórol', *Századok*, 1.
96 Orde, (1990), pp. 267-8.
97 Quoted in Péteri, (1995), p. 78.
98 BoE; G3/179, Norman to Sir J. Bradbury, 28 Apr. 1923.

99 BoE; ADM 34/12, entry 10 May 1923.
100 BoE; G3/179, Norman to Clegg, 26 May 1923.
101 Orde, (1990), p.268.
102 League of Nations, (1926), p. 11.
103 BoE; G3/179, Norman to Gaspard Farrer [Baring Brothers], 25 May 1923.
104 BoE; ADM 34/12, entries 25 Jun. 1923.
105 BoE; G3/179, Norman to Niemeyer, 7 Jun. 1923.
106 BoE; G3/179, Norman to Eyre Crowe, 27 Jun. 1923.
107 BoE; ADM 34/12, entries, 5, 11, & 12 Jul. 1923. Norman noted on 5 Jul. that: 'Benes is free to come to London - but the City takes no part in his domestic politics and is not ready to take future loans.'
108 BoE; G3/180 Norman to Siepmann, 14 Jun. 1924.
109 BoE; G3/179, Norman to Niemeyer, 23 Oct. 1923.
110 Janssen (Belgium), Bianchini (Italy), Parmentier (France), Pospisil (Czechoslovakia), Sekiba (Kingdom of the Serbs, Croats and Slovenes), and Ter Meulen (the Netherlands).
111 League of Nations, (1926), p. 13.
112 BoE; ADM 34/12, entry 9 Nov. 1923.
113 BoE; ADM 34/12, entry 20 Nov. 1923.
114 BoE; ADM 34/12, entry 21 Nov. 1923.
115 BoE; ADM 34/12, entries 22 & 26 Nov., 1923.
116 BoE; ADM 34/12, entry 29 Nov. 1923.
117 League of Nations, (1926), p. 13.
118 BoE; G3/180, Norman to Kindersley, 14 Jan. 1924.
119 BoE; G3/179, Norman to Niemeyer, 7 Dec. 1923.
120 BoE; G14/108 [Extracts from the Committee of Treasury], Hungary 1, 1924-, 9 Jan.1924.
121 BoE; G3/180, Norman to Niemeyer, 10 Jan. 1924.
122 BoE; G3/180, Norman to Baron Bruno Schröder, 11 Jan. 1924. On the question of setting a precedent see also ADM 34/13, entry 16 Jan. 1924.
123 BoE; ADM 34/13, entry 15 Jan. 1924.
124 BoE; ADM 34/13, entry 16 Jan. 1924.
125 BoE; ADM 34/13, entries 11, 16 Jan. 1924.
126 BoE; ADM 34/13, entry 31 Jan. 1924.
127 BoE; ADM 34/13, entry 11 Jan. 1924.
128 BoE; G3/180, Norman to Salter, 24 Jan. 1924.
129 BoE; ADM 34/13, entry 23 Jan. 1924.
130 BoE; G14/108, Memorandum, private, 23 Jan. 1924.
131 BoE; ADM 34/13, entries 31 Mar., 2 Apr. 1924. The League of Nations Union had been established in 1918 through the amalgamation of two pacifist organisations. Over the 1920s it became a popular movement so that its membership reached over 400,000 in 1931. See Boyce, (1987), p. 26.
132 League of Nations, (1926), pp. 13-4.

133 BoE; G14/108, 5 Mar. 1923.
134 BoE; ADM 34/13 entry 1 Apr. 1924; G14/108, 2 Apr. 1924.
135 BoE; G3/180, Norman to Strakosch, 16 Apr. 1921.
136 BoE; ADM 34/13 entries 1, 5 May 1924.
137 BoE; G14/180, 7 May 1924; Snowden to Norman, 7 May 1924.
138 BoE; G3/180, Norman to Vissering, 12 May 1924. Norman's emphasis.
139 BoE; ADM 34/13, entry 14 May 1924.
140 BoE; ADM 34/13 entry 6 May 1924.
141 BoE; ADM 34/13 entries 7, 8 May 1924.
142 BoE; ADM 34/13 entry 12 May 1924.
143 BoE; G3/180, Norman to Leese, 15 May 1924.
144 BoE; ADM 34/13, entry 19 May 1924.
145 BoE; ADM; 34/13, entries 26, 27, May 1924.
146 BoE; G14/108, 28 May 1924.
147 BoE; ADM; 34/13, entry 29 May 1924.
148 BoE; G3/180, Norman to Moll, Riksbank, 5 Jun. 1924.
149 BoE; G14/108, Snowden to Norman, 29 May 1924.
150 *A Magyar Nemzeti Bank Története*, 1, *Az Osztrák Nemzeti Banktól a Magyar Nemzeti Bankig 1816-1924* (Budapest, 1994).
151 BoE; ADM 34/13, entries 30 May, 3, 4, 12 Jun. 1924. See also G3/180, Norman to Neimeyer, 5 Jun. 1924.
152 BoE; OV 33/37 [Hungary], 14 Jun. 1924, f.2A.
153 The law for this new institution had been passed on 17 April, promulgated on 26 April and the Bank acquired its capital two days later. The Bank's articles required that $\frac{5}{6}$ths of its capital was held abroad and the markets of Amsterdam, London, New York and Zürich each took 10 million H. crowns. In addition the Banca Commerciale had a holding of $100,000 through the Hungarian-Italian Bank. See BoE; OV 33/37, Siepmann to Norman, 13 Aug. 1924, f.29; 28 Aug. 1924, f.39.
154 BoE; OV 33/37, 14 Jun. 1924, f.3.
155 BoE; G3/180, Norman to Siepmann, 14 Jun. 1924.
156 BoE; ADM 34/13 entry 31 May 1924.
157 BoE; G3/180, Norman to Moll, 5 Jun 1924.
158 BoE; G3/180, Norman to Vissering, 12 Jun 1924.
159 BoE; ADM 34/13. entry, 12 Jun 1924; G3/180, Norman to Stringher, 12 Jun. 1924.
160 Ultimately a guilder tranche was issued: see BoE; ADM 34/13, entries 13, 16, Jun. 1924; G3/180, Norman to Vissering, 25 Jun. 1924.
161 BoE; ADM 34/13, entry 18 Jun. 1924.
162 BoE; G3/180, Norman to Nathan, 16 Jun. 1924.
163 BoE; G3/180, Norman to Robineau, 19 Jun. 1924.
164 Orde, (1990), p. 273.
165 BoE; ADM 34/13, entries 19, 24, 27 Jun. 1924.

166 BoE; ADM 34/13, entries 28, 30 Jun. 1924. The Bank of England underwrote £2m of the issue on behalf of Popovics and the embryonic National Bank of Hungary. See G3/180 Norman to A. de Rothschild, 30. Jun. 1924; ADM 34/13, entry 1 Jul. 1924.

167 BoE; ADM 34/13, entry 1 Jul. 1924.
According to League of Nations, (1926), p. 220, part of the loan - £1,733,606 - was issued in the United States on 3 Jul. 1924.
The other tranches were:

Great Britain:	£7,902,700	2 Jul. 1924
Netherlands:	£433,605	4 Jul. 1924
Sweden:	£280,772	4 Jul. 1924
Italy:	£1,696,864	10 Jul. 1924
Switzerland:	£1,226,996	9 Jul. 1924
Czechoslovakia:	£568,845	Aug. 1924
Hungary:	£543,495	Aug. 1924

168 BoE; G3/180, Norman to Strakosch, 16 Apr. 1924; Norman to Moll, 8 May 1924.

169 BoE; G3/180, Norman to Strakosch, 23 May, 2, 4 Jun. 1924; Norman to Moll, 2 Jun. 1924.

170 *Who was who*, (1972), VI, *1961-1970,* London, p. 1032.

171 BoE; OV33/37, Siepmann to Norman, 24 Sep. 1924, f.52[A].

172 BoE; ADM 34/13, entries, 17, 18, Jul. 1924; OV33/37, Siepmann to Norman, 10 Jul. 1924, f.19[a].

173 Within two months, and after getting Jeremiah Smith's agreement, Norman was suggesting that Siepmann should come to London 'for a few days and talk some of your points out'. Siepmann protested that it would involve a long and expensive journey, which would cost him time and the National Bank money, which he further emphasised by stating 'I particularly don't want to be an unnecessary expensive luxury to the Bank'. By late November 1924 Norman had seven unanswered letters from Siepmann on his desk. BoE; OV33/37, Norman to Siepmann, 26 Sep. 1924, f.55; Siepmann to Norman, 30 Sep. 1924, f.55[A]; 'National Bank of Hungary' 27 Nov. 1924, f.101.

174 BoE; OV33/37, f.25[A].

175 BoE; OV33/37, Siepmann to Norman, 1 Aug. 1924, f.27.

176 BoE; OV33/37, Siepmann to Norman, 28 Aug. 1924, f.39.

177 BoE; ADM 34/9, entry 25 Nov. 1920.

178 BoE; OV33/37, Memorandum, Popovics, 8 Oct. 1924.

179 BoE; OV33/37, Memorandum, J. A. C. Osborne, National Bank of Hungary, 8 Oct. 1924.

180 BoE; OV33/37, Strakosch to Siepmann, 20 Oct. 1924, f.70.

181 BoE; OV33/37, Memorandum, Temporary borrowing by central banks [probably written by Strakosch], dated Oct. 1924, f.69.

182 BoE; OV33/37 Siepmann to Norman, 31 Oct. 1924, f.77.

183 BoE; OV33/37, Nov. 1924, f.86.

184 BoE; OV33/37, 'National Bank of Hungary', 26 Nov. 1924, f.96[C].
185 BoE; OV33/37, 'National Bank of Hungary', 25 Nov. 1924, f. 96[B].
186 BoE; OV33/37, Norman to Popovics, 28 Nov. 1924.
187 BoE; ADM 34/12, entry 4 Dec. 1924.
188 BoE; G3/177, Norman to Strong, 3 May 1921.
189 Guildhall Library, London: papers of A. Gibbs & Sons, merchant banker 3; MS. 11036/3, H. H. Gibbs' private letter book, III, to William Gibbs, 4 Dec. 1863.
190 BoE; OV 37/21, Strakosch to Clegg, 24 Oct. 1924.

CHAPTER FOUR

The relationship between the Bank of Poland and the government during the interwar period

Z. Landau

In any modern country, there are two authorities responsible for the direction of monetary policy - on one side, the treasury or ministry of finance and, on the other, the central bank. This was the situation in interwar Poland although, from 1929, if not from 1926, the respective positions and roles of the Ministry of Finance and the Bank of Poland in policy-formation changed substantially.

The formulation of monetary policy by two centres of expertise constitutes the norm in all capitalist countries and gives rise to advantages and disadvantages. The existence of two, parallel decision-making centres might improve the execution of policy to a greater extent than in an over-centralized system which, by its constitution, possibly lacks institutional safeguards against the taking of unduly biased decisions. It should be borne in mind that ministry of finance officials, by the very nature of their institution and its position within the state's administration, feel more responsible for implementing fiscal policy as opposed to securing the goals of monetary policy. Therefore, during periods of budget deficits, these civil servants might be more inclined to give a higher priority to the aims indicated by budgetary expenditure than to maintaining fiscal stability as the appropriate domestic context for the currency. Consequently, the ministry of finance may attempt, and on more than one occasion, to finance state expenditures, not covered by regular budget revenues, through issuing additional currency. For their part, central bank officials place considerably more emphasis on maintaining a stable currency because the central bank, again by its very nature, approaches macro-economic policy primarily from its monetary aspect as opposed to the goals indicated by state expenditure. It should also be remembered that the innate interests of the two centres formulating and managing monetary policy may differ, which is why each strives to secure a strong overall position - to enable the execution of that policy which its officials consider the most appropriate.

During the first years of independent Poland, the Ministry of Finance was paramount, with the central bank, the Polska Krajowa Kasa Pozyczkowa [Polish National Loan Bank] dependent upon its instructions. As this bank was state-owned, the Ministry held a decisive position within monetary policy formation, which led to the central bank being only an executor of policy guidelines formulated elsewhere. The situation changed in 1924 with the establishment of a new central bank, the Bank Polski S.A. [Bank of Poland]. This was founded as private, joint stock company in which the state initially held only one per cent of the share capital. The new central bank conducted its own monetary policy which, although it complied with the government's main objectives, none the less differed essentially with regard to many aspects of execution.

Within the Ministry of Finance of interwar Poland, the monetary circulation department was responsible for carrying out the country's monetary policy; its tasks included, among others, responsibility for the currency and public loans etc. The state treasury also played a role in the provision of loans to meet the needs of the domestic economy as well as performing supervisory activities (such as controlling usury).[1] In these circumstances, the establishment of proper relations between the Ministry of Finance and the central bank was a matter of great importance.

After the First World War banking theorists in Poland were divided. Some, including Stanislaw Karpinski, the Minister of Finance, saw merit in establishing a central bank of issue as a state-owned institution, whereas others preferred a central bank constituted as a private, joint stock company. Karpinski, in his draft statutes for a central bank which were submitted to parliament in May 1919, stipulated that the bank would be state-owned. The project was approved, but the projected bank was not established. In 1924, Wladyslaw Grabski, Prime Minister and Minister of Finance, decided to create a privately-owned central bank thereby taking the first step that led to the foundation of the Bank of Poland. He was anxious to protect the projected central bank against the undue influence of the Ministry of Finance in particular and of the government in general, a situation that might arise if the institution was state-owned. Grabski was especially concerned about pressures exerted for increasing the note issue and caused by the treasury seeking to meet demands for low interest-bearing loans for budgetary purposes etc. This had been precisely the situation of the previous central bank - the Polish National Loan Bank - whose policies and actions, through being a state-owned institution, had been largely determined by the Ministry of Finance. The Ministry had utilized this bank to implement its monetary policy, which consisted of financing the greater part of state expenditure by printing money.

More generally, international financial opinion during the first half of the 1920s largely favoured the creation of central banks as private joint stock companies. Both the Brussels (1920) and the Genoa (1922) international conferences recommended that central banks should be independent of state treasuries. Within Poland, the conception of a central bank as a private institution was supported by influential business circles which, with their outlook, were afraid of the state machine gaining an undue supremacy in economic life.

The statutes of the Bank of Poland approved on 20 January 1924 established the bank's relationship with the state,[2] especially with regard to several key issues. Article 12 stipulated that resolutions passed by general meetings of shareholders for increasing the Bank's share capital required the Finance Minister's approval. Article 15 laid down that the Bank's President and Deputy President were to be appointed by the President of the Republic of Poland while Article 35 specified the necessary procedures, with proposals for appointments being submitted through the Prime Minister. Article 37 was concerned with the procedure for dismissing the Bank's President. The Bank President would be required to resign by the President of the Republic on a motion from the Cabinet detailing the circumstances. Reasons for resignation included the Bank President not fulfilling his duties; or being unable to undertake his post; or combining his presidency with other offices, such as parliamentary membership, a paid state or a local authority position, a private appointment or membership of either the managerial or supervisory boards of a corporate business enterprise, or of a private business partnership. If the Bank President contravened the stipulations of Article 37 then, following an approach from the Ministry of Finance, the Cabinet was to appoint a special commission. This was to consist of three members, with each nominated by a different constitutional office: the Minister of Finance, the First President of the Supreme Court and the First President of the Supreme Administrative Tribunal. The Cabinet's motion for dismissal had to be based on the commission's statement of findings. The 1924 law also set down the procedures for appointing and removing the Bank's deputy president.

Furthermore, in terms of the relationship of the Bank with the state, Article 26 of the statutes of the Bank of Poland gave the Minister of Finance the ability to oppose the appointment of any member of the Bank's Council, or their deputies, within three days following elections to this body. Appointments to the Bank's board, made by the Council, required the confirmation of the Minister of Finance (Article 43). Moreover, the Minister of Finance had to ratify within three days the Bank President's decision to suspend the resolutions of the Council (Article 38). The Bank President was obliged to submit monthly reports on the Bank's activities to the Minister of Finance, whereas contact between the Minister and the Bank was ensured through the office of the Commissioner appointed by the Minister of Finance. The Commissioner could participate in meetings of the Council and the Board of Directors of the Bank in an advisory capacity, as well as require explanations of the activities and the current situation from the Bank's authorities (Article 39). Accordingly, the Commissioner was able to determine the timing of the obligatory replacement of the Bank's notes by gold, which was to be initiated by the Bank's senior management (Article 47), and ratified the resolutions of the Bank's Council regarding the nominal value of bank notes (Article 48).

The statutes also stated that the Bank, in return for receiving from the state the privilege of note-issuing for twenty years, was obliged to grant interest free loans, of up to 50 million zlotys in amount, to the government

(Article 52). Moreover, the Bank was required, on the request of the Minister of Finance, to receive and undertake, free of charge, payments for the account of the treasury. If the Bank lost its note-issuing rights, or if it was to be liquidated before its concession expired, the treasury had the right, by Article 80, to take-over, by the enactment of a special law, whole or a part of the Bank of Poland at its total balance sheet value as verified by the Ministry of Finance.

Article 90 specified the procedures for settling disputes between the government and the Bank of Poland:

> Any conflicts arising between the government and the Bank, resulting from application of these Statutes and the privileges granted by them, are to be settled finally by the Commission of Arbitration to the exclusion of any further legal steps. The Commission consists of the president of the Supreme Court and four members (of which two are appointed by the Prime Minister and two by the Council of the Bank). The Commission of Arbitration takes its decisions by simple majority of votes after giving prior hearing to the representatives of the Government and the Council of the Bank. In case of equal number of votes, the president has the casting vote. The Commission of Arbitration is not bound by any regulations for its activities, but is obliged to justify its sentence.

As can be seen, even from this short review, the power of the state administration with respect to the Bank of Poland was quite substantial despite the Bank having been constituted as a private company. Moreover, the scope of state's power could be extended further through the provisions of Article 93. This addressed the situation of the government having to increase its holding in the Bank's share capital due to it not having proved possible to distribute 600,000 shares, sixty per cent of the total, among individuals and private institutions. This all shows that, when Grabski established the Bank as a private joint stock company, he wanted none the less to secure a dominant influence for the state authorities in the membership of the Bank's managing board and in some areas of its activities.

Shortly after the Bank's creation, divisions developed between the Minister of Finance and the Bank's senior management. Before the first General Meeting of shareholders, convened to elect members of the first Council, Prime Minister Grabski met delegates of the different groups that made up the Bank's proprietary and came to an agreement regarding the representation of their various interests. There were twelve posts for Council members and three posts for deputies to be filled by election. In his memoirs Grabski wrote:

> as usual, every organisation wanted to have as many representatives as possible. Finally, I could not come to an agreement with the farmers, who, although had paid much less than 1/12 of the capital, wanted to have 2/12 seats. On the other hand, the officialdom and clerks paid together with co-operatives and the government almost more than 3/12, and therefore I booked three seats for those circles together with the government.[3]

At the General Meeting, a combination of the representatives of the landed gentry and of large-scale industry were able to carry their own list for Council membership. These nominations had not been previously agreed with Grabski. Instead of supporting a candidate backed by the Minister of Finance, the group formed by landed and industrial interests obtained the election of a further representative and, moreover, secured the election of three deputies from amongst their own candidates. This occurred despite Grabski having declared at the meeting that he would not agree to any nomination that he had not previously approved. Consequently, Grabski withheld his necessary agreement to the outcome of the Council elections and this was the only instance in the Bank of Poland's history when Minister of Finance vetoed the elections undertaken by the General Meeting.

In June 1924, at the next General Meeting, Grabski gave permission for the nomination of candidates that he had previously opposed - a de facto defeat of the Prime Minister and Minister of Finance. However, 'all subsequent by-elections were carried out only after agreement upon the candidate between the Bank and the Ministry'.[4]

This conflict over membership was not just a matter of personal prestige and public standing, as Grabski was anxious that the Bank's Council included representatives of interest groups closely allied with his government. The elections had provided some basis for such a linkage through the success of three Council members, as well as three deputies, which had his backing. However, in practice, it transpired that generally the Council had little cohesion since its members represented interests which were too diverse. As a result the Council was generally unable to agree upon ideas and guidelines acceptable to all its members. Although the Council felt responsible for the co-ordination of economic and monetary policy between the government and the Bank of Poland, its lack of consensus led to the situation that 'when any differences occurred which pertained to the parts of that policy, the Council yielded up to the postulates of the government and - beside the episode of 1924 - no conflicts arose between the Council of the Bank and the Ministry of Finance'.[5]

Yet, a greater uniformity of views between the dominant interest group within the Bank's Council and the Ministry of Finance may have been possible after the May 1926 coup d'état, when Jósef Pilsudski seized the power. Representatives of large-scale capital and the landed gentry within the Bank's Council established a very close relationship with the political regime, and also tried to avoid conflicts when they were a weaker party. At the same time, those acting on behalf of the Bank's small shareholders, who had been promoted by Grabski, withdrew from the Council and were replaced by leading businessmen. These new Council members included Andrzej Wierzbicki, managing director of the Centralny Zwiazek Przemyslu Polskiego [Central Union of Polish Industry]; Waclaw Fajans, president of the Zwiazek Bank6w Polskich [Union of Banks in Poland]; and Stanislaw Lubomirski, president of Bank Handlowy w Warszawie S.A. [Bank of Commerce in Warsaw S.A.]. Within the Council of the Bank of Poland, a microcosm of Polish economic life, small shareholders' representation declined, being replaced by that of business interests.

When Stanislaw Karpinski was the President of the Bank between 1924 and 1929, he endeavoured to pursue his own policy and attempted to protect the Bank's interests, even if this provoked conflict with the Minister of Finance. Tension between the Bank President and the Minister became very evident from summer 1925, when the government, facing an increasing budget deficit, began to meet state expenditures by an excessive issue of coinage. Bank officials, having decided that this might imperil the cover for the Bank's notes, refused to sell foreign currency for coins. These difficulties became greater at the end of July 1925 when, with a rapidly shrinking foreign exchange reserve, the Bank was forced to restrict the amount of foreign currencies sold on the foreign exchange market of the stock exchange. None the less, initially, Prime Minister Grabski demanded that the zloty's foreign exchange rate was maintained, but in August, following pressure from the Bank, was forced to give way.

This dispute between the government and the Bank also involved the methods used for sustaining the exchange rate of the Polish currency. Grabski required the Bank to intervene on the Warsaw stock exchange - to purchase zlotys with foreign exchange and hard currencies - and to follow a similar policy on foreign markets. This led to a rapid decline in the Bank's reserves, so much so that it threatened the cover for the note circulation and, therefore, Bank officials soon concluded that the policy was purposeless and, moreover, imicable to the Bank's interests. After a sharp decrease in reserves during the first ten days of November 1925, Karpinski refused to continue the support for the zloty's exchange rate. Although the Prime Minister pressurized the Bank, this was to no avail and, consequently, he sought the President of the Republic's arbitration. At the specially convened meeting, the President supported Grabski but was unable to convince Karpinski, who remained resolute in his opposition against continuing foreign exchange support operations. Karpinski's adamant stance led to the resignation of the Grabski Cabinet - one of very few known instances when a president of the central bank has caused a government's fall. This dispute also proved to be the apogee of the Bank of Poland's independence from the government. Thereafter, the Bank's freedom of action became increasingly restricted, step by step, although, even at the end of Karpinski's term of office in 1929, he still was struggling to sustain an independent role for the Bank.

The policy of Grabski's successors at the Ministry of Finance vis-a-vis the central bank consisted of presenting the Bank's senior management with decisions, as opposed to developed proposals for consideration and comment. For instance, in late 1925, the new Minister of Finance, Jerzy Zdziechowski, decided not to attempt to return to the zloty's foreign exchange parity of April 1924 but rather to initiate the so-called 'economic parity'. This was simply presented to the Bank as a firm decision. It is possible that this new relationship between Bank and Ministry arose from mutual personal and economic interests as the majority of influential members within the Bank's Council were now linked in various ways with business, while Zdziechowski was a leading entrepreneur. This common background may explain the lack of strong resistance displayed within the Bank towards the ideas of the new Minister of Finance.

Zdziechowski's concept for the Bank's development comprised an attempt to mount a policy of increasing its capital through issuing new shares overseas. This differed very greatly from Grabski, who had firmly opposed the Bank of Poland having foreign shareholders. Feliks Mlynarski, Deputy President of the Bank of Poland, twice went to London during autumn 1925, seeing, among others, Montagu Norman, Governor of the Bank of England. At the outset, it was thought that Norman was very much ill-disposed towards Poland, because of his close co-operation with Germany, but Mlynarski's discussions with the Governor of the Bank of England led to the possibility of British investment in the Bank of Poland. This outcome was placed on the agenda of the Bank of Poland's Council in December 1925, but the arising discussion produced no unanimity. In the end, despite Karpinski's verment opposition, agreement was reached for either Mlynarski or Konstanty Skirmunt, the Polish envoy in London, to clarify whether the Bank of England was prepared to indicate a financial group for undertaking a new issue of shares on behalf of the Bank of Poland. If the Bank of England agreed, then the Council of the Bank of Poland would invite a representative of either Norman or the group that he had nominated to come to Poland to examine the situation and discuss terms and conditions.[6]

The question of the Bank of Poland acquiring foreign capital was very seriously considered within Poland. Although there proved to be no English interest in the proposal, none the less Ministers of Finance continued to attempt to establish the conditions necessary for foreign interests to take an equity stake in the Bank of Poland. This, for example, led to a change in Bank's statutes in August 1926, which enabled its capital to be raised to 150 million zlotys. Moreover, Mlynarski returned to London to once more sound out Norman, but the Governor of the Bank of England continued to remain disinterested in the Polish government's intentions. In all this, the Bank of Poland was only an executor of government policy - its role was simply that of carrying out decisions.

After Pilsudski's May 1926 coup d'état, the Bank's role in the execution of monetary policy became very limited. The leading position was taken by the Ministry of Finance, with its officials preparing all the strategy required for the whole scope of monetary policy.

During autumn 1926 representatives of the Minister of Finance initiated talks for the issue of a Polish loan on the American market. Mlynarski, Deputy President of the Bank of Poland, was involved, but

> he was rather acting as a representative of the government, not of the Bank. The president of the Bank was not kept informed about all the details of the talks on a current basis and, according to the opinion of some members of the Council, behaved with much reserve towards the negotiations.[7]

The President was not the only person who was kept on the side lines, because members of the Bank's Council were only informed as and when it was necessary to have the formal approval of this body to enable the implementation of the government's loan policy. One Council member, a representative of the interests of the small shareholders, submitted, on behalf of a minority within the Council, a statement to be attached to the minutes. This commented, among other things, that 'facing the Bank of Poland with the accomplished facts concerning the matters which directly pertain to the Bank is against the basic principles of the Bank'.[8] It was a matter of fundamental importance.

The greater power possessed by the hand of the government became evident with its stabilization plan.[9] This was prepared during 1927 in co-operation with foreign banks which were to supply a stabilization loan for the zloty. It contained a provision for a representative of foreign capital to have a place on the Bank's Council as the financial advisor to the government. It is worth noting that, initially, the overseas interests required four seats on the Council - for an American and a British representative and the representatives of two neutral countries. The foreign representative was to publish a quarterly report on all his activities with a commentary, so producing public statements which would carry great authority with foreign investors.[10] Such a new Council member would automatically acquire an insight into all essential materials pertaining to the Bank, while he would also be able to influence the direction of its activities to some extent. It was difficult to predict how the foreign member of the Council might shape the Bank of Poland's conduct, but, even in this very essential matter, the Bank's senior management was not consulted.

A similar situation arose with regard to the question of making the Bank of Poland's notes convertible into gold. This raised considerable anxiety.

> There were no doubts against introducing the principle as itself into the Statutes. But the Council of the Bank considered it necessary to add some safety valve to such a strict resolution; in that connection,

> in the first draft version of the amendments to the Statutes passed by the Council of the Bank there was a statement saying that 'the obligation of exchange may be suspended in a legislative way'.

This amendment was opposed by the American bankers, who considered that it could weaken the most important principle of the whole plan which was to establish full confidence in the absolute stability of zloty. As a result the safety-valve rider was omitted from the final version.[11]

It can be seen from these developments that the government, even at the final stages of the planning for the stabilization of the zloty, failed to acknowledge the statutory rights of the Bank's management. This attitude arose from, on the one hand, the clear tendency of the Pilsudski camp to try and gain the centralisation of power within their hands. On the other, the President of the Bank of Poland was an opponent of the new leading political group, a marked stance which, to some extent, may have led to the Bank's opinion being neither sought nor considered. This observation is supported by available archival material. Three weeks after the approval of the stabilization plan in October 1927, Pilsudski spoke at the cabinet meeting which discussed changes in the central bank's statutes. He declared that he would propose, at the proper time, further amendments in order to give the government greater influence over the Bank's management. Pilsudski was seeking to ensure that the Bank President was obliged to submit monthly reports to the President of the Republic. Furthermore, he wanted changes in the procedures for dismissing the Bank President and Deputy-President so that all that was required would be a cabinet resolution as opposed to invoking the special commission stipulated in the 1924 statutes.[12]

It should be noted that the stabilization plan was based upon quite different views regarding the Bank's independence to those held by Pilsudski. The plan's basic principle was that the Bank should be fully independent of influence from the state administration. Gabriel Czechowicz, Minister of Finance, pointed this out to Pilsudski, emphasizing that the stabilization plan stipulated the Bank's autonomy through, as in the statutes of all central banks, the inviolable position of the Bank President. He also added, in terms of securing the government's proper influence over the Bank's activities, that this was possible on the basis of existing statutes 'provided only that the president of the Bank wants to co-operate loyally with the Minister of Finance, which, unfortunately, cannot be said about the current president of the Bank of Poland'.[13] But Pilsudski did not relent; he only agreed to postpone the introduction of the changes that he desired in the Bank's statutes until the stabilization plan's timetable expired in October 1930. But when so unfettered, he intended to use the occasion to 'fill the posts in the Bank of Poland with some people who would carry out the policy of the Bank also in the interest of the government'.[14]

Furthermore, Pilsudski opposed the resale of 50 million zlotys of Bank of Poland shares, which had been temporarily acquired by the government in accordance with the guidelines of the stabilization plan. Their transfer was the subject of a separate agreement concluded between Czechowicz, the Minister of Finance, and Bank President Karpinski. 'Reasoning of the Commander [Pilsudski] is as follows: an arrangement between Czechowicz and Karpinski obliging the sale of the shares of the Bank of Poland is considered by the Commander to be not binding on him'.[15] Pilsudski opposed the arising private sale of the shares as he wanted to make the Bank closely dependent upon the government. He argued that it was necessary to

> wait for the moment, when the advisor was to end his term of office, and then fight a battle for tighter dependence of the Bank of Poland on the government in spite of the American tendencies, and one must have the shares in the hands of the government at that moment, in order to use that as an argument and weapon for the purpose.[16]

As can be gathered from the above, the relationship between the Bank and the government was very uneasy after May 1926. The government's aim of subordinating the position of the Bank of Poland in the formation of macro-economic policy was not achieved between 1927 and 1929 solely due to the right of objection held by Charles Dewey, the government's financial advisor and foreign member of the Bank Council. This, in turn, gave rise to misgivings on the part of the government but, because of the situation arising from the stabilization plan, strife between the government and the Bank was postponed. Yet, the idea of the government gaining greater influence continued to be considered, although the Bank attempted not to fan the flames of conflict.

However, the situation exploded in April 1929, just after Karpinski's tenure of the presidency of the Bank had come to an end. The Prime Minister was concerned that the Bank should not increase its discount rate, since this would cause public difficulties for the new cabinet. The Bank's arising conflict with the government was described by Mlynarski, the Bank's Deputy President, in the following terms:

> I made it clear to the Council that the severe outflow of foreign exchange, which was still increasing, had to be halted, and that the rise of discount rate was the necessary means. I added that it would also be in the interests of the new cabinet to stop the outflow of foreign currency, because its scale gave rise to the anxiety on the market. The Council unanimously passed the rise.[17]

After a few days, Mlynarski was summoned by the Prime Minister, who told him that 'in the future such disregard of the will of the government should not occur again'.[18]

With the unfolding of events, it proved that there was no need to wait upon the expiry of the stabilization plan's timetable in order to increase the state's influence over the Bank. A possibility occurred as early as April 1929, with Karpinski's departure, followed by the completion of Deputy President Mlynarski's tenure. This gave the government the possibility of filling these two key posts with rather different personalities. The new President was Wladyslaw Wróblewski, previously Polish ambassador in London and Washington and who had no prior banking experience. According to widespread opinion, Wróblewski 'did not present any independent views on essential matters of the Bank, but became rather an executor of the wishes of the government and the Minister of Finance'.[19] In autumn 1932 Józef Pilsudski's brother, Jan, was appointed Deputy President; he was a lawyer and had had no previous involvement with banking. Consequently, the Bank's new leadership was not fitted to provide competent management, but instead the backgrounds of the President and the Deputy President guaranteed the Bank's full submission to the guidelines of the Ministry of Finance, which thereby acquired undisputed leadership in the execution of monetary policy. The Bank's only function in practice was undertaking the government's policy.

The executor of the new situation was Leon Baranski, the Bank Commissioner, who subsequently in 1932 became the Bank's deputy managing director and, in 1934, managing director. Furthermore, during the first half of the 1930s the board of directors came to constitute the real management and decision-making centre within the Bank, whereas the Bank's President and Deputy President were only figureheads.

Wróblewski left the Bank in February 1936, after a seven-year term of office, and was succeeded by Adam Koc, who was one of the leading personalities in the post-Pilsudski camp. Koc had been Deputy Minister of Finance for three years and had linked this government post with that of the Bank Commissioner, thereby obtaining knowledge and understanding of the Bank of Poland's problems and thinking. His leading political role created a potential for restoring the Bank of Poland's independence. It seems that Koc had plans in this direction, possibly to the extent that he intended to confront the policy of Eugeniusz Kwiatkowski, appointed Finance Minister in October 1935, who was also a confident of President Ignacy Moscicki.

Conflict between the Bank and the Ministry of Finance arose once more. On 21 April 1936 a consultation session for all the leading personalities in the country was convened by President Moscicki. The merits of devaluing the zloty were discussed, the main proponent of this policy being Koc, but almost all the other participants at the meeting opposed it. Summing up the discussion, Moscicki addressed Koc 'with a demand that he clearly told his staff at the Bank of Poland, with whom he had discussed the idea of devaluation, that this project has not been passed. The President considers devaluation a disaster'.[20]

However, with the rapid outflow of foreign currency reserves and gold from the Bank of Poland yet the Bank lacking permission to devalue, the only solution was to impose foreign exchange controls. These were introduced in April 1936 and Koc tendered his resignation in order to reinforce his protest against this policy. Justifying his decision to the Bank's Council, he said, among other things, that 'for a long time discrepancies could be seen in the views on financial policy between the president [of the Bank of Poland] and the Minister of Finance'.[21] Koc agreed to keep his resignation secret for a while in order that it should not undermine confidence in the government's economic policy. However, his departure from the Bank signified the Minister of Finance's victory, which meant a further submission of the central bank's activities to the Ministry's guidelines. Attempts to restore independence of the Bank had proved to be brief.

Between April 1936 and 1939 the Bank of Poland became more and more dependent upon the government. Its last president following Koc's resignation, Wladyslaw Byrka, possessed no real qualifications for filling the post. According to the distinguished economist Ferdynand Zweig, Minister of Finance Kwiatkowski's appointment of Byrka set such limits to the Bank of Poland's independence with respect to monetary policy and foreign relations that the formation of these policies were almost totally transferred to the Ministry of Finance. In Zweig's words, 'The Bank of Poland became only a submissive tool of the Ministry'.[22]

Bykra's appointment took place when there was a heated debate between supporters of the traditional methods of monetary policy, who argued that bank notes in circulation should be covered by gold, and proponents of moderate inflation. The former group was led by Kwiatkowski and Byrka, while the latter consisted of the military and their allies. At the outset the traditionalists had the upper hand but their opponents slowly gained predominance. As a result, in September 1938, issued notes exceeded the statutory limit and five months later the Bank's statutes were altered to authorise an uncovered note issue of 800 million zlotys and allowed this fiduciary issue to be increased to 1.2 billion zlotys. Resistance to these changes from the Bank's management was very weak, which resulted in, among other things, a stronger and stronger dependence on the part of the Bank upon the state administration.

The expansion of the money supply went hand in hand with increases in the amount of loans granted by the central bank to the state. This was in contradiction to the Bank's statutes where a maximum of 150 million zlotys was stipulated. This ceiling was maintained notionally, but the Bank in practice provided the state with funds on a large scale to finance its investment programme. Between 1931 and 1938 the state's indebtedness to the Bank of Poland, in terms of credits, rose by an additional 515 million zlotys and this financing was only formally approved, *ex post*, by the change in the Bank's statutes in 1939.[23] During the 1930s the Bank granted the government long-term loans on extremely favourable terms, far better than those obtainable on the private credit market. Furthermore, this had the consequence of giving rise to restrictions and limitations on the amount of loans provided for other investment purposes. This change in the behaviour of the central bank was all the result of the total dependence of the Bank of Poland on the Ministry of Finance.

Summing up, it is clear that, in the circumstances of interwar Poland, the founding of the central bank as a private joint stock company failed to secure its independence from the state administration, especially from the supremacy of, and pressure from, the Ministry of Finance. This situation largely arose from the great weakness of private capital within Poland, a frailty that became greater during the Great Depression. The slump forced private capital to seek on-going assistance from the government which consequently militated against any opposition on its part to economic and financial policy. In such circumstances, the Bank of Poland lacked the necessary support in its conflicts with the state authorities. It may be possible to extrapolate this into a more general conclusion that, in a country where private capital is weak, there is little possibility of securing by legal means the independence of the central bank from the state administration.

Another essential factor at work, which caused the weak position of the Bank of Poland vis-a-vis the government, was the political situation after May 1926. The new ruling political group sought to concentrate in their hands all the levers of power with respect to essential political and economic matters. This attitude and objective required, among other things, the submission of the Bank of Poland.

Personnel policy was used to make the Bank submissive to government. By filling critical posts within the Bank with those lacking proper professional qualifications, the Ministry of Finance's ability to gain a dominant position was facilitated. However, even when the Bank was headed by an experienced banker, like Karpinski, government representatives none the less strove to secure the Bank's submission. Karpinski managed to sustain the statutory independence of the Bank for only a short time as, from the close of 1925, the Bank's position was undermined, in a step by step process. This had the consequence that its increasingly circumscribed independence only came into play with respect to minor issues. Consequently, it was not simply a question of the particular characters and personal stances of presidents of the Bank that affected the relationship between the Bank and the government, but, rather, the country's underlying power structure.

Notes

1 B. Markowski, (1931), *Administracja skarbowa w Polsce,* Warsaw.
2 *Statut Banki Polskiego* (1924), Warsaw.
3 W. Grabski, (1927), *Dwa lata pracy u podstaw panstwowosci naszej (1924-1925),* Warsaw, p. 39.
4 Z. Karpinski, (1958), *Bank Polski 1924-1939. Przyczynek do historii gospodarczej okresu miedzywojennego,* Warsaw, p. 19.
5 Karpinski, (1958), p. 212.
6 Archiwum Akjt Nowych w Warszawie [hereafter AANwW]: Bank Polski t.70; Minutes, Meeting of the Council of the Bank of Poland, 16 Dec. 1925.
7 Karpinski, (1958), p. 50.
8 AANwW: Bank Polski t.70; Minutes, Meeting of the Council of the Bank of Poland.
9 J. F. Dulles, (1927), *Polish Stabilization Plan*, New York; and Z. Landau, (1963), *Plan stabilizacyjny 1927-1930,* Warsaw.
10 Compiled reprint of the *Quarterly Reports of the Financial Adviser to the Polish Government,* (1927), Fourth Quarter.
11 Karpinski, (1958), pp. 54-5.
12 AANwW: Protokoly Rady Ministrów t.40, p. 3; Minutes, Cabinet, 5 Nov. 1927.
13 Ibid.
14 AANwW: akta K. Switalskiego t.III, p. 128; Note of the discussions between Prime Minister Kazimierz Switalski, the President of the Republic Ignacy Koscicki, Commander Józef Pilsudski and Minister of Finance Ignacy Matuszewski, 8 Jun. 1929.
15 Ibid., p. 208; Note from the talks between Prime Minister Kazimierz Switalski and Commander Józef Pilsudski, 4 Oct. 1929.
16 Ibid.
17 F. Molynarski, (1972), *Wspomnienia,* Warsaw, p. 335.
18 Karpinski, (1958), p. 210.
19 Ibid.
20 H. Gruber, (1968),*Wspomnienia i uwagi,* London, p. 340.
21 AANwW: Bank Polski t.70; Minutes, Meeting of the Council of the Bank of Poland, 11 May 1936.
22 F. Zweig, (1944), *Poland between Two Wars. A critical study of social and economic changes,* London, p. 113.
23 *Dziennik Ustaw Rzeczypospolitej Polskiej,* (1939), 23, p. 142.

PART II

COMMERCIAL BANKING

CHAPTER FIVE

Bank-Industry networks: the Austrian experience, 1895-1940

Peter Eigner

Economic historians continue to debate the role and influence of banks within the processes of industrialization and economic growth. None the less, agreement has been reached in these scholarly interchanges regarding the establishment of a close relationship between universal banks and industry in central Europe by the close of the nineteenth century. Indeed, there is a consensus that the purest form of universal banking developed within the economy of the Austro-Hungarian Monarchy. It took the form of the major banks pursuing in tandem short-term deposit business with long-term engagements, the latter arising from acting as investors and stockbrokers.[1] Consequently, the period from the closing decades of the Habsburg Monarchy until the forced demise of the first Austrian Republic provides a clear historical example of the mutual interaction between bank and industrial capital, revealing both the positive and negative consequences of this relationship.

From the mid-1890s Viennese banks developed close contacts with manufacturing undertakings on the foundation of their well-established activities as providers of, or intermediaries for, credits. Such business led the banks to convert 'firms with the difficulties and risks of their early years already overcome' and which had 'favourable prospects' into joint stock companies. Moreover, during the fin-de-siècle period, the banks founded *de novo* joint stock companies and directly participated in share issues for established corporate enterprises.[2] The arising influence over industrial capital was frequently further strengthened by the banks' retention of majority shareholdings. While these ever closer links between Austrian banks and manufacturing over the half century after 1890 have often been regarded as having a 'symbiotic' nature, contemporaries considered the banks to be the dominant partner. Indeed, Hilferding developed his theory of *Finanzkapital* [finance capital] upon the premise that the banks had gained supremacy over industry as a result of observing Austrian and German financial developments during the 1900s.[3]

In their dealings with customers, managements of the Viennese 'great' banks tried to secure representation on the boards of directors, either the supervisory board [*Verwaltungsrat*], or the managing board [*Vorstand*], and the executives of industrial joint stock companies [*Direktion*]. The resulting substantial accumulation of industrial directorships by bankers (in some instances up to 50), has featured in historical studies of Austrian economic growth and banking development.[4] However, the stress given in commentaries on this practice has been mainly applied to illustrate and support the continuing assumption that finance capital had the upper hand in bank-industry relationships.[5] Indeed, this view has been so pervasive that, until very recently, a noticeable aspect of the literature was the lack of any empirical analysis. Consequently the banks' dominance is overestimated in the historiography if only because little, or no, distinction has been drawn between the potential given by their position and the actual extent of the influence that they commanded. It was the necessity for a more differentiated approach to bank-industry relationships, which has only come to the fore in some more recent considerations,[6] that constituted the starting point of the research underlying this contribution.

Although it must be recognized that the number of seats on boards of industrial joint-stock companies held by bank directors, or vice-versa, is not in itself decisive, the extent of interlocking directorships set the framework for the analysis of which the results are reported here. The personal relations of the ten largest Viennese commercial banks[7] with industrial joint stock companies constitute the focus of this study of the development of interlockings over the period from the 1900s until the 1930s.

Bank-industry relations, arising from personal connections, can be considered as networks. In the Austrian case, the 'great' Viennese banks collectively formed the centre of the web of links and were surrounded, institution by institution, by, first, a tightly bonded group of 'concern companies' and, second, an outer ring of more loosely related firms. (As will be shown subsequently, individual institutional networks overlapped to some extent since a number of industrial firms had personal links with more than one bank.) In these structures of personal relationships, a bank's industrial sphere of influence in general is mapped out by the extent and pattern of interlocking directorships. But, in order to go further, so as to bring more clearly into focus the closest relationships that the banks had with industrial undertakings, it is necessary to define a 'concern company' of a bank. An enterprise was considered to meet this definition when either a bank representative occupied a leading position within its management or at least three senior members of one bank sat on its board.

This approach to bank-industry relationships was developed, empirically, through compiling a database of the complete networks arising from bank board members' interlocking directorships with industry for four benchmark years: 1908, 1917, 1928 and 1937. Furthermore, it was combined with a longitudinal database of senior bankers over the whole period of investigation.[8] However, the impressive number of interlocking directorships which linked the Viennese universal banks and industry will have a relatively minor significance for historical analysis unless the functions that were exercised in practice by bankers can also be taken into account. Unfortunately, available source material provides little assistance. Yet, considering whether it was possible for a banker to have been an effective 'insider' agent with respect to as many as 40 industrial firms in some cases (through being fully and effectively informed about all their business activities), strongly suggests that there were factors in play which restricted the exercise of bank power. The limits on the time available to a banker for discharging his duties to all his industrial directorships, and the quality of his expertise, are some amongst many of the countervailing forces that may have been at work. In sum, these suggest, *a priori*, important restrictions on the extent of power that a bank might have wielded through the interlocking industrial directorships of its board members, and such constraints have to be continually borne in mind during the following discussion.

The remainder of this contribution consists of three major sections, an epilogue and some general conclusions. The first addresses the new era in the banks' financing of industry, that is the period from 1895 until 1918 in which the results of the analyses of the databases for 1908 and 1917 are considered and compared. The second consists of a discussion of the turbulent 1920s in terms of the changed circumstances that confronted the managements of the Viennese banks and to what extent, to use contemporary phrases, these institutions had either a 'big future' or were misled by a 'beautiful illusion'.[9] This section has two specific themes, namely, first, the impact upon bank-industry links of the nostrification of both parts of the banks' branch networks and their dependent companies, and second, the consequent result of the banks coming to head multi-national concerns, which are considered through the database for 1928. The theme of the third section is the process of 'Austrification' during the 1930s, its outcome being discussed through what is revealed by the database for 1937. This review of the insights yielded by analyses of bank-industry relationships in terms of four benchmark years has an epilogue, forming the fourth section, which briefly considers the major effects of the Anschluß upon Viennese banks. Lastly, some general conclusions are put forward with respect to the crisis in Austrian banking over the period from 1924 until 1934, that is from the collapse of the Depositenbank to the creations of the Creditanstalt-Wiener Bankverein and the Industrie-Credit AG as measures to salvage the system.

The Krach of the Vienna Börse in spring 1873 brought to a close the *Gründerzeit* [the founding years], a period of intense, wild speculation during which the banks had promoted a number of mainly weak industrial companies. The grave nature of this financial collapse led the managements of the Viennese joint stock banks to withdraw almost completely for nearly two decades from company promotion and other corporate operations on the stock exchange. The marked, general retreat from long-term engagements to industry after 1873 shows that bank managements did not continually display a 'missionary' eagerness to further industrialization as has often been stated.[10] Rather, commercial bankers only became once more substantially involved in the finance of industrial investment, including the founding of corporate companies, from the mid-1890s.

The return to medium- and long-term industrial engagements on the part of the banks occurred for very basic reasons. By the closing decade of the century past financial embarrassments had faded from memory while, on the one hand, the profits that the banks derived from issuing government loans had begun to diminish and, on the other, increased competition in the provision of short-term credits had become very evident. Moreover, by supporting manufacturing investment from the mid-1890s, the banks filled a vacuum created by the state's operation of economic and fiscal policies which were hostile towards industry. Legislation continued to hinder the development of an adequate capital market until 1899 when tax reforms were introduced.[11]

From 1904, during an economic upswing which coincided with good harvests, the Austrian universal banks increased their industrial commitments, thereby playing a major role in company promotions, the numbers of which reached peaks during 1905-7 and 1909-11. Such was the extent of the banks' involvement with the finance of manufacturing investment that they came to be called the 'pillars of rapid industrial development'.[12] Furthermore, the policies of bank managements altered with these renewed industrial relationships. Nurturing particular companies was increasingly overshadowed from the mid-1900s by the organisation of whole branches of manufacturing which resulted in the banks establishing impressive industrial concerns [*Industriekonzerne*]. Yet, it must be stressed that the banks' considerable equity interests in companies, and across industrial branches, were sometimes only held on a short-term and temporary basis. Moreover, the banks' involvement was in some cases involuntary, as with the sugar industry. Their forced engagements were brought about by the nature of the Austrian capital market arising from the little, or no, interest displayed by private investors in corporate securities.

The Austrian banks' closer relationships with industry during the fin-de-siècle period had two particular features. One was the establishment of sales departments [*Warenabteilungen*] within the banks' administrative structures, which undertook the sale of concern companies' products, an initiative that began with sugar and coal. The other was the banks' active role in the process of cartelization which got underway from 1896, when bank managements altered their strategies. Increasingly the emphasis was placed upon establishing powerful positions within whole branches of industry and to eliminate disagreeable competitors, rather than on measures concerned with the security of particular industrial involvements.[13] The cartel movement culminated in 1914 with the foundation of the Österreichische Kontrollbank, created jointly by ten Cisleithanian banks as a central institution to supervise and manage cartels and syndicates.

As a result, in 1914, operations of the 'concern companies' of the Viennese banks encompassed all the territories of the Dual Monarchy and Vienna was the undisputed financial centre of the Monarchy and the international transfer point for western capital in the Danube basin. This was in spite of Budapest and especially Prague having important capital markets, whose roles had increased in importance through the rise of national sentiment and consequent ethnic emancipation since the turn of the century.[14]

Data for the first benchmark year, 1908, shows that the board members of the ten banks chosen for analysis had in total 599 interlocking directorships with 307 industrial joint stock companies. In the arising networks, bankers had, by the definitions applied in the analysis, leading positions in the case of 126 companies,[15] while about one third of enterprises linked with the banks fulfilled either definition of a concern company. Through its senior staff having 162 interlocking directorships (27 per cent of all personal relations) with 86 companies, the Österreichische Credit-Anstalt für Handel und Gewerbe was at the fore front of links with industry, followed by the Niederösterreichische Escompte-Gesellschaft which had 96 interlocks with 64 companies. The rest of the centre field was filled out, in rank order, by the Wiener Bank-Verein (78 interlocks with 55 companies), the Österreichische Länderbank (71; 45), the Anglo-Österreichische Bank (68; 41) and the Allgemeine österreichische Boden-Credit-Anstalt (54; 35). The four other institutions investigated - the Unionbank, the Allgemeine Verkehrsbank, the Bank und Wechselstuben-Actien-Gesellschaft 'Mercur' and the Allgemeine Depositenbank (in rank order of number of interlockings) - were 'middle' as opposed to 'great' banks and, moreover, during the mid-1900s were still in the process of establishing their industrial concerns .

An analysis of bank links by industrial branch revealed that those with engineering and metal-working were the most important (88 interlocks), although very closely followed by connections to mining and metallurgy (84). Surprising in an international context, textiles occupied third position (66) and was the only branch where interlocks of all ten banks investigated could be found. This outcome was not anticipated since, globally, textiles was one of a number of industrial branches during the early twentieth century that in relative terms displayed little technological and capital intensity. Compared with other industrial undertakings, textile firms during the 1900s were usually financially self-sufficient and therefore normally less dependent on banks for the provision of long-term finance.

Despite the banks having only begun to re-develop medium- and long-term engagements during the 1900s, some specialisation of their industrial interests is evident within the database for 1908. Directors of the Credit-Anstalt constituted 36 of the 88 interlockings with engineering and metal-working and almost one third of all interlocks with the mineral oil industry. The board of the Niederösterreichische Escompte-Gesellschaft had 23 (of 84) interlocks with mining and metallurgy, whereas senior staff of the Boden-Credit-Anstalt formed 22 out of the 64 interlocks with textiles. As well as the banks focusing upon certain industries, there was also some regional concentration of bank links with, for instance, the Anglo-Österreichische Bank being to the fore in the Trieste area. However, it is necessary to place these spatial nodes within the context of the enlargement of the banks' branch networks from the turn of the century. This largely took place in the Czech Crown Lands, the industrial heart of the Monarchy.

In 1908 the number of so-called 'multi-functionaries' or 'major linkers', defined as those bankers having more than 15 interlocking directorships with industry, was relatively small. Maxime Krassny, executive [*Direktor*] and member of the managing board [*Vorstandsmitglied*] of the Niederösterreichische Escompte-Gesellschaft, held 20; Ludwig Neurath, industrial consultant of the Credit-Anstalt, 16; and Ludwig August Lohnstein, the general manager of the Länderbank, 15. With regard to the location of interlocks within bank administrative hierarchies, executives and managers formed the majority of links, although precise patterns varied between institutions.

The composition and structure of the banks' boards of directors and executives in 1908 reflected the growth of industrial business that had taken place over the past decade or so. The new relationship with manufacturing was most clearly marked by the banks' recruitment of industrial experts with, for example, Neurath's appointment as a consultant to the Credit-Anstalt. It was also displayed in the motives for the Boden-Credit-Anstalt seeking the services of Julius Deutsch. 'On the occasion of his appointment it was announced that Deutsch was designated for industry, as the Boden-Credit-Anstalt had decided to [abandon] its previous tradition to devote [the bank] to the intensive care of industry'.[16] Moreover, numerous industrialists, mainly bank customers, were brought onto the banks' boards. There were other changes in the composition of bank boards, particularly the co-option of private bankers. Leading examples are Julius Petschek in the case of the Anglo-Österreichische Bank; Siegwart Mayer Freiherr von Ketschendorf, a representative of Gebrüder Gutmann, with regard to the Niederösterreichische Escompte-Gesellschaft; and Dr. Heinrich Miller von Aichholz joining the Boden-Credit-Anstalt. However, the demise of private banking that this marked was lamented by bankers, especially with respect to its consequences for the training of future staff members.[17] Aristocracy's continuing representation, with family names like Hardegg, Hohenlohe, Hoyos, Kielmannsegg, Montecuccoli, Pallavicini and Thurn und Taxis being prominent on their boards, guaranteed the status of the joint stock banks and, likewise, the presence of former high state officials and ministers amongst directors.

The process of concentration, with regard to either industrial or finance capital, was not halted by the First World War as the number of the banks' personal links with industry almost doubled from 599 to 1,195 between 1908 and 1917. The major role undertaken by the Viennese banks during the hostilities was the placing of war loans, while the demands of the war economy also led to bankers being seconded to war central offices [*Kriegszentralen*]. Furthermore, the banks were substantially involved in financing the armaments industry, a business which initially proved to be a source of profit. This commitment to munitions production led to an increase in bank personal links with engineering and metal-working companies, and the arising 213 interlocking directorships in 1917 constitute by far the most important field of bank activity during the 1910s. Engineering and metal-working continued to be the domain of the Credit-Anstalt (indicated by 51 interlocks), but the Niederösterreichische Escompte-Gesellschaft and the Anglo-Österreichische Bank established sizeable connections, 38 and 30 respectively, with this industrial branch during the war. The other industries prominent in the personal connections of the banks in 1917 were sugar, textiles and chemicals. Interlocks with sugar totalled 136 and largely consisted of bankers from the Länderbank (38) and the Boden-Credit-Anstalt (34). There were 132 interlocks with textiles, of which more than one fourth were constituted by representatives of the Boden-Credit-Anstalt, while there were 117 interlocks with chemicals, one of the industrial growth points of the early twentieth century.

It has often been maintained that the war led to the further specialisation of the industrial interests of particular banks, but this development has to be considered very carefully. If the shares of the three industries with the highest number of interlockings per bank are taken, then (with the exceptions of the Credit-Anstalt and the Länderbank) a lesser extent of concentration in links with industries is evident. It is only with respect to industries where there was a relatively small number of interlocks that the particular positions of some individual banks can be considered as being relatively dominant in 1917. This was the case in the food industry (but excluding sugar and brewing) where the Anglo-Österreichische Bank held 24 out of 42 interlocks, and the brewing and distilling industry in which the Credit-Anstalt had 22 of 64 interlocks. The overall pattern can be explained by the banks' business policies, which appear generally to have aimed at achieving a broad distribution of commitments, being shaped by the principles of risk minimization. As a result, the banks had interests in almost all industries, with only shoe and leather, and glass and porcelain, lying outside of their spheres of influence as indicated by personal relationships.

With regard to the distribution by bank, in 1917 the Credit-Anstalt's representatives held in total 240 interlocking directorships, comprising one fifth of all links and which involved 132 companies. Senior bankers from the Anglo-Österreichische Bank (168 interlocks with 103 companies) occupied second place, followed, in order, by their peers at the Niederösterreichische Escompte-Gesellschaft (147; 87), the Boden-Credit-Anstalt (145; 93), the Wiener Bank-Verein (125; 81) and the Länderbank (117; 70). However, by 1917 every bank of the ten considered, and therefore including the 'middling' institutions, had a substantial industrial concern. Amongst them, the senior staff of the Anglo-Österreichische Bank and the Boden-Credit-Anstalt display the greatest increase in the number of industrial directorships between 1908 and 1917.

A revision of the Boden-Credit-Anstalt's statutes in 1899 had enabled the growth of its industrial business. This, in turn, was related to the influence of two of its governors - Theodor Taussig and Rudolf Sieghart - but they represented two very contrasting styles of banking. Taussig was a gentleman of the old school and was regarded by contemporaries as omnipotent and omniscient, authoritarian, paternal and patriarchal. 'He tolerated no strong personalities beside him but only executive bodies [*ausführende Organe*]. He knew at every hour of the day, what every officer of his bank was doing'.[18] Sieghart was a new and very different type of banker, being described as power hungry and unscrupulous. He had been in the civil service, a somewhat unusual background for a Viennese banker, and which was pointed up by the public comment that his move to the Boden-Credit-Anstalt provoked.[19]

Comparison of the data for the first two benchmark years, 1908 and 1917, also reveals some functional changes. By 1917 industrial experts were common place on bank boards. However, Georg Günther, a director of the Boden-Credit-Anstalt, not only represented the 'pure' bank representative on an industrial board, but also might be regarded as the prototype *Sanierer* [reconstructor]. Some companies facing emergencies consulted Günther, with such approaches facilitated by his presence on their boards. The geographical expansion of the banks' businesses was reflected on their boards by individuals possessing the relevant local expertise as, for instance, Felix Kuranda, a specialist on the Balkans at the Wiener Bank-Verein. None the less, it remains difficult to determine the extent to which these personal links allowed the banks to shape the business policies of industrial companies, even those with which they were most closely connected. Without doubt, the banks held some sway since they organised mergers and reconstructions, or concluded cartel agreements, amongst their concern companies. However, there were limits to the extent of influence wielded by bank managements.

There are indications that the number of banks represented on a particular industrial board played a significant part in the arising relationship. Consequently, it is important to differentiate between those industrial companies whose boards contained delegates from only one bank and others which had representatives from a number of banks. In 1908 it was exceptional for boards of industrial companies to have representatives from more than one bank. One of the few examples is the Österreichisch Alpine Montangesellschaft, whose board membership included seven directors from three of the banks investigated. Before the war, companies, with multi-bank representation on their boards, were to a very great degree financially self-sufficient, a situation which enabled their managements to select their banking partners and so avoid one-sided power relationships. By 1917 more companies had a number of banks represented on their boards and, furthermore, these enterprises no longer largely relied on internal financing. These changed relationships had their origin in the growth of the scale of business transactions which, in turn, had generated increases in capital requirements beyond an individual company's internal capacity. The arising financial demands could only be met by co-operation between the

Viennese banks through syndicates and consortia. This changed situation led in 1917 to representatives of four banks being found on some industrial boards, like those of the Vereinigte Maschinenfabriken Rüsch-Ganahl AG and the Vereinigte Brauereien Schwechat, St. Marx, Simmering-Dreher, Mautner, Meichl AG. The greatest number of banks (nine) was represented on the board of Hirtenberger Patronen- Zündhütchen- und Metallwaren Fabrik, vormals Keller & Comp.

In both contemporary and current discussions of the relationship between banks and industry, the exercise of power and influence is generally attributed without question to the banks - banks dominate industry. However, this conclusion does not take into account the number of firms before 1914 that were independent of the banks because they generated sufficient profits to be financially self-sufficient. Furthermore, there seems to have been a period in Austrian economic history when 'industrial giants' were able to influence the business policy of 'their' bank. This can be illustrated by the example of the so-called Wittgenstein group, named after Karl Wittgenstein, the most prominent Austrian iron master at the turn of the century. Wittgenstein often operated secretly, by working through his confidants, and here just two of his representatives, Wilhelm Kestranek and Max Feilchenfeld, and, in turn, their connections with the Niederösterreichische Escompte-Gesellschaft, will be considered. Kestranek, an important personality within the Austrian iron cartel and general manager of the Prager Eisen-Industrie-Gesellschaft, eventually became the vice-president of the Niederösterreichische Escompte-Gesellschaft. In 1917 he was president of three companies: the Österreichisch Alpine Montangesellschaft, Hofherr-Schrantz-Clayton-Shuttleworth, Landwirtschaftliche Maschinen-Fabrik AG (an engineering enterprise) and Österreichische Stickstoffwerke AG; and was also chairman of the Schlesische Kohlen- und Cokes Werke AG. Feilchenfeld was president of both the Niederösterreichische Escompte-Gesellschaft and its subsidiary the Böhmische Escomptebank. He was also vice-president of the Alpine, of the Skodawerke, AG in Pilsen and of the Prager Eisen-Industrie-Gesellschaft, as well as being chairman of Poldihütte, Tiegelgußstahl-Fabrik and deputy-chairman of the Schlesische Kohlen- und Cokes-Werke. These personal links provided the context for Sieghart's comment that the Niederösterreichische Escompte-Gesellschaft was controlled by Kestranek and the Wittgenstein group.[20]

There is evidence of greater competition between the banks during the 1910s. For instance, Sieghart, on behalf of the Boden-Credit-Anstalt, managed to penetrate parts of the Credit-Anstalt's industrial domains such as Leitenberger's textile empire, the engineering undertaking Ringhoffer-Werke A.-G. and the wide-ranging sugar interests of the Schoeller business dynasty. Sieghart's success was due to his web of personal acquaintanceships and relationships which underlay the business links that were publicly evident. These private connections were often consolidated and strengthened by marriage through the instrument of 'Heiratspolitik'.[21]

More generally and to place such links in perspective, it should be recognised that, in spite of their often different origins, bankers and industrialists belonged to the same social stratum constituted by the business élite of Austria-Hungary. However, whilst they all sat alongside one another at various board meetings, a wide social gulf separated bankers and industrialists from members of the leading aristocratic families.

Economic disintegration, arising from the collapse of the Habsburg Monarchy in 1918, not only led to changes in Austria's industrial structure but also largely shaped the fate of the Viennese banks. With the national revolutions of autumn 1918, about half of the concern companies of the Viennese banks, together with many of their own branches, came to be situated on the territories of the newly established successor states. One effect of the post-October 1918 geo-politics of the region was that the Viennese banks headed multi-national concerns. Furthermore, the successor states reacted rapidly to the changed political environment of central and eastern Europe through establishing national currencies and applying the process of nostrification. Nostrification legislation and policies required company head offices, most of which were located in Vienna, to be transferred to the territories of the states where enterprises' operations were sited. In this process, companies were reconstituted under the legal codes of the successor states. Furthermore, in the case of companies which had plants distributed across the new states, nostrification caused their break-up into numbers of autonomous national firms. This aspect will also be considered below - in terms of post-war losses amongst the concerns of the Viennese banks.

The actual impact of the nostrification ran even deeper since the relocation of head offices from 1918 often resulted in property transfers. This development led to the establishment of new credit links, a restructuring of financial relationships which was also shaped by differentials in the impact of the post-war inflations and hyper-inflations. Inflation forced the Vienna banks to relinquish their roles as credit guarantors to what were, following nostrification, foreign companies and, for instance, in 1919 the Boden-Credit-Anstalt transferred a major part of its current business in the new Czechoslovakia to the Živnostenská banka, although both banks agreed to co-ordinate their future activities.[22] Albeit following some delay, the effects brought about by nostrification and inflation on bank-industry relations led to new personal links. Although there was discontinuity since the historical actors (banks and board members) changed, the structure of the bank-industry relations in most successor states was none the less similar to the pre-war Austrian pattern, so giving rise to continuity. Indeed, the Viennese banks reacted to the consequences of the national revolutions by establishing a system of confidantes in order to re-establish former personal relations.

The managements of the Viennese banks faced two alternative

conceptions for the future business policies of their institutions. One consisted of withdrawal from central and south-east Europe in order to concentrate by and large on meeting the financial demands of the Austrian economy. The other comprised a strategy which aimed at maintaining the banks' wide geographical spheres of influence that had been established from the late nineteenth century.[23] Generally, bank managements opted for the latter by deciding to try and maintain 'business as usual'.

Some Viennese banks were able to constitute friendly institutions out of segments of their former branch networks now located in the successor states and, in most such cases, retained participations in these new banks. An example is the creation in 1921 of the Všeobecná česká bankovní jednota from the 18 branches of the Wiener Bank-Verein that after 1918 were situated in Czechoslovakia. It involved the intermediation of Belgian partners (Société Générale and Banque Belge pour l'Étranger) whereas the Bank-Verein was able to hold an interest of 35 per cent in the new Czech institution.[24] Another possibility for Viennese banks was to transfer their branches in the successor states to foreign, sympathetic banks, but this was not always an operation in which totally equal partners were involved. Whereas the Credit-Anstalt and the Niederösterreichische Escompte-Gesellschaft each took an interest of 22.5 per cent in the Česká eskomptní banka a úvěrní ústav which acquired their Czech branches, these Vienna banks were of minor importance in the founding syndicate which was headed by the Živnostenská banka. Consequently, with nostrification, a Viennese bank that was able to continue to retain a fully-related office in one of the successor states proved to be a rare exception, with the most important being the Wiener Bank-Verein's Budapest branch. All in all, with regard to the ten Viennese banks investigated, only nine of their branch offices were still under direct control from Vienna in 1924 out of a total of 144 that had been operating at the end of the war.

Losses were equally unavoidable in the case of the links that the banks had with industry. The breaks caused by nostrification were very significant since many of the companies affected were those that constituted the 'kernels' of the banks' concerns. Significant lesions arose, for instance, with the nostrification-induced reconstitution of the Österreichische Berg- und Hüttenwerks-Gesellschaft, which had belonged to the concern of the Boden-Credit-Anstalt, so that its Czech title,[25] Báňská a hutní společnost, became its leading legal name. Similarly, the Prager Maschinenbau-AG turned to its Czech legal title, Pražská akciová strojírna, while the Credit-Anstalt also lost the Stabilimento Tecnico Triestino. Further leading examples are the Skodawerke, AG in Pilsen [A. S. dříve Škdovy závody] in the case of the concerns of both the Credit-Anstalt and the Niederösterreichische Escompte-Gesellschaft, and the Prager Eisen-Industrie-Gesellschaft [Pražská železářská společnost] with respect solely to the Niederösterreichische Escompte-Gesellschaft. In some instances, industrial share interests had to be sold, with those held immediately post-war by the Czech branches of the Credit-Anstalt purchased by the Česká eskomptní banka a úvěrní ústav. The

Viennese banks attempted to minimise such losses by establishing holding companies in neutral European countries.[26]

Vienna's importance as the financial and banking centre for central Europe could only be sustained with the assistance of west European capital.[27] Foreign banks were attracted by the expectation that participations in the equity capitals of the Viennese banks constituted an ideal basis for developing or expanding their interests in the central and south-east Europe. This, in turn, arose from the underlying assumption that the economic entity of the region would survive.[28] Moreover, share interests in Viennese banks avoided the risks arising from direct participations in industrial companies with uncertain future prospects. For instance, Schneider et Cie through its holding company, the Union Europeénne industrielle et financière, acquired a stake in the capital of the Niederösterreichische Escompte-Gesellschaft, banker to the Österreichisch Alpine Montangesellschaft and the Pražská železářská společnost [Prager Eisen-Industrie-Gesellschaft]. On the other hand, the Viennese banks' eagerness to attract foreign participations in their capitals was heightened by the consequences of the giddy post-war Austrian inflation and the stipulations of the Treaty of St. Germain. These push and pull forces led to the internationalization of the Viennese banks. Foreign participations in the share capitals of the Viennese banks increased from 10.4 per cent in 1913 to 30.5 per cent in 1923 (excluding the Anglo-Österreichische Bank and the Länderbank which had to transfer their head offices to London and Paris respectively because of high indebtedness dating from August 1914).[29]

Managements of the Viennese 'great' banks not only had to try and resolve the problems arising from the dissolution of the imperial economy, but also those of the transition to a peacetime economy. Reconstruction after 1918 proved to be a problem of greatly widening proportions, since Austria experienced growing economic difficulties, indicated most graphically by the growing size of the budget deficit and the precipitous decline of the Austrian crown on the foreign exchanges. Nevertheless, the close relationship between banks and industry, inherited from the pre-1914 period, survived to put its particular stamp on the inflation of 1918 to 1922. But a new type of actor entered the stage since the inflation period was the time of 'sharks', as Karl Kraus named the nouveaux riches and the speculators in his *Fackel*. The most prominent were Camillo Castiglioni, president of the Depositenbank, and Siegmund Bosel, who gained control of the shares of the Unionbank.

During the inflation of the early 1920s, the Viennese banks continued to acquire industrial shares, but the subsequent development of financial conditions did not permit their later disposal, with the result that their industrial participations increased secularly. Inflation allowed the banks to generate what proved to be doubtful profits, often from involvements in issuing syndicates. Although the deflationary effect of currency stabilization from 1922/3 caused the demise of most companies that had been established during the inflation, speculation continued for a further year. The banks to varying degrees participated in the feverish speculation that took place in foreign currencies, goods and securities during 1923/4 which gave rise to a post-stabilization boom on the Vienna stock exchange. Capital, that returned to Austria with reconstruction based upon the 1922 Geneva protocols, was employed in speculative foreign exchange operations, such as the bear attack on the French franc in spring 1924. However, the failure of the selling manoeuvres against the franc produced in its wake a high degree of illiquidity. In these circumstances, bank managements were either forced, or felt that they were being forced, to maintain dividends and offset previous losses by drawing upon hidden internal reserves. Consequently, bank balance sheets deviated further and further from reality.

There was continuing crisis in the Austrian banking sector from spring 1924 until 1934 and the difficulties experienced by particular institutions became publicly evident through collapses and by mergers to salvage at least in part foundered banks. These crashes and fusions include the failure of the Depositenbank in 1924, so removing one of the ten banks that comprise the database, whereas the subsequent unfolding of events give rise to further reductions in the number of banks that compose it. In 1926 the Austrian business of the Anglo-Austrian Bank was transferred to the Credit-Anstalt, a step which Cottrell considers to mark 'the inception of the Credit-Anstalt becoming the sole commercial bearer of the burdens of sustaining the industrial 'concerns' developed by the Austrian system of investment banking'.[30] Mergers continued with the Unionbank and the Verkehrsbank fusing with the Boden-Credit-Anstalt in 1927. Alongside the warnings given by bank collapses and mergers, there were other signs of danger as the post-inflation, opening balance sheets of 1925, based on gold, revealed a shrinkage of the banks' capitals and reserves.

The demand for externally-supplied funds from manufacturing companies increased substantially during the second half of the 1920s, but the Austrian capital market remained weak and bond issues only played a subordinate role in industrial finance. Industry's demands were met by the banks but they, in turn, became increasingly dependent upon short-term foreign borrowing so giving rise to a growing indebtedness to western Europe and the United States.[31] 'Borrowing short, lending long' came to characterise the business policies of the banks which were able once more, but on the basis of foreign-provided facilities, to grant long-term credits to their old clienteles in the successor states. The extent of the debts of even individual components of the banks' impressive industrial concerns escalated, in some cases to overshadow the banks' share capitals. This was a sign of extreme negligence on the part of the senior bankers, who, with rose coloured glasses, continued to view the business world in terms of the optimistic expectations conceived in 1918/19 although, with the subsequent passage of time, these had become more and more mis-placed.

To what extent are these developments and tendencies evident in the data for the third benchmark year, 1928? There were more interlocks in the late 1920s than in 1917. However, it proved necessary to consider very carefully the extent and nature of interlockings displayed in the 1928 data. This was because the internationalization of the Viennese banks since 1918 had resulted in the presence on their boards of foreign directors, but these individuals were also involved in the corporate management of industrial enterprises which had no contact with the Austrian economy. Even when proper allowance is made for this, the Viennese banks had prominent positions in 1928 but, in some cases, their impressive personal representations on Austrian industrial boards disguised actual power relations. For instance, Anton Apold, the general manager of the Österreichisch Alpine Montangesellschaft, was a director of the Niederösterreichische Escompte-Gesellschaft and, moreover, this bank's manager, Wilhelm Kux, was president of the mining giant. However, these personal links merely reflected that the Niederösterreichische Escompte-Gesellschaft was the prime bank connection for the Alpine's current business since during the mid- and late 1920s the majority of the Alpine's shares was held by the Vereinigte Stahlwerke AG, a German company.

With regard to the rank order of the banks' industrial directorships, the Boden-Credit-Anstalt occupied second position to the Credit-Anstalt, its increased importance compared to 1917 arising from the take-overs of the Unionbank and the Verkehrsbank which had substantially augmented the Boden's industrial holdings.[32] An analysis by industry shows that textiles had maintained their position in the number of interlocks, being second to engineering and metal-working, and that the Boden-Credit-Anstalt was the locus of one third of all textile interlocks. The electrical industry (where the Niederösterreichische Escompte-Gesellschaft held the most links) experienced the biggest increase of bank interlocks over the 1920s. Electricity-generating enterprises were mainly located in Austria and the augmentation of the banks' links with this industrial branch could be interpreted as the first indication of the execution of policies that concentrated on the requirements of the domestic economy. However, the personal presence of Viennese bankers on boards of industrial companies located in the successor states continued to be very significant, still being of an impressive extent during the late 1920s. Over the decade Austrian bank managements had been able to compensate for some of their immediate post-war losses by establishing new companies in the successor states.[33] Yet, this had not produced uniform outcomes across industrial branches with, for instance, sugar, an industry mainly located in Czechoslovakia and Hungary, having a declining importance for the Viennese banks by the late 1920s.

The boards of the Viennese banks became international meeting-points over the 1920s, with the large number of representatives of foreign banks (between 25 and 60 per cent of directors) being their most salient feature. For instance, in 1928, seven of the 27 directors of the Boden-Credit-Anstalt represented west European or North American financial groups, like Robert Hankar-Solvay of the Belgian Solvay chemical combine, or Eugène

Schneider of the French Schneider group, or Baron Bruno Schröder, head of J. Henry Schroder & Co., the London merchant bank. Furthermore, in the dislocation of the post-war period, two representatives on this bank's board had taken Czechoslovak nationality. Internationalization during the 1920s had gone hand in hand with the banks' expansion by merger. By 1928 growth, arising from fusions, was reflected not only in the increased sizes of some of the banks' industrial concerns but also in inflated administrative hierarchies, especially the much greater number of deputy executives.

During the late 1920s, the increasing tally of industrial directorships held by bankers, to 40 or more, reached its peak for the period being considered. Perhaps not accidentally, the absolute 'multi-functionary' of the overall database is Friedrich Ehrenfest, manager and executive of the Credit-Anstalt. In 1928 he sat on the boards of 49 industrial joint stock companies. However, in the wake of the 1931 collapse of the Credit-Anstalt, Ehrenfest was accused of fraud and this may be a pointer to the changing nature of personal links and also how they were established. Although the field of action open to the Viennese banks became more restricted over the post-war period, some of their managers, like Ehrenfest, through not being effectively controlled, seemed to have found or created enough elbow-room to make their own personal profits. This points to internal managerial and organizational problems while, externally, there was a lack of regulating legislation.

In 1929, the bank merger movement of the decade reached its climax with the take-over of the Boden-Credit-Anstalt by the Credit-Anstalt. Bank mergers over the 1920s had two effects for the database: a decrease in the number of universal banks investigated but a widening of the surviving banks' networks of dependent companies, arising from their absorption of the dependent companies connected to the banks that they acquired. However, mergers appear to have taken place during the 1920s without any searching investigations of the current affairs and, consequently, the actual financial positions of either the concern companies, or the banks, that were taken-over. The myopia displayed by Viennese bankers, subsequently to be combined with the consequences of the world economic crisis of the early 1930s, led to an increase of illiquidity which caused further banking insolvencies and mergers.

The most spectacular was the foundering of the Credit-Anstalt in spring 1931[34] which, through its acquisitions of other banks since 1926, had accumulated stakes in the most important Austrian industries. If the companies connected with the Credit-Anstalt had been liquidated from spring 1931, as part of the process to salvage the bank, then thousands of workers would have been made redundant. It was this potential consequence, with its political as well as economic dimensions, that forced the state to intervene and rescue the universal banking system from summer 1931. The wave of bank mergers that had got underway in 1924 came to an end in 1934, when the Wiener Bank-Verein was fused with the Credit-Anstalt to form the Österreichische Creditanstalt-Wiener Bankverein. This fusion also involved the Creditanstalt-Wiener Bankverein acquiring the current banking business of the Niederösterreichische Escompte-Gesellschaft, while the illiquid industrial interests of the Escompte-Gesellschaft were placed in a special company analogous to a holding - the Österreichische Industrie-Credit AG. Consequently, Austria had almost in practice a one-bank system from 1934.

Whereas the economy experienced stagnation or even a shrinkage during the 1930s, the financial sector underwent a process that can best be described as 'Austrification'.[35] During the 1930s the Creditanstalt, the only surviving important bank in Vienna which was Austrian-owned, strengthened its controlling position. It was used to bring about measures of industrial concentration and rationalization. The Creditanstalt's senior staff arranged recovery strategies, usually involving industrial mergers, on behalf of its heavily indebted related companies, but they liquidated those firms where there seemed to be no possible other resolution of their difficulties. Most of the bank's remaining interests and participations in the successor states were sold, while current credit business from 1931 lost its multinational character for a second time since 1918/19. Moreover, 'Austrification' in banking during the 1930s also affected the composition of the banks' boards. One of the immediate consequences of the Credit-Anstalt crash in 1931 was the withdrawal of all of the bank's non-Austrian directors. This proved to mark the start of a complete change in the composition of the Credit-Anstalt's board as the seats of the bank's Austrian directors in May 1931 were occupied two years later by former ministers and state functionaries, which reflected the changes in the bank's ownership during the early 1930s.

Mergers within Austrian banking has the result that the 1937 database comprises only four banks. When compared with the 1928 data, it shows that the number of joint directorships had decreased by almost 70 per cent, with losses evident across all industrial branches. For example, the number of bank interlocks with textiles shrank from 183 in 1928 to 35 by 1937. Although the Creditanstalt-Wiener Bankverein headed the rank order of number of interlocks, its position in 1937 was not so dominant as might have been expected. In 1937 both the French-owned Länderbank and Österreichische Industrie-Credit AG had nearly as many interlocks with industry as the Creditanstalt. The German-owned 'Mercur' Bank was in fourth position. An analysis by industrial branch produced a surprising result. In 1937 the electrical industry occupied first position (with half of the interlocks constituted by representatives of the Österreichische Industrie-Credit AG), closely followed by engineering and metal-working. 'Austrification' over the 1930s had the result that the majority of interlocks in 1937 were with joint stock companies situated in Austria. More than half of the interlocking directorships and, among them almost all leading positions, were held by members of the banks' managing boards. The development of this particular pattern had got underway from the 1920s and could be interpreted as an indicator that decision-making was being increasingly concentrated within the hands of the banks' most senior managements.[36]

Although the personal ties between banks and their concern companies proved generally to be remarkably durable, the period investigated has a number of political turning-points (1918, 1938) as well as being marked by structural changes in the organization of banking (as with years of major mergers and the banking crisis of 1931). These discontinuities had affected the composition of bank boards even before the crisis of the early 1930s, as can be shown by the following examples. In 1913 seven of the 23 directors and executives of the Credit-Anstalt had been on the bank's board since 1894, but in 1919 only two out of 19 of the bank's senior staff had this longevity of tenure. With respect to the exchange and the co-option of personnel arising from banking mergers, this can be demonstrated through the example of the Boden-Credit-Anstalt. In 1928, five former members of the Verkehrsbank, and four of the Unionbank, sat on the Boden-Credit-Anstalt's board, following the acquisitions of these banks the previous year. One year later, with the Credit-Anstalt's take-over of the Boden-Credit-Anstalt, 14 Boden-Credit-Anstalt directors were co-opted onto the Credit-Anstalt's board.

When the interlockings of all four benchmark years are aggregated, it shows over the half century from the mid-1890s that firms engaged in engineering and metal-working had by far the strongest attraction for the Viennese banks, followed by those in mining and metallurgy and textiles. Other main fields of bank activity, in terms of industrial directorships, were the electrical and chemical industries, both of which were growth points in the secondary sector from the turn of the century and whose importance increased during the 1920s. The sugar industry, through nostrification, lost its pre-1918 significance for the Viennese banks as most of the refining companies came to be situated in the successor states. The results of investigating the structure of the network between banks and Austria's 'big' business (defined by equity) in 1937 revealed that the Creditanstalt-Wiener Bankverein was by far the most central and thus the most important actor. Overall, this outcome verified the hypothesis that banks held the central positions within the Austrian bank-industry networks.[37]

The last discontinuity within bank-industry relationships over the period investigated was that caused by the Anschluß in 1938. The enlargement of the Credit-Anstalt's shareholdings in the most important Austrian industries between 1926 and 1934, through its transformation by first absorbing other banks and then its post-1931 reconstitution, gave this bank a strategic, key position in German plans. Indeed, the Creditanstalt's post-1934 industrial and other interests enabled the invaders to 'Germanize' the Austrian economy.

Following the Anschluß, the Austrian banking system was fully integrated into that of the Third Reich. While the organization of banking was not changed, the Anschluß claimed numerous victims through the replacement of Jewish and other 'disagreeable' (such as representatives of the Austrian Ständestaat) senior bankers and industrialists by German and Austrian Nazis, and by sympathisers with the new regime. These changes in the composition of bank boards had been heralded, first, during the Credit-Anstalt crash when Jewish bank executives were pilloried and then the 'aryanization' of the staff of the German-owned 'Mercur' from 1933.[38] Comparing the composition of bank boards, before and after the Anschluß in 1938, shows that only 24 out of 70 directors continued in post. Some of the directors, managers and industrialists that were removed from office were able to emigrate, but others were not so fortunate and were incarcerated in prisons or concentration camps.[39] As well as victims of the Anschluß, there were also perpetrators and camp followers. Some revealed their sympathies for the Nazis, while others at least managed to come to an accommodation, and this was especially the case with regard to technical and economic specialists, whose expertise was most required by the new regime. This segment of bank staffs comprised of technocrats fused, or rather became interwoven, with a new network of bank links with industry which was dominated by representatives of the Deutsche Bank, the Dresdner Bank, the Reichswerke 'Hermann Göring' and IG Farbenindustrie AG.

Bank-industry networks, formed by interlocking directorships, are often comprehended and interpreted as tools of bank control and power. However, they seem to have a greater importance through minimizing and directing competition, by their facilitation of information acquisition and through their more general provision of communication media. None the less, the Austrian experience between the mid-1890s and 1938 provides abundant evidence that even these attributes of the underlying relationships failed to be articulated as an economic/financial system. Rather, Austrian networks of personal relations give predominantly an insight into the construction of the economy's élite and its changing nature. In addition to a social dimension, Austrian networks of the first half of the twentieth century also include an important political aspect. Lastly, with regard to general considerations, the accumulation of interlocking directorships, at the level of an individual actor, was a profitable source of money-making, especially during the 1920s.

The situation of the Austrian banks during the interwar period was characterised by increasing difficulties caused by a severe financial crisis, which was aggravated by the pursuit of short-sighted policies on the part of bank managements who failed to heed danger signs. The breakdown of the Austrian system of finance capital was due to an interplay of factors. First, if the origins of the banking crisis of the period 1924-1934, do not lie before 1914, then its seedbed was prepared and further developed by the economy's immediate post-war structural problems and thereafter by the effects of inflation and hyper-inflation. Industrial companies and banks were equally affected by the nostrification measures of the early 1920s but these failed to constitute the crux of the crisis. Second, in retrospect, bank managements' decisions to maintain their old spheres of influence were misguided. During the 1920s the Viennese banks faced pressure from two interrelated directions. Demands for accommodation from established clienteles at home and in the successor states led to the Viennese banks' growing dependence on foreign capital. Furthermore, such was the extent of these demands that ultimately it sapped the banks' capacities. By the mid-1920s, following the tocsin sounded by the first, post-stabilization wave of bank mergers and liquidations and with the further warning contained in any analysis of the gold opening balance sheets of 1925, Viennese bankers should have recognized their worsening situation. Third, the subsequent deterioration of the banks' positions, which led up to the foundering of the Credit-Anstalt in 1931, was not caused solely or simply by either macro-economic developments in terms of the consequences of the growing world economic crisis, or political factors, such as the withdrawal of the French capital in 1931. These destabilizing developments contributed to the banking crisis but were not in themselves decisive; rather they added to the difficulties caused by the banks' managements themselves. These self-generated problems arose from the pursuit of business policies which, with some exceptions, disregarded sound principles so that, for example, dividends were maintained from undisclosed reserves. Fourth, the banks faced unresolved managerial and organizational problems,[40] generated in part during the 1920s due to the lack of an effective legislation framework curbing unsound banking and excessive speculation. The progressive collapse of Austrian universal banking from 1924 to 1934 was, thus, aggravated by the absence of legislative controls and the failure of crisis management.[41]

Notes

1 A. Teichova, (1992), 'Rivals and Partners: Reflections on Banking and Industry in Europe, 1880-1938', in P. L. Cottrell, H. Lindgren & A. Teichova (eds), (1992), *European Industry and Banking Between the Wars. A Review of Bank-Industry Relations*, Leicester, pp. 17-18.

2 R. L. Rudolph, (1976), *Banking and Industrialization in Austria-Hungary. The Role of Banks in the Industrialization of the Czech Crownlands, 1873-1914*, Cambridge, p. 104. See also W. Reik, (1932), *Die Beziehungen der österreichischen Großbanken zur Industrie*, Vienna, p.20. Many contemporaries were, and a considerable number of historians remain, convinced that the essential point of the bank-industry relationship is the link arising from the provision of credit and not the banks' share participations. Credits were often funded by either share issues, made by the banks, or the conversion of firms into joint stock companies undertaken by the banks; see, for example, D. Stiefel, (1989), *Finanzdiplomatie und Weltwirtschaftskrise. Die Krise der Credit-Anstalt für Handel und Gewerbe 1931*, Frankfurt-am-Main, p. 86.

3 Rudolf Hilferding's main work, *Das Finanzkapital* was first published in Vienna in 1910.

4 E. März, (1981), *Österreichische Bankpolitik in der Zeit der großen Wende 1913-1923*, Vienna, especially pp. 73-5; and D. F. Good, (1986), *Der wirtschaftliche Aufstieg des Habsburgerreiches 1750-1914*, Vienna, especially pp. 188-9.

5 See *Die Frage des Finanzkapitals in der Österreichisch-Ungarischen Monarchie 1900-1918* (1965), Bucharest; and I. T. Berend & G. Ránki, (1960), *The development of the manufacturing industry in Hungary (1900-1944)*, Budapest.

6 For Germany, see, for example, V. Wellhöner, (1989), *Großbanken und Großindustrie im Kaiserreich*, Göttingen; for Austria-Hungary, see Rudolph, (1976) and D. Stiefel, (1984), 'Die österreichischen Banken am Höhepunkt von Macht und Einfluß', *Bankhistorisches Archiv. Zeitschrift für Bankengeschichte*, 1.

7 The Anglo-Österreichische Bank, the Allgemeine Österreichische Boden-Credit-Anstalt, the Österreichische Credit-Anstalt für Handel und Gewerbe, the Allgemeine Depositenbank, the Österreichische Länderbank, Bank und Wechselstuben-Actien-Gesellschaft 'Mercur', the Niederösterreichische Escompte-Gesellschaft and its post-1934 successor, the Österreichische Industrie- Credit AG, the Unionbank, the Allgemeine Verkehrsbank and the Wiener Bank-Verein.

8 For a more detailed description, see P. Eigner, (1994), 'Interlocking Directorships between Commercial Banks and Industry in Interwar Vienna', in A. Teichova, T. Gourvish & Á. Pogány (eds), (1994), *Universal Banking in the Twentieth Century. Finance, Industry and the State in North and Central Europe*, Aldershot, pp. 260-93. Subsequently

the sample has been enlarged, through the inclusion of all branch managers with interlocking directorships, giving rise to a more detailed pattern. The direction of these links, i.e. whether, as in most cases, a bank representative sat on the board of an industrial company, as opposed to an industrialist being present on the board of a bank, was not investigated in detail. However, it can be shown that the majority of interlockings related to the banks' managers.

9 In retrospect, Sieghart wrote about the expectation held within financial circles after 1918 that Vienna and Austria would have a significant future as indispensable intermediaries between the west and the chaos of newly established states in central and east Europe, and that Austrians in general shared this 'beautiful illusion'. See R. Sieghart, (1932), *Die letzte Jahrzehnte einer Großmacht*, Berlin, p. 195.

10 E. März & K. Socher, (1973), 'Währung und Banken in Cisleithanien', in A. Wandruszka & P. Urbanitsch (eds), (1973), *Die Habsburgermonarchie 1848-1918*, I, *Die wirtschaftliche Entwicklung*, Vienna, p. 347.

11 K. Bachinger & H. Matis, (1973), 'Österreichs industrielle Entwicklung', in Wandruszka and Urbanitsch, (1973), p. 216; and A. Mosser, (1980), *Die Industrieaktiengesellschaft in Österreich 1880-1913*, Vienna, p. 184.

12 März & Socher, (1973), p.358. According to Reik (1932), p. 15, 59 per cent of industrial company promotions (accounting for 67 per cent of the total capital involved) between 1907 and 1913 took place with the help of the banks.

13 Bachinger & Matis, (1973), pp. 134-40. In 1910 36 cartels, and among them the most important, were directed and controlled by the Viennese 'great' bank; ibid., p. 139.

14 Ibid., p. 134.

15 It proved to be necessary to differentiate between at least two, if not three, levels within bank administrative hierarchies: the supervisory board of directors [*Verwaltungsrat*], and the management of the bank, but with the latter consisting of the board of executives [*Direktion*] and the managing board [*Vorstand*]. Leading positions were defined as president of the board of directors, chairman, general manager or owner.

16 R. Kola, (1922), *Rückblick ins Gestrige*, Vienna, p. 151.

17 See the articles by K. Morawitz (president of the board of directors of the Anglo-Österreichische Bank): 'Der Mangel an Bankdirektoren', pp.115-25, and 'Der Nachwuchs an Bankleitern', pp. 126-35, both in Morawitz, (1911), *Aus Arbeitstagen und Mußestunden. Neue Folge*, Vienna/Leipzig. With regard to the importance of private banks as places of banking education, Michel notes that, at the beginning of the twentieth century, fifty-five per cent of the leading personalities of the Austrian banking world came from the 'school' of private banks; B. Michel, (1976), *Banques et banquiers en Autriche au début du 20e siècle*, Paris, p. 320. The educational function performed by the private banks was increasingly replaced by young managers getting accustomed

to all possible sorts of banking business in the banks' branches.

18 Sieghart, (1932), p. 156.

19 The same was true for Alexander Spitzmüller, who was placed at the top of the management of the Credit-Anstalt. He could be taken as representing a third type of banker, since his own conception was to create a 'social type of banker fulfilling the public interest' while being a 'servant of state and society'. A. Spitzmüller, (1955), '... *Und hat auch Ursach, es zu lieben*', Vienna, p. 112.

20 Sieghart, (1932), p. 182.

21 For example, Kestranek's father-in-law was the commercial executive [*kommerzieller Direktor*] of the Prager Eisenindustrie-Gesellschaft, while his sister Anna was married to Johann Blaschczik, owner and central executive of the Königshofer Zementfabrik. Both men belonged to the Wittgenstein group. See G. Günther, (1936), *Lebenserinnerungen*, Vienna, pp. 70-1.

22 Ibid., p. 160; F. Weber, (1991), *Vor dem großen Krach. Die Krise des österreichischen Bankwesens in den zwanziger Jahren*, Habilitation thesis, Vienna, pp. 411; V. Lacina, 'Banking System Changes after the Establishment of the Independent Czechoslovak Republic', in Teichova et al, (1994), p. 132.

23 See H. Kernbauer & F. Weber, 'Die Wiener Großbanken in der Zeit der Kriegs- und Nachkriegsinflation (1914-1922)', in G. D. Feldman et al., (1984), *Die Erfahrung der Inflation im internationalen Zusammenhang und Vergleich* [The experience of inflation: international and comparative studies], Berlin/New York, p. 151.

24 Such co-operation with banks from beyond central Europe was not restricted to the establishment of new local institutions to meet the demands of nostrification. Banks based in America and western Europe were often also involved in the inflation-induced increases of equity capital undertaken by the Viennese banks and thus Western financial institutions pursued from 1918 a two-sided business strategy in central Europe.

25 Before 1914 companies that operated across the Monarchy frequently had both a German title and titles in the local languages of the regions where they operated.

26 These holdings took over share participations in those concern companies which, from 1918, had had their nationalities changed as a result of nostrification, in exchange for their equities, thus only formally changing the ownership. The Fanto holding company (the Vereinigte Fanto Petroleum AG), established by the Boden-Credit-Anstalt, temporarily controlled shares of, and participations in, seventeen companies located after 1918 in ten states. Other examples are the Tarbouches Trust, the Färbereien und Druckereien Trust in the textile industry, and the Mundus Allgemeine Handels- und Industrie AG in the wood industry (all created for the interests of the Credit-Anstalt). Kernbauer & Weber, (1984), p. 156; and Weber, (1991), p. 90.

27 Regarding foreign capital participation, see Kernbauer & Weber, (1984), pp. 156, 162 and especially 165; Weber, (1991), p. 106; A. Teichova, (1974), *An Economic Background to Munich. International Business and Czechoslovakia 1918-1938*, Cambridge, p. 279; and idem, (1988), *Kleinstaaten im Spannungsfeld der Großmächte*, Vienna, p. 87.

28 M. L. Recker (1976) quotes the English ambassador: 'Any cooperation with the Boden-Credit-Anstalt means an entrance into the most important industries and companies of Central Europe', in *England und der Donauraum 1919-1929*, Stuttgart, p. 72, fn. 137.

29 Kernbauer & Weber, (1984), p. 166.

30 P. L. Cottrell, (1994), '"Mushrooms and dinosaurs": Sieghart and the Boden-Credit-Anstalt during the 1920s', in Teichova et al, (1994), p.173.

31 Teichova, (1992), p. 25. Banks took special care of large-scale enterprises, although great combines were less dependent on credits of a single bank and were the only undertakings that could obtain credits from abroad. This was especially the case during the 1920s, when larger industrial clients could raise western credits without the intermediation of their Viennese banks. Therefore, the often stated paradigm of a constant credit squeeze has to be analysed more carefully - in terms of the size of industrial companies. On the other hand, low investment and the low reinvestment of profits seemed to have contributed to the poor economic conditions. See A. Mosser, 'Financing Industrial Companies in Interwar Austria: Working Capital and Liquidity', in Teichova et al, (1994), pp. 208-14.

32 Companies like Veitscher Magnesitwerke AG, Schoeller-Bleckmann-Stahlwerke and the paper industry-imperium of Neusiedler AG now belonged to the industrial concern of the Boden-Credit-Anstalt.

33 März, (1981), pp. 534-5.

34 Regarding the crash of the Credit-Anstalt, and its consequences in general, see Stiefel, (1989).

35 D. Stiefel, (1983), 'The Reconstruction of the Credit-Anstalt', in A. Teichova & P. L. Cottrell (eds), (1983), *International Business & Central Europe, 1918-1939*, Leicester, p. 427.

36 For example, in 1937 Franz Rottenberg, manager of the Creditanstalt, had seats on 36 industrial boards and held 18 leading positions. Erich Heller, a member of the managing board, was found on 28 industrial boards, acting as president in 11 enterprises. The absolute 'multi-functionaries', arising from the 1928 data, were also concentrated within the ranks of executives or managers.

37 Results of an analysis of the situation of the banks operating in Austria in 1937, and of their joint directorships with industry especially Austrian big business, are contained in a comparison of three small economies - Austria, Greece and Sweden - and will be published in *Financial History Review*, 3.2 (1996) in an article co-authored with M. Dritsas & J. Ottosson.

38 L. Wittek-Saltzberg, (1970), *Die wirtschaftlichen Auswirkungen der*

Okkupation, Dissertation, Vienna, p. 141.

39 G. Clare's (1981) *Last Waltz in Vienna*, London, describes the despairing but relentless efforts of Henry Reuter, the French general manager of the Länderbank in Paris, to save the lives of his Jewish employees working in Vienna. George Clare's father, Ernst Klaar, was an officer of the Länderbank authorized to act and sign on behalf of the bank. His flight from persecution failed and Ernst Klaar died in Auschwitz in 1942.

40 See D. Stiefel, (1994), '"For Better, for Worse ...": the Credit-Anstalt and its Customers in 1931', in Teichova et al, (1994), pp. 178-93.

41 See G. Enderle-Burcel, (1994), 'The Failure of Crisis Management: Banking Laws in Interwar Austria', in Teichova et al, (1994), pp. 116-28.

CHAPTER SIX

The financial system following the establishment of Czechoslovakia, 1918-1929

Vlastislav Lacina

The maintenance of an effective banking system was of the utmost importance for the economic development of the fledgling Czechoslovak Republic. The financial structure, inherited from the Habsburg economy, had two major components: one consisting of the commercial banks and the other comprised of secondary institutions, such as savings banks and small loan companies. This was filled out by the activities of private banking houses, together with those of provincial and mortgage banks, but, none the less, these particular institutions played only minor roles in the functioning of the system. In 1918 the banks already performed the tasks of accumulating and mobilizing capital, whereas the major institutions also played a very important role in the allocation of capital. This integration of the financial market was due to the predominance of universal banks, which since the late nineteenth century had provided a broad range of services spanning the provision of credit and capital.

This contribution will focus upon the development of commercial banking during the 1920s, but the significance of secondary institutions will be briefly considered in its concluding paragraphs. It begins by outlining the banking system immediately prior to the creation of Czechoslovakia. Thereafter, it considers the changes that came about by the creation of a separate Czechoslovak currency and the process of nostrification. These are placed within the context of the post-war expansion in the number of banks, a development which came to an end in 1924. The relative size of individual banks in 1929 is then reviewed, followed by a brief survey of the business of banking during the 1920s.

Before 1918 Vienna was the business and banking centre of the Dual Monarchy, including the Czech Crown Lands, to the extent that the financial system of the 'imperial' economy was dominated by 22 major Viennese banks. These institutions collectively accounted for 71.4 per cent of total banking capital within Cisleithania, the Austrian half of Austria-Hungary, while the ten 'great' Viennese banks had 76 branch offices and 26 agencies in Bohemia, Moravia and Silesia. The major banks had links with most leading industrial and commercial enterprises through meeting their requirements for credits and by the substantial equity interests that they held in these companies.[1]

Local banking in Prague, which further developed from 1900, was essentially a provincial business. Before 1914 Czech capital was weaker than Austrian, yet during the fin-de siècle period it developed more rapidly, to penetrate Slav areas within the Dual Monarchy and to have a presence in the Balkans and Russia. None the less, it was difficult for local capital to succeed even within the Czech Crown Lands and, in 1900, the capital of four Czech banks only accounted for 7.9 per cent of total Austrian bank capital. However, by 1913, the share of Czech banks, now arising from the capital invested in 13 institutions, had increased to 13.3 per cent.[2]

With the creation of the Czechoslovak Republic, significant changes took place in the economy's banking system, arising from currency separation, nostrification and organic economic growth, which differentiated it to some degree from the Austrian and Hungarian financial sectors. None the less, the general pre-war trend of financial development, established in the territories of the future Czechoslovakia, persisted within the now separated Czechoslovak credit system, except for some minor modifications.

During autumn 1918 the decisive influence within the banking system of Czechoslovakia was exerted by major Viennese banks, namely the Allgemeine österreichische Boden-Credit-Anstalt, the Anglo-Österreichische Bank, the Bank und Wechselstuben-Actien-Gesellschaft 'Mercur', the Niederösterreichische Escompte-Gesellschaft, the Österreichische Credit-Anstalt für Handel und Gewerbe, the Österreichische Länderbank and the Wiener Bank-Verein. Following the national revolutions, managements of these seven had attempted to pursue multinational banking policies through trying to continue the activities of their institutions in all the successor states. However, these plans failed since they directly clashed with the aims of those who framed economic policy in almost all of the new republics. In Czechoslovakia, financial and industrial interest groups supported the introduction of government policies designed to secure their new country's full economic independence and which therefore sought financial separation from Vienna.

Although branches of Viennese banks were allowed to continue their operations within Czechoslovakia, their position, especially with regard to credit intermediation, became more adverse after the introduction of a Czechoslovak currency on 25 February 1919. This step had been undertaken by the Prague government in order to try and prevent the Czechoslovak economy from being further affected by the accelerating Austrian inflation.[3] Lacking sufficient quantities of the new currency, branches of Austrian banks within Czechoslovakia were unable to provide their local clients with credits to the extent required. These customers turned to domestic banks which possessed larger capital resources. This was particularly the case with respect to the Živnostenská banka [Industrial Bank], which had the largest capital reserves amongst Czech banks and, furthermore, enjoyed close contacts with state institutions and the Prague government. The Boden-Credit-Anstalt concluded an agreement with the Živnostenská banka in July 1919 and, nine months later, both the Credit-Anstalt and the Niederösterreichische Escompte-Gesellschaft followed suit in allowing the Živnobank to participate in credits provided to their major clients.[4] The establishment of these links constituted a basis for domestic institutions gaining a greater influence in the banking system and within the national economy of the Czechoslovak Republic. However, it was the process of nostrification that brought about the most significant changes in the Czechoslovak credit market and banking system.

Legislation for the nostrification of corporate commercial, industrial and transport undertakings was enacted on 11 December 1919 and nostrification was extended to financial institutions, in particular the branches of Viennese banks, by a decree of the Ministry of Finance issued in September 1920.[5] Although the 1919 law only required the transfer of the head offices of joint stock companies to Czechoslovak soil, the practical consequences of the nostrification went much further. After their reconstitution to meet the requirements of nostrification, companies established new credit links with Czechoslovak banks which, normally, also became responsible for making new share issues on their behalf. Through acting as issuing houses, the banks undertook share allocations and thereby could influence the distribution of new issues amongst investors.[6] Nostrification not only influenced the nature of the credit market but also had a strong impact upon the banking system. One of the most important effects came in 1919, even before legislation was passed, with the Credit-Anstalt transferring its branches in Czechoslovakia to the then provincial, German-owned Bömische Escomptebank in Prague. The consequent restructuring of this Prague bank involved the participation of the Živnostenská banka which, together with its clients, purchased 52 per cent of the shares that were issued. The arising institution, mixed by language and ethnicity, Czech-German, Česká eskomptní banka a úvěrní ústav [Böhmische Escomptebank und Creditanstalt], became the second biggest bank in Czechoslovakia and came to be the locus for co-operation between Czech and German speaking bankers and industrialists throughout the 1920s.[7]

The Ministry of Finance's decree of September 1920 called for the establishment of independent head offices for the Czechoslovak branches of Viennese banks. This led to the creation of the Česká komerční banka [Bohemian Commercial Bank], which took over the branches of the 'Mercur', the Všeobecná česká bankovní jednota [General Bohemian Bank Union], established to acquire the branches of the Wiener Bank-Verein, and the Banka pro obchod a průmysl [Bank for Commerce and Industry], the successor institution to the branches of the Länderbank. All of these were ethnically mixed, Czech-German financial institutions, but the Banque de Paris et de Pays-Bas held a decisive influence in the Banka pro obchod a průmysl.[8] Furthermore, as a result of an agreement between the British and the Czechoslovak governments made in 1922, all the Czech branches of the Anglo-Österreichische Bank were acquired by the Anglo-československá banka [Anglo-Czechoslovak Bank], formed for that purpose. Its capital remained exclusively British held until 1927, when the British interests involved, now represented through the Anglo-International Bank, sold 25 per cent of their holdings to the Czechoslovak state and 50 per cent to a group of Czech companies (including the Škoda Works, the agrarian Kooperativa, J. Schicht and F. Petschek), and the Prince of Liechtenstein.[9] In 1929 the remaining British interest was relinquished while, a year later, the Anglo-Czechoslovak Bank merged with the Pražská úvěrní banka and the Česká komerční banka. This fusion created the Anglo-Prague Bank, with the Czechoslovak state holding 40 per cent of its capital.[10]

Nostrification in Slovakia led to the establishment of only one bank, the Slovenská všeobecná úvěrná banka [Slovak General Credit Bank], out of the branches of the Credit-Anstalt and the Magyar Általános Hitelbank [Hungarian General Credit Bank]. During the 1920s branches of other Hungarian banks in Slovakia (formerly Upper Hungary) were mostly taken over by local and Czech financial institutions.[11]

Changes in credit links and within the banking system, arising from nostrification, took place when the Czechoslovak financial system was rapidly developing. The number of commercial banks in the Czech Lands increased from 22 to 38 between 1918 and 1922, whereas total banking share capital rose over the same period from 529 to 1,905 million Czech crowns [Kč].[12] However, save for the Banka československých legií [Bank of Czechoslovak Legions], none of the large number of banks that were founded during the postwar years subsequently rose to any position of prominence. The core of the banking system was constituted by former provincial banks, some of which managed to develop into large-scale institutions.

The Czechoslovak banks were affected by a short-term crisis during 1923/4 to the extent that a number had to be salvaged by the state. Stability returned to the credit market after 1925. Four main groups, by language and ethnicity, can be distinguished in the Czechoslovak banking system during the second half of the 1920s: Czech, mixed Czech-German, German and Slovak. In 1929, there were 22 banks with a total capital of 1,845 million Kč operating in the Czech Lands, whereas small financial institutions prevailed in Slovakia, the province having 76 banks with an aggregate capital of 375 million Kč .[13] Table 6.1 details the principal banks.

In 1929, before the Great Depression began to have an impact, seven Czech, three Czech-German, two German and two Slovak banks, in terms of nationality by language and ethnicity, featured among large and medium-size financial institutions. The extraordinary economic power wielded by the Živnostenská banka arose from not only the volume of its own capital but also from the balances placed with it by savings banks and loan companies.

Table 6.1: Capital stock and balance sheet totals of the main commercial banks (in millions of Czech crowns)[14]

Bank	banking group, by language	Capital 1919	Capital 1922	Capital 1929	Balance sheet total, 1929
Živnostenská banka [Industrial Bank]		120	200	300	5,676
Pražská úvěrní banka [Prague Credit Bank]*		50	75	235	4,509
Česká průmyslová banka [Bohemian Industrial Bank]		80	120	210	2,448
Moravská agrární a průmyslová banka [Agrarian and Industrial Bank of Moravia]		36	120	120	1,919
Česká banka [Bohemian Bank]		20	60	60	637
Agrární banka [Agrarian Bank]		12	60	60	913
Banka československých legií [Bank of Czechoslovak Legions]		-	70	70	1,020
Česká eskomptní banka [Bohemian Discount Bank]	C-G	48	175	250	4,397
Anglo-československá banka [Anglo-Czechoslovak Bank]	C-G	-	120	-	-
Banka pro obchod a průmysl [Bank for Commerce and Industry]	C-G	-	80	160	1,966
Böhmische Bank Union [Bohemian Bank Union]	G	80	160	200	4,404
Deutsche Agrar- und Industriebank [German Agrarian and Industrial Bank]	G	-	-	60	750
Tatra banka [Tatra Bank]	S	2	-	75	730
Slovenská banka [Slovak Bank]	S	9	-	70	692

Notes
* In 1930, Anglo-Prague Bank
C-G Czech-German banks
G German banks
S Slovak banks

In spite of the considerable importance of popular savings institutions, commercial joint stock banks formed the most significant component of the Czechoslovak money market. They held in aggregate 57 per cent of all financial institutions' balances and directed their businesses, first and foremost, towards large- and medium-size industrial enterprises and the wholesale trade. The commercial and credit activities of the banks grew considerably over the first decade of the existence of the Czechoslovak Republic. This was reflected in the expansion of branch networks and by increases in their capitals, reserves and total balances. Czechoslovak banks were universal financial institutions through combining deposit and investment banking, together with the provision of mortgage loans. In addition, they undertook extensive trading activities, especially the wholesale marketing of sugar and coal and, when the bank laws of 1924 forbade such activities, wholesaling was transferred to subsidiary commercial enterprises. The creation of the Czechoslovak Republic led to the banks undertaking the finance of imports and exports, which previously had been the preserve of the 'great' banks and trading companies of Vienna, together with merchant houses in Trieste and Hamburg.[15]

Over the entire interwar period commercial banking activities consisted mainly of concentrating financial resources and granting credits to industry and the wholesale trade. The banks' liabilities largely fell under four heads: deposits, current accounts, entrusted money and equity capitals and reserves.

Table 6.2: Capital sources and credits of commercial banks in the Czech Lands, selected years (millions of Czech crowns)[16]

Year	Savings	Current accounts	Credits
1919	1,299	767	8,551
1922	5,803	19,590	19,551
1926	8,022	14,848	17,165
1929	8,927	18,416	20,643

The vast majority of credits consisted of short-term loans. Largely, this form of accommodation comprised credits to provide working capital; advances to enable the purchase of raw materials (principally cotton, wool and oil); credits to finance stocks of finished products; lombard credits; and a heterogeneous group of facilities supplied to other banks together with commercial companies. The range of bank clients obtaining such credits varied widely but, predominantly, credits went to regular customers, who also featured prominently with regard to other services provided by the banks. However, the outstanding financial feature of the 1920s was the numerous promotions undertaken by the banks. Companies were founded to meet the needs of the newly created Czechoslovak economy and to reconstruct industry and transport. The banks were involved in the establishment of nearly every joint stock company, with only two industrial enterprises, Osram and Explosia, being created with the participation of foreign capital.[17]

Savings banks and small loan companies also played a major role in Czechoslovakia's financial system. They fulfilled two important tasks: the concentration of capital generated by small enterprises and the amassing of private savings. These liabilities grew rapidly with, in 1929, the deposits of these financial institutions totalling 25.1 billion Kč, as opposed to the mere 10.1 billion Kč held by the banks.[18] The institutions of the secondary financial sector entrusted some of their resources to the banks for the facilitation of major investments, with the balance being mobilised as credits to small entrepreneurs such as peasants, craftsmen and traders. Savings banks and small loans companies were two of the five types of institutions which made up the Czechoslovak secondary financial sector, the other three being civic and trade loan companies, Raiffeisen banks and, in Slovakia, co-operative credit unions. Each type of institution concentrated upon a particular social stratum. Savings banks and small loan companies were the financial institutions of the urban middle classes. District loan companies and Raiffeisen banks undertook their business in the rural economy. The dense network and the capital power of these institutions is shown in table 6.3.

Table 6.3: Savings banks and small loan companies, 1929

	Number	Resources (millions, Kč)
Savings banks	368	16,586
District loan companies (B)	171	3,465
Small loan companies	1,866	11,129
Raiffeisen banks	4,190	4,905
Co-operative credit unions (S)	1,002	538

Notes
B In Bohemia only
S In Slovakia

The pressing lack of capital during the first post-war years was partly met by the resources of the secondary financial sector. The institutions that comprised it not only accumulated significant resources but mobilized them through credits to small businesses, so playing a very important role in the country's national economy.

Notes

1 R. L. Rudolph, (1976), *Banking and Industrialisation in Austria-Hungary. The Role of Banks in Industrialisation of the Czech Crownlands, 1873-1914*, Cambridge.

2 C. Nečas, (1957), *Na prahu české kapitálové expanze* [On the threshold of Czech capital expansion] (Brno, 1987), pp. 43-114; and Z. Jindra, (1957), 'K rozvoji českého bankovního kapitálu před první světovou válkou' [Development of Czech bank capital before World War I], *Československý časopis historický*, 5, pp. 506-526.

3 V. Lacina, (1990), *Formování československé ekonomiky 1918-1923* [The formation of the Czechoslovak economy 1918-1923], Prague, pp. 81-88.

4 Czechoslovak National Bank Archives [hereafter ASB] ZB-S-I.c, Minutes of Živnostenská banka Executive Committee meetings of 30 Sep. 1919, 9 Oct. 1919 & 20 Apr. 1920.

5 V. Lacina, (1994), 'Nostrifikáce podnike a bank v prvním desetiletí Československé republiky' [Nostrification of enterprises and banks during the first decade of the Czechoslovak Republic], *Česky časopis historický*, 92, pp. 77-92.

6 Ibid, pp. 81-87.

7 Ibid, pp. 87-8.

8 A. Pimper, (1929), *České obchodní banky za války a po válce* [Czech commercial banks during and after the war], Prague, pp. 485-527.

9 *Hospodářská politika, 1930* [Economic Policy], pp. 232, 233.

10 Ibid.; and see also A. Teichova, (1974), *An Economic Background to Munich*, Cambridge, pp. 350-6.

11 *Almanach československého peněžnictví* [Almanac of the Czechoslovak banking system], Prague 1928, pp. 106-7.

12 Ibid., p. 108.

13 *Statistická příručka RCS* [Statistical Survey of the Czechoslovak Republic], 4, Prague, 1932, pp. 257-9.

14 Ibid, p. 259.

15 ASB; ZB-S-V. a-13/9. Cotton Syndicate.

16 *Statistical Survey*, 1932, Part 2, p. 214; Part 3, p. 158; Part 4, p. 258.

17 For further details about the participation of foreign capital in Czechoslovak industry see Teichova, (1974).

18 *Statistical Survey*, 1932, Part 4, p. 258.

CHAPTER SEVEN

The financial sector in Yugoslavia and Slovenia during the interwar period

Franjo Štiblar

This contribution is concerned with the economic development of Slovenia, and especially the growth of the financial sector, during the interwar period. The discussion and analysis considers the region's changing comparative position within the economy of the Kingdom of Yugoslavia. While Slovenia was the leading manufacturing area within the Kingdom, it was not a dominant pole of trade and finance. Zagreb was the financial centre of Yugoslavia during the interwar period, whereas Belgrade also had some prominence in trade and finance, especially during the 1930s when Yugoslavia was further centralized.

The first section of this contribution considers the place of Slovene inhabited territory within the economy of the Austro-Hungarian Monarchy immediately prior to 1914, and also reviews the region's relative position within Yugoslavia during the interwar period. Post-war reconstruction is addressed in the opening paragraphs of the second section, which thereafter surveys the macro-economic history of Yugoslavia during the 1920s and 1930s. The focus of the third section is the growth of the real economy, domestic trade and international trade over the interwar period. The first three sections provide the necessary context and background for sections four and five which concentrate upon the development of Slovenian banking from 1900 until 1939. Finally, some general conclusions are drawn, as well as some parallels with current experience.

Before the First World War, the lands populated by Slovenes were part of Cisleithania, the Austrian half of the Dual Monarchy.[1] The areas inhabited by Slovenes constituted one of the least developed regions of the Empire, with agriculture and mining being the main branches of its economy. On the basis of this structure, the Slovenian areas supplied raw materials and food to other parts of the Dual Monarchy, as well as to Italy and Germany. Manufacturing in Slovenian territories, particularly the production of capital goods, was predominantly controlled by the German-speaking population resident within this region or from Austria and Germany. However, in autumn 1918 with the collapse of the Dual Monarchy, the *relative* economic position of Slovenian populated areas changed dramatically since they were the most developed parts of the newly constituted Kingdom of Serbs, Croats and Slovenes. This relative change was to have important consequences for the future development of the Slovene economy's structure. With the new, post-war political and economic boundaries of central and eastern Europe, Slovenian agriculture lost its former markets and came to face strong domestic competition from Voivodina, Dalmatia and other provinces. These changes led, positively, to a further increase in the importance of its trade in manufactures and which, in turn, resulted in Slovenia becoming, technologically, the leading region of the new Kingdom.[2]

The economic, political and cultural aims of the programme for a 'Unified Slovenia', which had developed over the nineteenth century, spoke only of autonomy for the Slovene nation, not full independence. During the collapse of the Dual Monarchy at the end of the war, south Slavs formed the State of Slovenes, Croats and Serbs and then, on 1 December 1918, joined Serbia and Montenegro in the new Kingdom of Serbs, Croats and Slovenes ruled by the Serbian Karadjordjevic dynasty. Within the Kingdom, Slovene inhabited territory constituted two provinces: Ljubljanska oblast and Mariborska oblast. In 1929 the Kingdom of Yugoslavia was established, following which the state's organization became more centralized and its government increasingly autocratic. With these changes, the territory of Slovenia was renamed Dravska banovina.

The Slovene population rose from 1.060 million in 1921 to 1.144 million in 1931 and to 1.209 million in 1938, comprising 7.73 per cent of the total population of Yugoslavia in the latter year. Although the name, Slovenia, was never used, the Slovene population, and the territory they occupied, was always clearly delimited, nationally and geographically, from other parts of the Kingdom, which was not the case, for instance, with Croatia or Serbia.

The post-war economic situation of Slovene territories was similar to that elsewhere in central and eastern Europe. There was a dire shortage of food and raw materials while machinery was affected by a previous lack of repair and maintenance. These problems were expressed financially in a weak currency and rapid inflation, in turn, augmented by the Austro-Hungarian crown continuing in circulation.

Immediately following the war, Slovenian inhabited areas had partial autonomy and the National Council, established on 16 August 1918 as the 'Slovene Interim Government', had an economic section among its departments. The major problem that the economic section had to resolve was the post-war transition. Along with improving the supply of goods and economic resources, post-war policies included the nostrification of enterprises, currency reform and the concentration of co-operatives. A special administrative body for trade and industry was formed during December 1920 in Ljubljana, the Slovene capital, to address economic matters, including trade and finance, and a transitional office was established to deal with a range of concerns, including exports and imports. Both the National Council - the provisional government in Slovenia - and its economic section dealt at length with the problems arising with the nostrification of those enterprises on Slovene territory which had been previously owned by foreigners. Equally, tax reform occupied a leading position on the agenda of economic issues.

The post-war transition period in Yugoslavia came to an end in 1924, with the stabilization of the currency and the balancing of the budget. These measures were rounded out by the signing of international treaties and the introduction of a new customs regime. Some difficulties were eased by good harvests during the mid-1920s, but two attempts had to be made at agricultural reform - in 1919 and again in 1931. The external debt, arising from loans obtained during the war and over the transition period, continued to pose a problem.

After the establishment of the kingdom in December 1918, currency reform came to be the first major task of the central authorities. Monetary and fiscal policies were developed by the central government and the central bank in Belgrade. However, until 1924, four currencies had circulated in Yugoslavia - crowns in the regions which had been formerly part of the Dual Monarchy, and dinars, levs and perpers in Serbia and Montenegro. After several attempts at reform, an exchange rate of 4 crowns/1 dinar was introduced, to the detriment of holders of crowns, and a restrictive monetary policy was initiated which led to the appreciation of the dinar from 1924. The stronger dinar stabilized the economy, but brought to an end the post-war period of a revival in economic activity and which in part had been spurred by inflation. The world economic crisis and the introduction of the gold standard in 1931 (but for what proved to be for only a few weeks in Yugoslavia), further strengthened the dinar. However, this restrictive monetary policy failed to revive the economy during the early 1930s. The volume of all financial aggregates decreased substantially and were not to regain their previous magnitudes until outbreak of the Second World War, as shown for instance in the deposits and credits of Slovene financial institutions displayed in table 7.10.

The structure of M1 in table 7.1, with the share of cash exceeding 80 per cent over the whole period, is an indication of the extent to which the financial sector of Yugoslavia was underdeveloped.[3] Throughout the interwar period the volume of savings exceeded M1. Standing behind these developments, the amount of outstanding credits, granted by central bank to the government for budgetary purposes, was 3.2 billion dinars in 1920 (88 per cent of M1), thereafter until 1925 stood about 4.5 billion dinars (75 per cent of M1 or seven per cent of national income), but during the second half of the decade then contracted to 4.1 billion dinars (60 per cent of M1 or 7.5 per cent of national income). However, this accommodation substantially decreased over the 1930s, with the amount ranging between 1.6 to 1.8 billion dinars (ten to 30 per cent of M1 or four per cent of national income).

The world economic crisis had several major effects upon the Yugoslav financial sector and the Slovene region, with the financial aggregates decreasing coupled with a decline in the number of financial intermediaries. Moreover, there were significant changes in the structure of financial aggregates. As can be seen from the table 7.1, during the first half of the 1930s the share of demand deposits within M1 fell substantially (a typical sign of a crisis of credibility), and saving deposits in Yugoslavia (as well as deposits and credits in Slovenia, see tables 7.8 and 7.10), contracted and never recovered to their 1930 level.

Table 7.1: Yugoslavia, monetary aggregates 1920-1940 (millions of dinars)

Year	Cash	Demand deposits	'Narrow' M1*	Saving deposits	'Broad' M (M1 + savings deposits)
1920	3,344	258	3,602		
1921	4,688	372	5,060		
1922	5,040	460	6,008		
1923	5,790	460	6,250		
1924	6,001	630	6,631		
1925	6,062	532	6,595		
1926	5,811	640	6,452		
1927	5,743	1,254	6,997		
1928	5,528	1,179	6,707	10,306	17,013
1929	5,817	1,510	7,328	11,790	19,118
1930	5,396	922	6,319	13,880	20,199
1931	5,172	416	5,589	12,170	17,759
1932	4,772	698	5,471	10,226	15,697
1933	4,327	1,031	5,358	9,662	15,020
1934	4,383	866	5,250	9,780	15,030
1935	4,889	1,386	6,276	10,120	16,396
1936	5,409	1,629	7,038	10,671	17,709
1937	5,834	2,459	8,393	11,770	20,163
1938	6,920	2,093	9,014	11,228	20,242
1939	9,697	1,718	11,416	10,145	21,561
1940	13,843	3,531	17,365		

* Cash and demand deposits
Source: D. Potocnik, 'Slovenško denarnistvo, 1919-1938', in *Spominski Zbornik Slovenije 1919-1939* (Ljubljana, 1939), and *Statistički godišnjak Jugoslavije* (Belgrade, 1919-1941).

Precise budgetary details for the period 1919 to 1922 are unavailable. However, there are indications that there were large deficits during these years, resulting in an expansionary fiscal policy during the period of postwar reconstruction. Following stabilization, the Yugoslavian authorities pursued prudent monetary and fiscal policies between 1924 and 1934, which might provoke surprise among some commentators. Even when the accounts of the state enterprise sector were included, the balance of the budget was usually positive. The possibility of stimulating the economy through a combination of a monetary and fiscal policies (especially by a budget deficit in the case of the latter), was neither generally known nor appreciated as most economists adhered to classical principles during the interwar period. As can be seen from table 7.2, the state budget was in surplus, except between 1931 and 1934 when the world crisis affected the country. The budget of Dravska banovina, as Slovenia was called after 1931, comprised only one per cent of the Yugoslav budget.

Table 7.2: Public Sector Expenditure: State Budget and Budget of Dravska banovina (millions of dinars)

	Yugoslavia			Dravska banovina	
	Total expenditure of the public sector	Government budget			
Year		Expenditure	Balance	Budget	State enterprises
1919/20	1,574	1,558			
1920/21	4,815	3,994			
1921/22		4,660			
1922/23	8,134	6,934			
1923/24		10,344			
1924/25	11,765	10,540	+298		
1925/26	12,251	11,777	+286		
1926/27	12,900	11,592	+13		
1927/28	11,477	10,983	+336		
1928/29		11,146	+240		
1929/30		11,817	+1,632		
1930/31		12,470	+436	136	31
1931/32		11,530	-627	105	56
1932/33		9,969	-422	110	49
1933/34		9,663	-30	97	43
1934/35		9,379	+380	90	40
1935/36		9,562	+439	98	38
1936/37		10,058	+512	103	41
1937/38		11,083	+903	115	42
1938/39		12,180	0	121	63
1939/40		12,942	0	128	73

Source: D. Potocnik, 'Slovenško denarnistvo, 1919-1938', in *Spominski Zbornik Slovenije 1919-1939* (Ljubljana, 1939).

A general overview of the interwar period shows that prices doubled in Yugoslavia between 1914 and 1924, then halved over the ensuing ten years, but increased by 25 per cent between 1935 and 1940. These medium-term movements were related to the stance of monetary and fiscal policies. These were expansionary between 1914 and 1924, but were restrictive until 1934 with their effects upon the economy being also augmented by the influence of the world economic crisis from 1929/30. Macro-economic policy then became expansive to a moderate degree during the six years until 1940. Variations in the exchange rate followed the movement of prices. The dinar depreciated against the dollar and sterling until 1924 but then appreciated against these two key currencies until 1934. After an official devaluation of 28.5 per cent in 1935, the dinar once more fell on the exchanges, especially against sterling (see table 7.6).

Movements in interest rates display a broad sympathy with changes in the price level and the dinar's exchange rate. In 1920, when there was an expansive economic policy, the passive bank rate was four per cent, while the active rate reached seven to eight per cent. The introduction of a restrictive monetary policy in 1924 caused an increase in the passive interest rate to 12 per cent and raised the active rate to 18-20 per cent. From 1927 interest rates fell to more normal levels, the passive rate declining to a band between 4.5 to eight per cent, the active to nine to 12 per cent. With the measures of reform associated with the 1935 devaluation, the National Bank of Yugoslavia decreased its discount rate from 6.5 to five per cent and limited the passive Bank rate to a maximum of five per cent and the active to ten per cent.

Yugoslavia was one of the least developed European economies during the interwar period. Agriculture was the dominant activity while another indication of backwardness is that most of the economy was controlled by foreign owners.

Table 7.3: Sectoral shares of the Yugoslav economy, 1923, 1939 (per cent)

	1923	1939
Agriculture and fishing	52.8	46.0
Forestry	7.5	5.7
Manufacturing and mining	13.4	20.6
Crafts	9.6	8.4
Trade, tourism, catering	12.3	11.6

Source: Various annual volumes of *Statistički godišnjak Jugoslavije* (Belgrade, 1919-1941).

Table 7.3 indicates that the Yugoslav economy experienced little structural change during the interwar period. Although the share of manufacturing and mining increased by seven per cent between 1923 and 1939, this sector's contribution to GDP at the end of the interwar period was still only half of that generated by agriculture. Furthermore, whereas the share of transport and communications expanded, those of trade and tourism and craft contracted. The extent of structural change brought about by economic development during the interwar years is indicated by the contraction of the role played by forestry, crafts and agriculture. From the mid-1930s the growth and orientation of the economy was affected by the likelihood of war, leading to an emphasis in manufacturing upon armaments and steel and producing a stronger dependence upon trade with Germany.

The Kingdom was a common economic area in which prices, interest rates and exchange rates did not differ significantly between its constituent regions, despite there being wide disparities in levels of provincial economic development. As indicated by the standard of living or the extent of industrialization, Slovenia was the most developed part of Yugoslavia throughout the interwar period. Slovenia experienced its first 'Gründerzeit' [founding period] during the years from immediately after the war until 1925. The industrialization of Slovenia involved the further development of mining and construction coupled with the growth of manufacturing, especially with regard to the output of textiles, wood products, steel, chemical, food, paper and glass. A major feature of these developments was the shift to electricity as the main source of power. After 1925, despite the increasingly centralized government in Belgrade, dominated by Serbian interests,[4] directing flows of credits towards the south and east of the Kingdom, other regions of Yugoslavia did not reach the Slovenian level of economic development. With regard to establishing Slovenia's relative economic position amongst the constituent regions of the Yugoslav Kingdom, the only available data relate to Dravska banovina (Slovenia) in 1931. This region comprised 6.43 per cent of Yugoslav territory and contained 8.21 per cent of Yugoslav population. Kresal, a historian, has estimated that the province's share of Yugoslav total manufacturing was 26 per cent. In 1938, Slovenian national income per capita was 4,000 dinars as opposed to 2,400 dinars with respect to Yugoslavia.

The development of trade and finance in Slovenia was strongly influenced by the geo-political changes within central and south-eastern Europe as well as by world economic cycles, including the Great Depression. Unfortunately it is very difficult to mount an evaluation of the role of trade and finance in Slovenia as compared to Yugoslavia or other countries. Essential statistical data, such as those for Slovenian national product, exports and imports, are not available.

Some pointers regarding Slovenian trade and finance can be gleaned from the census. In 1931 6.8 per cent of the Slovenian population was employed in trade, finance and transport as opposed to 4.6 per cent within all Yugoslavia. In terms of occupations of solely heads of households, in 1921 3.65 per cent were in trade and credit within Slovenia as opposed to

3.18 per cent within Yugoslavia, and in 1931 the shares engaged in this sector were 2.99 and 2.88 per cent respectively.

Table 7.4: Number of business undertakings within commerce and finance in Slovenia and Yugoslavia, 1937 and 1939

	1937		1939	
	S	Y	S	Y
Wholesale trade	1,223	5,658	657	5,635
Food shops	358	18,262	343	17,025
Mixed shops	3,199	34,143	3,390	39,185
Other retail shops	295	25,670	302	30,258
Agents and commission brokers	93	1,806	76	1,920
Banks	573	1,333	16	1,308
Insurance companies	16	109	16	105
Other financial enterprises	-	200	-	-
Hotels	74	450	75	473
Other catering companies	6,053	39,575	6,169	43,131
Forwarding agents	26	438	30	490
International trading agents	15	129	14	123
Urban transport companies	456	2,660	503	3,443
Carriers	126	1,423	124	1,683
Other transport companies	533	3,389	607	3,770
Bureaux	4	353	3	364
Other undertakings	3,137	16,181	3,719	12,962
TOTAL	16,181	144,080	16,629	162,033

Key: S = Slovenia; Y = Yugoslavia
Sources: Various annual volumes of *Statistički godišnjak Jugoslavije* (Belgrade, 1919-1941) and *Indeks* (Zagreb, 1938).

Table 7.4 gives some pointers to the enterprise structure of domestic trade. Domestic trade and travel in Slovenia had a relatively small share as compared with Yugoslav overall, not exceeding ten per cent in most branches that comprised this sector of economic activity, with the only exceptions being hotels and restaurants, and transport. However, this has to be understood in the context of Slovenia having a share of 26 per cent of manufacturing, while the region only accounted for six per cent of the population of Yugoslavia. The data in table 7.4 can be fleshed out to some extent from other available sources. These point to the number of commercial travellers in Yugoslavia during the 1930s being not very substantial although the Slovenian share of such marketing activity was between 20 and 30 per cent. Equally, during the 1930s depression, there was a contraction in this form of selling, with the number of such representatives declining between 1929 and 1933 from 2,964 to 1,802 in the case of Yugoslavia, and from 841 to 387 within Slovenia. By 1937 their numbers had recovered to 1,673 (Yugoslavia) and 414 (Slovenia). Table 7.5 gives some indicators as to the respective levels of the formalized distribution of goods within Slovenia and Yugoslavia and the extent of change over the interwar period. However, the data contained in the table are fragmentary, arising from being constructed out of a variety of sources, each of which used various definitions.

Table 7.5: Distribution - shopping outlets in Slovenia and Yugoslavia, 1922, 1925-31, and 1934-9

	Service shops in manufacturing (Ljubljana Chamber of Trade, Craft and Industry)	Commerce shops (Ljubljana Chamber of Commerce)	Retail shops		Wholesale shops	
			S	Y	S	Y
1922	12,389					
1925		12,425				
1926		12,745				
1927	14,464	12,954				
1928		12,930		124,323		
1929		12,798				
1930		12,923				
1931		12,935				
1934			903	63,948	1,290	6,583
1935			732	69,157	1,204	6,652
1936	9,900		4,048	73,188	1,655	7,919
1937			3,852	78,075	1,223	5,658
1938	10,365		4,019	77,914	608	5,922
1939			4,035	86,468	657	5,635

Key - S = Slovenia; Y = Yugoslavia
Source: D. Potocnik, 'Slovenško denarnistvo, 1919-1938', in *Spominski Zbornik Slovenije 1919-1939* (Ljubljana, 1939), and *Jugoslavija 1918-1988,* (Belgrade, 1939).

In the case of foreign trade, only aggregate data for the whole Kingdom are available and these are displayed in table 7.6. Generally, exports exceeded imports, with the largest visible trade surplus occurring in 1924 when exports were greater than imports by 18 per cent. Trade deficits were only experienced between 1920 and 1923, and in 1927, 1928 and 1930. Total trade (exports plus imports) reached a maximum during the period of $

(current) 250 million, while the sum of total current receipts and payments (flows in the current balance of payments) peaked close to $ (current) 350 million. Estimates place annual national income at between $800 million and $1,000 million. This all suggests that the trade coefficient (exports + imports/national income) was between 25 and 30 per cent. Balance of payments data, available for 1930 to 1936, indicate that the current balance was slightly positive only in 1933 and 1936.

Table 7.6: National Income and Foreign Trade of Yugoslavia, 1920-1939, millions of dinars

Year	National Income		Exports	Imports	Exchange Rate Dinar/$	Exchange Rate Dinar/£	Import Price Index
	Current prices	1938 prices					
1920			1,321	3,466			
1921			2,461	4,122			90
1922			3,691	6,442	73.57	328.1	192
1923	65,223	34,470	8,049	8,310	93.86	432.5	158
1924	70,080	36,515	9,539	8,222	78.48	347.2	145
1925	63,282	40,147	8,905	8,753	58.79	284.3	142
1926	56,156	38,709	7,818	7,632	56.64	275.7	145
1927	53,328	37,624	6,400	7,286	56.78	276.4	138
1928	59,629	41,079	6,445	7,835	56.85	276.8	117
1929	59,966	43,471	7,922	7,595	56.73	276.1	107
1930	50,418	43,062	6,780	6,960	56.44	274.9	95
1931	45,100	42,071	4,801	4,800	56.49	257.8	93
1932	36,481	38,333	3,056	2,860	56.67	199.3	84
1933	36,117	38,945	3,378	2,883	46.38	190.6	88
1934	34,066	40,398	3,878	3,573	34.11	173.0	91
1935	34,602	39,271	4,030	3,700	43.62	215.1	99
1936	40,744	44,885	4,376	4,077	43.41	217.4	100
1937	45,027	45,122	6,272	5,234	43.35	215.5	104
1938	48,476	48,476	5,047	4,975	43.44	213.7	
1939	52,784	50,988	5,521	4,757	44.19	196.9	

Sources: Various annual volumes of *Statistički godišnjak Jugoslavije* (Belgrade, 1919-1941) and *Jugoslavija 1918-1988* (Belgrade, 1989).

Formal financial intermediation was evident on Slovene inhabited territories from the early nineteenth century. It was undertaken by private bankers and, more importantly, by credit co-operatives in the countryside and regulated, or self-managed, savings institutions in urban areas. Generally the business of these houses and institutions was restricted to short-term transactions.

Following the Austro-German approach, universal banking developed with the introduction of corporate banking in 1900. As a result, joint stock banks became directly involved in the ownership and management of enterprises. The first was the Ljubljanska Kreditna Banka, established in 1900, followed by the Jadranska Banka, formed in Trieste in 1905.

The development of corporate universal banking had features related to the ethnic composition of the population and, in turn, the economic activities of various ethnic groups. Even in the provinces of Austria which had a Slovene majority within their populations, ethnic German entrepreneurs dominated the business scene. However, they did not establish their own banks so that before 1914 there were no 'German' banks with head offices located on Slovene territory. Rather the German business community dealt with branches of the Viennese banks, which had been opened as a response to the early success of local corporate banks founded by Slovenes. None the less, foreign personnel played a major role in banking, not only through the branches of extra-regional banks on Slovene inhabited areas, but also in the first Slovene bank which had Czech managers due to an initial lack of domestic expertise.

In terms of the adaptation of corporate banking to Slovene conditions, domestic Slovene banking was 'relation banking', through the close ties that these institutions had with domestic enterprises. This was not the case with respect to branches of banks from outside the region, as they largely undertook 'transaction' business by transferring deposits to the main branches out of the region, and bringing back some of the financial assets as investments through different channels. Thus, branches of Austrian banks transferred saving deposits to their head offices in Vienna while, at the same time, drew in capital to finance investments in German-dominated industries. During the Balkan Wars and the First World War, the financial power of the Slovene banks decreased to a lesser extent than that of Austrian banks. This was because the Slovene banks were located within the vicinity of war transfers, while their business clientele predominantly consisted of entrepreneurs involved in small-scale industries producing consumer goods, which were relatively more prosperous during the war. The hostilities influenced the structure of the balance sheets of the Slovene banks, decreasing the shares of savings deposits and the real value of capital stock among their liabilities and, at the same time, increasing the share of cash on the asset side. The extent of the financial relationship between Slovene territory and Vienna was reduced in 1918 as, following the war, the newly established state of the South Slavs did not permit the incorporation of foreign banks. None the less, financial links with Vienna were to remain of some importance until the 1930s.

With the loss of Trieste as a result of the peace treaties of 1919 and 1920, Ljubljana became the sole financial centre for Slovene territory. A stock exchange was established in the city in 1924, on which trading was initially in commodities and securities, foreign exchange dealings not taking place until 1927. By size, it was, by far, the smallest of the three financial stock exchanges in Yugoslavia (the other two were in Zagreb and Belgrade) and the smaller of the six produce exchanges (the remaining three were in Sombor, Novi Sad and Skopje). The relative position of the Ljubljana stock exchange can be appreciated from the data displayed in table 7.7.

Table 7.7: Yugoslav stock exchanges, volume of operations, 1929, 1933, 1937, 1939 (millions of dinars)

	State securities		Shares		Foreign exchange		Produce	
	L	A	L	A	L	A	L	A
1929	0.7	656	0.3	50.4	978	5,923	2.4	1,314
1933	0.3	256	0.1	23.0	126	836		
1937	0.4	298	0.6	26.4	376	3,544	3.4	1,212
1939	2.9	365.7	1.7	32.9	516	8,500	8.9	1,060

Key - L = Ljubljana; A = Ljubljana, Belgrade and Zagreb exchanges.
Source: Various annual volumes of *Statistički godišnjak Jugoslavije* (Belgrade, 1919-1939).

Total turn-over on the Ljubljana exchange increased from 34 million dinars in 1926 to 418 million dinars in 1927 and to over 1 billion dinars in 1928. The wider, positive effects of the creation of the Ljubljana Exchange on trade and commerce were shown in the education of exchange employees, the adoption of exchange provisions (usance) and the setting up of an exchange court of arbitration.

The Drustvo bancnih zavodov [Society of Banking Institutions] was formed in Ljubljana in 1920 with the goal of securing uniform rules and policies, such as restricting interest on deposits to a maximum of five per cent. Following the war, the number of corporate banks in Slovenia increased from three to nine (whereas their affiliates rose from eight to 31), and within Ljubljana there were also six affiliates of banks which had their head offices in other cities. None the less, there was competition - from Yugoslav banks with special privileges, beginning with the Ljubljana branch of the Postal Savings Institute which opened in 1919, and most especially from unincorporated credit co-operatives and savings institutions. Moreover, the establishment of the Society of Banking Institutions did not mean strong monopolization because of the continuing significant competition arising from both local branches of banks based in other Yugoslav territories and unincorporated financial institutions.

Table 7.8: Slovene Banks, 1918-1937 (millions of dinars)

Year	Number	No. of subsidiary offices	Total no.	Total capital	Aggregate balance sheet total	Aggregate profits	
						Net	Total
1918	10	9	19				
1919	10	9	19	7.5	107.3	0.78	
1920	14	15	29	24.0	295.7	4.27	
1921	14	20	34	37.6	593.0	7.97	
1922	14	33	47	66.3	912.7	9.97	
1923	15	43	58	103.2	1092.7	1.59	
1924	16	41	57	117.0	1,284.1	17.17	
1925	15	40	55	118.0	1,498.3	15.8	
1926	13	28	41	112.6	1,542.0	12.97	
1927	12	26	38	98.3	1,512.1	11.4	11.95
1928	12	26	38	98.3	1,601.5	11.7	12.34
1929	12	26	38	101.3	1,688.3	11.8	11.33
1930	12	26	38	101.3	1,836.2	11.8	12.41
1931	13	26	39	103.3	1,520.6	9.5	10.21
1932	13	24	37	103.3	1,312.7	6.0	9.29
1933	12	21	33	98.3	1,193.8	4.4	8.48
1934	10	21	31	74.7	1,076.3	3.1	3.88
1935	10	18	28	84.7	1,072.8	6.7	7.49
1936	10	18	28	84.7	1,104.9	5.8	6.66
1937	10	18	28	84.7	1,116.7	8.9	10.3

Source: D. Potocnik, 'Slovenško denarnistvo, 1919-1938', in *Spominski Zbornik Slovenije 1919-1939* (Ljubljana, 1939).

Following the war, the Ljubljanska Kreditna Banka quintupled the size of its nominal share capital; the share issue was taken up locally while this capital increase also enabled the bank to retain its position as the largest Slovene financial institution. The Jadranska Banka, previously the major Slovene financial institution, had been decentralized during the war into three separate operations: the Adriatische Bank in Vienna, the Banco Adriatico in Trieste and the Jadranska Banka with a head office in Belgrade. The first two successor banks of the Jadranska subsequently got into difficulties due to outside pressures and mismanagement and were liquidated in 1925, whereas the third was later merged with another institution. The various fates of these successor banks meant that what had been the strongest Slovene bank before 1914 disappeared from the banking scene over the 1920s.

Nostrification had some effect upon the structure of Slovene banking. In 1920, the Ljubljana branch of the Vienna-based Credit-Anstalt was transformed through nostrification into a Slovene institution, the Kreditni Zavod za trgovino in industrijo [Credit Institution for Trade and Industry], but the Viennese bank continue to hold 30 per cent of its capital. As Tosti has explained in detail,[5] this bank, which pursued universal banking, played an important role in the Slovene economy during the 1920s. Like other Slovene financial institutions, it was affected by the crisis of the 1930s but the Kreditni Zavod za trgovino in industrijo managed to survive even the stresses and strains of the Second World War. A similar process of reorganization arising from nostrification[6] led to the formations of the Hipotekarna Banka Jugoslovanskih Hranilnic in Ljubljana, the Mariborska eskomptna banka and some smaller corporate banks in Prekmurje.

As well as reconstitutions due to nostrification, new banks were incorporated in Slovenia. The most important was the Zadruzna Gospodarska Banka [Cooperative Economic Bank] which was established in 1920 as a result of an initiative from co-operative institutions. Local popular savings institutions also created the Zadruzna Banka [Cooperative Bank], formed in Ljubljana in 1920, and the Celjska Posojilnica [Celje's Credit Institutions], established in Celje in 1922. At the same time, Slovene entrepreneurs founded several new smaller corporate banks, each tailored to their specific needs. These included the Obrtna Banka [Craftsman's Bank], the Slovenska Banka, the Prometna Banka [Traffic Bank] and the Trgovska Banka [Trade Bank] all established in Ljubljana, and the Merkantilna Banka set up in Kocevje and the Kreditna Banka created in Murska Sobota.

The number of Slovene corporate banks, and their branches, reached a peak in 1923. The 'founding euphoria' evaporated thereafter as a result of the deflationary monetary policy of the Yugoslav government and the arising difficulties of the Slavenska Banka Zagreb. This bank had a Slovene manager and close business connections with several Slovene banks and its collapse, due to improper post-war speculations, caused the liquidation of several Slovene financial institutions while some others decreased their total assets by clearing dubious claims. Among the institutions that ceased business, which was not in every case due to the fall of Slavenska Banka, was the Mariborska eskomptna banka which left the industrial centre Maribor without a local financial institution. The other institutions that ceased business were the Slovenska Banka, the Hipotekarna Banka, the Ilirska Banka (which had been established in 1916), the Trgovska Banka and the Merkantilna Banka Kocevje, together with some smaller banks. None the less, their liquidation, along with the dubious claims of others, contributed to the consolidation of the Slovene banking sector during the second half of the 1920s which thereby, in turn, established a more solidified banking structure when the effects of the world economic crisis were first felt in 1930.

Table 7.9: Joint stock banks in Slovenia and Yugoslavia, 1929, 1933, 1936, 1938

Year	Banks (total)		Branches (total)		Capital (m dinars)		Aggregate balance sheet total (m dinars)		Profit (m dinars)	
	S	Y	S	Y	S	Y	S	Y	S	Y
1929	9	637	26	272	94	2,192	1,809	18,419	6.8	264.3
1933	12	619	20	209	75	2,785	1,367	14,840	3.5	-133
1936					86	2,503	1,249	13,296	7.1	29.1
1938					84	2,416	1,347	13,063	5.2	85

Key - S = Slovenia; Y = Yugoslavia
Source: Various annual volumes of Statistički letopis ZStat (Belgrade, 1919-1941).

In 1930, Slovene banking capital was concentrated in Ljubljana, while the three largest financial institutions in the city, the Ljubljanska Kreditna Banka, the Kreditni Zavod za Trgovino in Industrijo and the Zadruzna gospodarska banka Ljubljana, accounted for over 88 per cent of the assets of all Slovene banks. Total banking assets reached a peak in 1930 and the subsequent contraction, that ran its course until 1934, was due to the operation of a wide variety of factors. The most important were the Yugoslav government's ill-fated decision to adopt the gold standard in 1931 and the collapse of the Credit-Anstalt in Vienna, as this bank still had strong financial ties with Slovenia during the early 1930s. Both the outflow of capital from Austria and Germany and the Hoover moratorium on reparation payments (with Yugoslavia being a recipient), also had an impact.

The major Slovene banks came under severe pressure during the first half of the 1930s as they were closely connected with the banking sectors of Austria and Germany, which were those most affected during the world economic crisis. According to Hocevar's calculations,[7] the total assets of Slovene banks decreased at an annual rate of between ten to 20 per cent from 1931 to 1934, which had the result in 1935 that, in nominal terms, they were half of their pre-crisis level. The amount of outstanding bank credits declined at a somewhat slower rate, but the volume of saving deposits fell faster. Although the contraction of Slovene banking ceased from 1935, the years before the Second World War brought little more than a mere stagnation of banking assets.[8] From 1935 until 1940, total assets of Slovene banks increased by approximately ten per cent, within which outstanding credits rose by ten per cent whereas cash holdings more than doubled, while on the other side of the balance sheet equity capital increased by a fifth. Profits rose steadily, from eight per cent in 1935 to nearly ten per cent in 1940. However, in relation to the levels pertaining before the crisis, total Slovene banking assets in 1940 were much smaller. This indicates a substantial contraction of Slovene banking activity, even when deflationary movements during the 1930s are taken into account. The following table illustrates the trends.

Table 7.10: Deposits and credits of Slovenian financial institutions, 1919-1939 (millions of dinars)

	Deposits				Credits			
Year	B	S	C	Total	B	S	C	Total
1919	96		96	94		94		
1920	255	37	292	246	20	266		
1921	531	114	645	507	29	536		
1922	811	228	332	1,371	810		201	1,011
1923	951	260	324	1,535	958		189	1,147
1924	1,121	350	442	1,913	1,123	198	244	1,565
1925	1,333	483	589	2,405	1,331	269	385	1,985
1926	1,428	624	984	3,036	1,374	378	705	2,457
1927	1,358	728	939	3,025	983	473	650	2,106
1928	1,420	861	1,060	3,341	1,124	604	781	2,509
1929	1,524	1,025	1,307	3,856	1,254	741	1,148	3,143
1930	1,649	1,182	1,688	4,519	1,415	902	1,299	3,616
1931	1,169	1,269	1,723	4,161	1,247	1,005	1,367	3,619
1932	1,049	1,193	1,651	3,893	1,080	971	1,316	3,340
1933	912	1,139	1,564	3,615	880	936	1,261	3,077
1934	787	1,101	1,505	3,393	773	901	1,213	2,887
1935	788	1,072	1,454	3,314	7,89	863	1,138	2,790
1936	819	1,053	1,396	3,268	820	758	1,064	2,642
1937	837	1,045	1,374	3,256	817	723	890	2,430

Key - B = Banks; S = Savings institutions; C = Cooperatives
Source: D. Potocnik, 'Slovenško denarnistvo, 1919-1938', in *Spominski Zbornik Slovenije 1919-1939* (Ljubljana, 1939).

The corporate banks faced competition on the Slovene financial market from two different groups of financial institutions: the larger and more protected privileged state banks, and the smaller and less organized, regulatory savings institutions in conjunction with savings and credit cooperatives.

The state privileged banks were, by value of assets, more important than the joint stock commercial banks (see data in table 7.11). They were established in Belgrade and were subject to greater regulation from the central bank and government than corporate banks. They were formed to meet specific financial needs, as their names indicate: the Hipotekarna banka [Mortgage Bank], the Obrtna banka [Craftsman's Bank], the Agrikulturna banka [Agricultural Bank] and the Postna stedionica [Postal Saving Institute]. On some occasions they provided long-term finance and supported investment. A comparison between the privileged banks and other banks in 1938 shows that, despite their smaller number (4 against 20), they were more important in terms of the aggregate value of assets. Collectively, they had larger equity capital - by 40 per cent, greater total balance sheets - by 34 per cent, and higher profits - to the extent of 63 per cent.

Table 7.11: Privileged banks in Yugoslavia, 1938 (millions of dinars)

Bank	Capital	Balance sheet total	Profits
Agricultural	700	2382	18.3
Mortgage	2,700	10,572	49.4
Craftsman's	71	326	3.1
Postal Savings		4,295	68.2
Total	3,471	17,575	139.0
Private banks	2,416	13,063	85.0
Total	5,887	30,638	224.0

Source: *Statistički godnišnjak Jugoslavije* (Belgrade, 1939).

The privileged banks opened branches in Ljubljana, beginning in 1919 with the Postal Savings Institution, which had a pre-war tradition. Similarly, the Mortgage Bank, also established before the war, set up a branch in Ljubljana in 1927, followed by the Craftman's Bank (founded 1927) in 1931 and the Agricultural Bank (established 1929) in 1937.

The somewhat heterogeneous group of savings institutions were organized in Slovenia under three bodies: the Cooperative Association in Ljubljana, the Union of Slovene Cooperatives and the Cooperative Association, both of which were located in Celje. With regard to changes in both the amassing of deposits and the disbursing of credits, the corporate banks were first affected by changes in the economic environment with the other financial institutions following with a lag of a year or two. The joint stock banks felt the impact of the world economic and financial crisis in 1930/1, before savings institutions and cooperatives, but the banks were also the first to benefit from the revival of financial activity in 1935/6. However, it should be noted that unincorporated savings institutions were stronger than joint stock banks in Slovenia, in terms of both the number of establishments and the volume of transactions and assets. In that regard Slovenia differed from other provinces or countries. Table 7.12 provides an indication of the strength of the popular savings movement at the end of the 1930s in Slovenia and Yugoslavia.

Table 7.12: Popular saving institutions in Slovenia and Yugoslavia, 1936 and 1938 (millions of dinars)

	Number		Balance sheet aggregate		Profits	
	S	Y	S	Y	S	Y
1936	29	63	1,134	2,512	1.3	10.6
1938	29	61	1,210	2,871	-20.0	-7.0

Key - S = Slovenia; Y = Yugoslavia
Source: *Statistički godnišnjak Jugoslavije* (Belgrade, 1939).

In order to round out this review which has focused upon domestic developments, it is necessary to point out that there were a number of branches of foreign banks in Yugoslavia, while there was also a significant extent of foreign ownership within a number of domestic banks. According to some estimates, during the late 1930s about 80 per cent of the banking sector of the Kingdom of Yugoslavia was controlled by foreigners.

A number of concluding points arise. First, the available data show that the Slovene corporate banking before 1914 was only at its initial stage of development in comparison within Cisleithania to the higher developmental stage of Czech banks and the mature stage of Austrian banks. Slovenia's share in Austrian banking was less than proportionate with respect to the shares in population and economic power of Slovene inhabited territory during the first decade of the twentieth century. Similarly, the subsequent share of Slovene financial intermediation in Yugoslavia during the interwar period was less than Slovene territory's share of economic potential, as indicated at the beginning of the 1930s. Both the sub-proportional shares of Slovene corporate banking in Cisleithania, and thereafter in Yugoslavia, were more than offset by the over-proportional shares of Slovene unincorporated financial intermediaries - lending cooperatives, saving institutions etc.

Second, the role of government and state measures in banking had been important before the mid-1920s crisis, when the restrictive monetary policy of the central government in Belgrade caused financial contraction and, at the same time, the consolidation of the banking sector. During the crisis, additional government regulation had not as severe an impact on the performance of banking sector as in other, more developed world financial countries, although this was not to be the case during the unsuccessful, short-term introduction of the gold standard in 1931.

Third, the question of the correlation between banking and nationalism has a specific answer in the case of Slovenia, which was a less developed region where the population desired autonomy, if not independence. In countering the economic dominance of Austrians and Germans and establishing an economic foundation for political autonomy, the independent Slovene universal banks provided some of the first footings. This was not an expression of nationalism, but merely the creation of financial institutions in order both to preserve national identity and to prevent economic and political subordination to major powers lying beyond the region. As an illustration, in Yugoslavia during the interwar period, foreign capital had a share of between 70 and 80 per cent in the banking sector. Analysis shows that the development of Slovene banking can be considered as a relevant part of the history of the Slovene nation through the important contribution that financial institutions gave to developing the economic foundations of rising Slovene self-awareness.

Fourth, there are implications from the historical experience which are quite instructive for banking in Slovenia during the 1990s. Many questions and problems, relevant for the current development of the Slovene banking sector, were raised at the beginning of the twentieth century. A similar situation has now arisen during the 1990s with regard to the entry of Austrian banks into Slovenia and, to some degree, by the indirect presence of German banks and the less than successful arrival of Italian banks. Currently, banks from other countries have not shown the same extent of interest in either establishing branches, or founding new institutions, in Slovenia. At the same time and similarly echoing the past, the foreign ownership of real property (land, housing, enterprises) is once more high on the political agenda.

Notes

1 The territory predominantly inhabited by Slovenes included Carniola (capital Ljubljana), Styria (southern), Carinthia, Pomurje, Dolenjsko, Primorsko and Trieste.

2 Present changes in the status of Slovenia, including separation from Yugoslavia (so losing 60% of its market) and the proclamation of independence, coupled with a subsequent tendency towards integration into Europe has, interestingly, similar effects. However, Slovenia was the most developed republic in Yugoslavia, but remains one of the least developed states in the (future) Western European economic alliance. Will trade patterns and experience with internal trade and finances follow previous changes, although this time in the opposite direction? This would mean concentration again in primary sectors and stronger economic dependence on technologically advanced industries and some services (including trade and finances) from more developed West European countries, especially neighbouring states.

3 Separate data for Slovenia within the common monetary area of Yugoslavia could not be obtained.

4 The central bank was also strongly influenced by Serbian interests.

5 A. Tosti, (1989), *Denarni zavodi v Sloveniji po prvi svetovni vojni* [Monetary institutions in Slovenia after World War I], Ljubljana.

6 Nostrification after World War I should be distinguished from the post-World War II nationalization in Slovenia. In the first case it meant the transfer of ownership from foreign to Slovene (private) ownership; in the second case it involved the transfer from the Slovene private to the state, and later social ownership. In relation to current discussion of ownership transformation in Slovenia, it could be observed that the policy towards foreign ownership of Slovene firms and banks was relatively restrictive immediately after World War I .

7 T. Hocevar, (1984), 'Slovensko poslovno bančništvo, 1913-1941' [Slovene business banking, 1913-1941], *Bančni Vestnik*, 33.7-8, p. 271.

8 J. Jonker & J. L. van Zander, (1992), 'Method in the Madness? Banking crises between the wars: an international comparison', in Department of Economic History, Budapest University of Economic Sciences, *20th Century Universal Banking: International Comparisons, Report from the International Conference Budapest, 2-5 September 1992*, I, Budapest.

Further reading

'Gospodarstvo med vojnama', *Zgodovina Slovencev*, Ljubljana, 1988.

S. Granda, (1987), 'Poskus organiziranja slovenske Ljubljanske obče banke, 1872' [An attempt to establish a Slovene Ljubljana General Bank, 1872], *Zgodovina denarstva in bančništva na Slovenskem*, Ljubljana.

T. Hocevar, (1986), 'Financial Intermediation in a Multilingual State: the Case of Slovene Corporate Banking in Austria, 1900-1912', *Slovene Studies*, 8.1.

T. Hocevar, (1987), 'Slovensko poslovno bančništvo kot inovacijski dejavnik' [Slovene Business Banking as an Innovation Factor], in *Zgodovina denarstva in bančništva na Slovenskem*, Ljubljana.

B. Michel, (1976), *Banque et banquiers en Autriche au début du 20e siècle*, Paris.

F. Šink, (1939), 'Razvoj trgovine, in *Spominski zbornik Slovenije 1919-1939*, Ljubljana.

I. Slokar, 'Valutne razmere, devizna politika in bankarštvo', in J. Mal (ed.), *Slovenci v desetletju 1918-1928.*

Zavod SR Slovenije za statistiko, *Slovenija 1945-1975*, Ljubljana 1975.

'Slovenija in Slovenci', in *Enciklopedija Jugoslavije*, Zagreb, 1958.

Splošni pregled Dravske banovine, Ljubljana, 1939.

Statistika spoljne trgovine kraljevine Jugoslavije, Belgrade, 1930.

F. Štiblar, (1992), 'Universal Banking on Slovene Territory, 1900-1945', in Department of Economic History, Budapest University of Economic Sciences, *20th Century Universal Banking: International Comparisons, Report from the International Conference Budapest, 2-5 September 1992*, IV, Budapest.

CHAPTER EIGHT

The role of finance in Romania's quest for modernization: insights from the interwar period

Daniel Daianu

A question has remained in my mind from the moment when the invitation to participate in this conference arrived. What is the relevance of the past, especially the interwar period, for the post-communist transformation of the economies of central and eastern Europe in general, and for Romania in particular? There are, at least, two explanations for having succumbed to the temptation of pursuing this nagging question in my endeavours to frame this contribution, instead of resorting to the approach of an economic historian. One is related to the exceptional nature of the process of post-communist transformation in humankind's history which has made, almost inescapably, most eastern European economists 'intellectual opportunists'. By the latter phrase, I mean the overwhelming and compelling intellectual appeal of contemporary events, because this has guided and almost established the research agenda since 1989.[1] The second explanation concerns the role played by history in teaching. On the one hand, the flow of historical events and their analytical interpretation directly feeds the kernel of theoretical and policy-oriented knowledge. On the other, history has influenced the development of current events in terms of what is meant by path-dependency in development theory and where this refers to the burden of the past. In the case of central and eastern Europe, path-dependency encapsulates the legacy of the region's backwardness bequeathed over a long historical period. Consequently, this contribution attempts to address continuities and discontinuities within the secular quest for modernization in Romania as well as the specifics of the interwar period, which is the focus for particular scrutiny here. Albeit timidly, this opening points to some of the following discussion, but with it also shaped by the author's own perceptions and, unavoidably, his intellectual biases.

The central concern of this contribution is the role of finance as an engine for modernization, as a means for catching-up with the advanced economies of the West. With this perspective, the extraordinary handicap of the transforming economies looms large because, due to the long communist interregnum, they start almost from scratch with regard to the financial sector. Paradoxically for these countries' economies, what should lie under the terminological umbrella of institutional modernization appears, bearing in mind what has been left in the memory of society, as grand institutional (societal) innovation. This constitutes a change more profound than that highlighted by Trygvee Haavelmo.[2] Consequently, there are a number of related issues which also need to be explored here. These involve the general, congenital institutional fragility of the banking and financial system, and of the economy, arising from backwardness. A second issue is the nature of banks as institutions required and shaped by the dynamics of reality and which, in turn, lies well beyond the aims of institutional designers. Third, it is necessary to consider the impact of shocks arising from the international environment and the weak counter-response on the part of policy-making. Fourth, there are the peculiarities of stabilization policies and the role of foreign capital, and banks, and their relationship with the domestic capital. And last, but not least, there is the 'war of ideas' as a source for either accelerating progress or inducing policy mistakes.

The last sentence of a leading student of the history of eastern Europe, made at a conference in Sofia several years ago, took the form of: 'If a lesson is to be learned from the functioning of the region's interwar capital markets, it would more likely be what to avoid rather than what to emulate'.[3] I share much of the motivation which prompted this message but also feel the need to pose a related question.[4] It is agreed that farsighted and innovative individuals (or groups) can shape events and institutions under certain circumstances - in Hayek's perspective that these human actors can singly or collectively be effective *constructivists*. However, is there not also continually at work the powerful and impersonal power of *structure*[5], conceived as the very product of history, and which has a considerable bearing upon the evolution of large socio-economic aggregates? Furthermore, this force appears to be directed by a logic of motion embedded in, and emerging from, the flow of historical experience. An important inference is that, inexorably, there is much in the dynamic of reality which lies beyond that which political and institutional 'would-be wizards' assume they are able to design and control. When so much depends on structure, official designers of transformation policy are confronted by a haunting and daunting challenge posed by the problems of how to construct (or reconstruct) institutions seen also as rules (norms) which enjoy social acceptability,[6] and of how to undertake 'societal re-engineering'.[7] Or, in other words, how is it possible to escape the grip of history when, currently, there is such a unique case of, or a window of opportunity for, societal reconstruction? It is to be hoped that this will usher in economic miracles but not in terms of what eastern Europeans have become accustomed to understand by the possibly misleading syntagma of 'recovering normalcy'.

The power of structure articulates the burden of the past. On the one hand, it affects the way that institutional constructs function in, as in our case, relatively, less developed societies. On the other, it affects the very choice of institutional devices. Should decision-makers at both macro- and micro-levels be cognisant of what best fits the environment? For example, the current debate over the efficacy of 'universal' as opposed to 'narrow' banks in transforming economies loses its relevance to the extent that the reality of unfettered social and economic forces determines the pace and the quality of institutional change, and imposes its own solutions. More significant than new formal institutional constructs in themselves is their functioning and here the burden of the past - the legacy of backwardness - makes its presence heavily felt.

Institutions cannot but reflect society, particularly its level of overall development. For instance, since the second half of the nineteenth century, numerous prestigious Romanian intellectuals have time and time again decried the structural syndrome of 'form without substance' in all spheres of social and economic life. Yet, it should be acknowledged that this feeling of disenchantment was warranted to a degree since the role model provided by western institutions could only have been very imperfectly replicated locally and, moreover, not fully in sympathy with that required to uplift entire social bodies.[8] It is noteworthy that this feeling of bewilderment, *vis-à-vis* the difficulties of the post-communist societies to accommodate or absorb change, still currently pervades the thoughts of intellectuals. Furthermore, it leads to frustrations similar to those felt by our grand- and great-grandfathers, although more acutely due to the ardent desire to be able to join the European Union as soon as possible.

The current quest for catching-up with the West, through post-communist transformation, therefore, has to be judged within the larger time frame of the secular quest for modernization, and of the potential for society to learn. An astute observer of the region has recently remarked that 'Eastern Europe was in some sense economically backward long before it was absorbed into the broader Western world market. This backwardness has roots in the very distant past'.[9] Likewise, Ivan Berend pointed out that 'What is missing in most of these analyses is a deeper understanding of long-term historical trends in East-Central Europe'.[10] Possibly, due to the new information age and the high degree of literacy in the European post-communist societies, an upward shift in their long-term learning curve may (or may have) occur(ed), a phenomenon which might facilitate transformation. Moreover, the gravitational power of western Europe is very likely to exert a positive pull in this respect. But, still, ignoring the legacy of backwardness is counterproductive for understanding and assessing the real dynamics of change in the region. It also needs to be comprehended that the desire to close the economic gap with the West has long fuelled intense doctrinal debates and influenced economic policy.

During the interwar period, two, intricately intertwined tracks can be detected in economic thought and in modernization policies, which reverberated to a very great degree upon the role of finance as an agent of societal change. These consisted of a *sui generis* structuralism, which provided a vision, a set of basic presuppositions,[11] and of attitudes towards state intervention in the economy in terms of either interventionism or laissez-faire .

Structuralism directed attention to structure, to the structural deformities within, and the constraints afflicting, an underdeveloped economy. What is striking is the emphasis that was placed on the characteristics of an agrarian economy, namely, a large rural overpopulation subject to the vagaries of the harvest. There were two opposing schools of thought: the agrarians and the industrialists. The first searched for a remedy basically within agriculture itself, whereas the second sought a way out of underdevelopment through a drive for industrialization. The main spokesman for the agrarians was V. Madgearu, who was one of the most prestigious economists of interwar Romania and the leading theoretician of the National Peasants Party. (The National Liberal Party and the National Peasants' Party were the main political formations during the interwar period.) He questioned the appropriateness of Sombart's scheme for explaining the advance of capitalism in eastern Europe and, to this end, emphasized the so-called 'agricultural question'.[12] It was argued that the extent to which this problem might be satisfactorily resolved would affect the progress of the whole economy. In this context, the agrarian economists favoured the creation of specialized financial institutions to cater for the particular needs of Romanian agriculture, a view which had some affect upon the development of the financial system. The setting up of the Creditul Rural in 1934 was due, to a large extent, to this type of advocacy. The agrarians also supported an 'open door' policy due to Romania's significant exports of cereals. It is noteworthy that after his emigration to the United States, N. Georgescu-Roegen, returned to the problems posed by overpopulated agrarian economies and highlighted an arguably related misuse of neo-classical economics.[13]

The 'agricultural question' has once more become prominent since 1989 because the reform of property rights in itself is insufficient to turn to good account the huge potential of Romanian agriculture. Moreover, the impact of agriculture on the conduct of monetary policy in a primitive financial environment has to be considered. For instance, currently, most of the refinancing needs of the banking system relate to agriculture, while one of the worst debt portfolios is held by the Banca Agricola [the Agricultural Bank]. This compounds a situation already complicated by the bad debts of the banking sector arising from provisions to eastern Europe's, including Romania, large industrial facilities - indeed, Jeffrey Sachs talks about an 'over-industrialization' of the region.

In a different vein, industrialists emphasized the need to develop manufacturing in order to change structure by seeing this as a means to do away with the legacy of backwardness. To this end, finance was asked to play a special role and banks were regarded as the carriers of the seeds of modernization. Either through the prodding of state policy, or as the sheer consequence of being in the whirls of the psychological boom that followed the country's unification in 1918, banks maintained, or acquired, large equity stakes in industrial companies. In this context should be mentioned the crucial role played by the central bank, the National Bank of Romania, which supported the drive for industrial development from its creation in the 1880s.[14] The central bank's policy in this direction was staunchly supported by the Bratianu family, who were the brains and the soul of the Liberal party. They had considerable sway in the formulation of the policies of the National Bank (only partially state-owned) and controlled the Banca Romaneasca, the then largest commercial bank in Romania[15] and the most able to compete with the major foreign banks that were operating within the country. When considering the role of this family - in particular, Vintila Bratianu, who was Finance Minister during the 1920s - in the political and economic history of Romania, it is tempting to make a comparison, however stretched, with either that played by Dr. Hermann Abs, former Chairman of Deutsche Bank, in the reconstruction of Germany after the Second World War, or by the Wallenbergs in Sweden.

Industrialists promoted a vigorous policy under the slogan 'Through Ourselves'. They emphasized the need for strengthening the Romanian entrepreneurial class and urged the creation of strong Romanian banks to support industrialization. However, the banks' involvement in the economy through being large equity-holders was not without its risks. Thus, during the early 1920s, due especially to poor lending, the mushrooming banking sector experienced a logical sequence of boom and bust. The plight of banks was subsequently much accentuated by the consequences of the Great Depression, in particular capital flight. From 1934, there was a period of intense consolidation, while the banks embarked upon policies of partial disinvestment in industry to improve the quality of their assets. Furthermore, the National Bank introduced very strict regulations aimed at preventing banks from indulging in reckless lending behaviour.

The doctrine of protectionism was discussed vigorously[16] and became even more prominent with the Great Depression as major European economic powers closed their markets to exports from less developed countries.[17] Protectionism was closely inter-twined with the idea of state intervention in the economy.

What is striking about the interwar period is that the Liberal Party, which governed the country for most of these years, adamantly favoured an activist state policy of fostering industrial development. This was equally true of the party's main theoreticians, while this policy stance was reinforced by the experience of the Great Depression. Consequently, M. Manoilescu's theoretical work[18] was not an intellectual curiosity but a reflection of an evolving collective train of thought which had direct implications for policy formation.[19] One could argue that this was a response to the protectionist tendencies of Romania's main trading partners, primarily the continental powers, which were grossly amplified after the Great Depression.

Moreover, Keynesian-type ideas were beginning to spread throughout Europe and their influence on policy may, very likely, have been increased by the darkening skies heralding a new European military confrontation. But, although having a logical development with empirical support, such interpretations ignore the long-held views among the Liberals advocating a quasi-state industrial strategy.

State intervention to promote industry was the policy of the Liberals of the 'old vintage' and it contrasts markedly with the prevailing attitudes among the Liberals of the 'new vintage', who have appeared since 1990. Certainly, the peculiarities of post-communist transformation explains much of this difference over policy. The ideological winds blowing throughout the world during the 1980s, starting with the so-called Thatcher revolution in the United Kingdom and supply-side economics in the United States, have an explanatory power as well, but, notwithstanding, this contrast provides considerable food for thought.

The development of commercial policy after the Great Depression provides an example of interventionism, in terms of regulation, and is markedly different to the current policy regime in Romania and in other post-communist countries. Given the parallel goal of maintaining the stability of the national currency on the foreign exchanges but with a relative scarcity of reserves due to the above-mentioned protectionistic tendencies, commercial policy during the 1930s involved the very strict regulation of foreign trade through the use of licences. What may sound strange in the 1990s is that the National Bank was the institution empowered to implement commercial policy. Although surely plagued by considerable 'rent-seeking' and inefficiencies, this arrangement directly facilitated the functioning of a regime of foreign exchange surrender. The role of the central bank in this respect is being highlighted since one of the most important reasons, prompting the Romanian authorities to resort to a foreign exchange regime of full retention rights in spring 1992, was the extremely liberal trade regime introduced during the aftermath of the explosion of December 1989. This motivation was strengthened by a policy credibility problem revealed by substantial capital flight.

There are several issues whose exploration allow a judgement of the financial system and a comparison of the interwar period with the first years of post-communist transformation. These are the need for capital; the need for adequate financial institutions, in particular banks, which should channel capital to its most profitable use; and the links between banks and the real economy.

At the end of the First World War, Romania's shortage of capital was made more acute by the financial needs of reconstruction, including monetary unification, industrial development within a unified territory and the consequences of rural reform. Apparently, the economy was 'underbanked' both in quantitative and qualitative terms and this was certainly accentuated by the kinds of operations that were being undertaken by major foreign banks. According to the *Enciclopedia Romana*, foreign banks were less interested to a significant degree in providing facilities for investment,[20] although their contribution to the institutional modernization of Romania was widely acknowledged. Stimulated by the euphoric climate of the peace, the banking sector expanded in terms of the numbers of institutions[21] and such new creations became more involved in lending to, and acquiring equity stakes in, industrial companies. Moreover, the National Bank took part in this frenzy through its readiness both to cover large budget deficits and refinance commercial banks.

Competition among banks for deposits became ferocious, while their rates charged on advances rose sharply despite the National Bank's discount rate hovering around six per cent during the 1920s. The discount rate policy of the National Bank failed to arrest the marked rise in lending rates, which increased by about 20 per cent for the banks' prime clients during the late 1920s. This was because the central bank was restraining to a considerable degree the flow of credit within the economy in order to re-value the national currency. It goes without saying that very high commercial lending rates were detrimental to investment in production and, very probably, encouraged adverse selection. The crunch occurred in conjunction with the Great Depression[22] and the resulting consolidation within banking was accompanied by the establishment of specialized financial institutions.

The 1920s provide an image of an intense learning experience for both banks and the policy-makers. Policy-makers reacted vigorously to the effects of a decade of almost 'free banking', and then of the Great Depression, by imposing stringent regulatory measures upon banking. This took place within a framework of a radical change of policy regime which meant a significantly greater reliance upon controls.

The substantial capital flight, triggered by the collapse of several leading western banks and the domino effect that this had on Romanian banks, aroused misgivings about the utility, under any circumstances, of foreign capital. The run on Romanian banks is clearly indicated by their loss of almost 43 per cent of their deposits in 1931. An increasingly influential line of reasoning cautioned policy-makers against too greater a reliance on short-term and portfolio capital inflows, and stressed the need to increase domestic savings for financing investment in production.[23] Domestic savings came to be seen as essential for fostering growth during a period of increasing uncertainty in the international environment. The way I read the events of this period suggests that, because of the bitter experience of the Great Depression, scepticism *vis-à-vis* the working of capital markets, including the stock exchange, was equally increasing. When placed in the current debate over which system is better for corporate governance, the tendencies initiated by the effects of the Great Depression seem to provide conflicting signals. In any case, resolving this dilemma during the 1930s became irrelevant because of, first, the war and then the advent of the all-encompassing command system.

A major paradox and a challenge facing post-communist economies arises from the assumed status, and functions, of banks as agents of change. Apart from institutional construction, change means essentially the restructuring of economies which have, as a legacy of the command system, a very substantial mis-allocation of resources. It is beyond contention that restructuring is a prerequisite for the durable stabilization of these economies, bearing in mind the existing high degree of cross-subsidization and the entrenched behavioural patterns and routines of enterprises. A crucial question therefore emerges: should and can banks be in the forefront of change in the sense of providing the thrust for restructuring and the arising technical support required? An immediate, but possibly unconsidered, answer might be in the affirmative since the financial system is presumed to be the main vehicle for resource reallocation in a market environment. Because capital markets are very much in their infancy and non-bank financial institutions are primitive or non-existent, banks gain a high profile in a compelling fashion.[24] However, a sceptical answer would pay attention to the inherent primitiveness and fragility of the banking sector and would, in turn, question the realism of vesting so much of a role, through performing an allocative function, in it.[25] An answer framed in these terms might point to an enhanced 'financial instability hypothesis'[26] being applicable to the dynamics of post-communist, transforming economies. Moreover, the wide-ranging privatization programmes are relevant to the issue, since via a 'Big-Bang' approach to the creation of capital markets, they would seem to favour the Anglo-Saxon model of corporate governance.

The '"narrow" versus "universal" banks' debate is also directly related to this concern. The discussion is still current and may have a greater operational relevance for the position of Russia and other former soviet republics. With regard to central and eastern Europe, its significance in terms of institutional design has been considerably diminished by the flow of events.[27] None the less, both the way that banks actually operate in real terms, and the tension between the two viewpoints in the debate discernible all over the region, need to be considered. The real functioning of banks is clearly shaped more by the dynamics of the environment than by the intentions of policy-makers. In this context, it can be argued that 'the less attuned to a market environment the economy is, the more ineffective the would-be universal banks are and the more inefficient resource allocation is'.

The experience of post-communist Romania gives support to the last statement. The Romanian banking system is confronted by a shortage of human skills, the slowness of institutional reform and the lack of a 'banking culture'. With the common problems of segmentation, concentration and an antiquated payments system, it also faces the extraordinary pressure exerted by the magnitude of required resource reallocation, amply illustrated by the steady reproduction of bad debts (and, implicitly, of much of the old resource allocation) and by the structural phenomenon of inter-enterprise arrears.[28]

However, banks learn and improve their skills. It would seem that what banks do now is, comparatively, less related to the skills of their staff than to what was defined as the power of structure and government policy. Therefore, on one hand, banks need to pursue their liberation from the malign grip of structure and of non-banking constraints. On the other hand, because of their high fragility as financial institutions and the high risks they pose to the functioning of the entire system (the systemic risk), they need to be under the tight rein of prudential regulations and supervision. Apart from the extraordinary pressure exerted by structure, if it is assumed that skills will improve quite significantly, and twinning with foreign banks (a strategy pursued by Romanian banks) will compensate for (and complement) local resources, then the fuzziness of the environment proves to be the comparatively harder issue that has to be surmounted. As the experience of foreign banks operating in the area shows, banks may and do perform surprisingly poorly in a post-command economy. Fuzziness and uncertainty explain why banks show a very low propensity to provide long-term credit, behaviour which concatenates with low domestic savings. All this indicates the need for steady and substantial foreign capital inflows - but those committed to the restructuring of the economy.

Personally, I detect the main common feature of the interwar period and the first years of post-communist transformation, as far as the activity of the National Bank is concerned, to be its role as an institutional builder. In both periods the National Bank emerges as a large-scale designer, as a powerful force, for modernization.

On one hand, it is not surprising that, due to the backwardness of the country, the vision and the drive of the people at the helm of policy-making made the National Bank the main pillar of modernization policy during the interwar period. This hypostasis for the National Bank only reinforced a pre-war policy commitment. On the other hand, amazement might arise from the diversity of the tasks which the National Bank was asked to take over directly, and of the needs to which it was asked to respond. The issues ranged from a designed development of the financial system to the extensive support of industry[29] and, after the Great Depression, to the management of commercial policy. Surely, the wisdom behind placing so much weight on the National Bank can be questioned, especially as it ran the risk of diverting the attention of its staff from their main task: defending the value and stability of the national currency. In fact, policy-makers were conscious of this risk and constantly tried to relieve the National Bank of the 'borrowed' tasks.[30] However, the difficulties facing the country, particularly after 1934, aborted such attempts to a large extent. It seems that the main factor which impeded the normal streamlining of the tasks of the National Bank was the sequence of major and reverberating shocks which rocked the national economy. These arose from, in chronological sequence, war financing, the needs of post-war reconstruction, the Great Depression and the demands of rearmament in the anticipation of a new war.

Similarly, the National Bank during the 1990s is engaged in a substantial effort directed towards building the financial system. It is obvious that the current endeavour has a wider scope and greater depth than that of the interwar period. Likewise, the inherited huge mis-allocation of resources has put the economy under a tremendous strain. This is a continuing and very troublesome pressure which complicates to a great degree the conduct of monetary policy and undermines the effectiveness of stabilization measures. This is especially the case when the lack of capital markets, budget deficits, low domestic savings rates and meagre capital inflows are taken into account.

When focusing on the impact of the international environment, four issues can dominate the discussion of the role of finance in an open economy. These are: the relative level of economic development as a determinant of the need for foreign capital; the mechanism of interaction with the international environment; the sizes of domestic disequilibria; and the dynamics of the international environment.

In the case of the Romanian interwar economy, its level of development and the insufficient domestic savings called for substantial capital inflows. The gold exchange standard[31] provided the functional channel for the free interaction between the domestic economy and the international environment. It can be argued that this mechanism lent a deflationary bias to the conduct of monetary policy, which was supposed to be targeted on the exchange rate, and this became evident when the National Bank embarked upon a revaluation policy in 1925. This policy, which meant a very strict control of credit, led to a substantial jump in the lending rates of commercial banks, which were forced to compete ferociously for deposits; these rates moved in the range of 18-20 per cent for prime borrowers, whereas the discount rate of the National Bank was about 6 per cent. But such interaction, which implied free capital movements, was called into question by the substantial capital flight experienced by Romania during the Great Depression. As pointed out previously, this led after 1934 to a new policy which relied on controlling foreign exchange and trade.

Capital flight came as a very severe blow since it occurred soon after Romania initiated its stabilization programme in 1929,[32] a programme which relied considerably on foreign loans. Some questioned the timing and the preparation of the programme,[33] whereas others criticized the level chosen for the exchange rate. However, what is certain is that the onset the Great Depression had a decisive impact on the expected outcome of the programme. Looming here as a policy issue is the vulnerability of the economy, which also depended heavily on the nature of capital movements.

Vulnerability is very much an issue for the post-command economy. The sizes of disequilibria and the ensuing strain, against the background of the scarcity both of organizational capital and of domestic resources for investment with respect to restructuring, pose a daunting dilemma for policy-makers. On one hand, they need to mould an environment which should be attractive to foreign capital. On the other, under certain circumstances, large movements of portfolio capital can be very destabilizing. It should not be forgotten that this capital has a short-term focus and is extremely volatile. Therefore, the likelihood of this capital being over-sensitive in a post-command, transforming environment is very high because this is perceived by investors as highly uncertain and risky.

The interwar period can reveal interesting lessons for the designers of financial systems in post-communist economies.

One is that *natura non facit saltum*, that making institutions function properly takes time, since it is extremely difficult to release the grip of structure, of the product of history. One can detect a 'clash of visions' regarding the model of financial system - over which would arguably best fit the conditions of the European post-communist countries. The evolution of real financial systems will depend on real dynamics, which are not necessarily under the control of those who design the transformation policy. It would be naive to assume that the institutions of the post-communist economies can and will perform according to the standards of the role-model. They need time to grow in order to perform. Realism is needed not only in order to work out proper design policies but also in order to make balanced judgements as to 'what are good performances' and 'what is to be done next'.

Another lesson is that institutions in the making are fragile and that their fragility makes the economic system more vulnerable to both internal and external shocks. This institutional fragility magnifies the strain in the system caused by the resource mis-allocation inherited from the command economy. Furthermore, all over the world, including the advanced market economies, financial innovation subjects economies to pressure. A good example is financial derivatives against the background of increasingly interdependent capital markets. In the case of post-communist countries, the creation of financial systems is the equivalent of a large-scale financial innovation. Consequently, there is a relatively high degree of systemic risk unless proper regulations and prudential rules are enforced by the monetary authorities. There is much need for foreign capital, when it acts as a powerful force for modernization and restructuring. The more that this capital is committed on the long-term, the easier it will be for post-communist economies to weather the inherent risks of a market environment. Policy-makers in post-communist countries need to remind themselves constantly that the competition for capital is intensified by the effects of the redistribution of economic power in the world space.

Building up financial systems in eastern Europe has to be seen in the perspective of a double challenge facing Europe. The quest of western Europe for regaining vitality is doubled by the quest of eastern Europe for creating viable economic entities. The danger for both western and eastern Europe lies in the inability of policy-makers to conceptualize, and make operational, the intricate connections between these two processes. The overall challenge for Europe is how to accelerate its adjustment as a means to cope with the trends in the world space.

Notes

1 Nearly three decades ago, N. Georgescu-Roegen remarked (1960) that every economist who has won a place in the history of economic thought 'has been intellectually opportunistic in the sense that each has been exclusively preoccupied with the contemporary economic problems of the society in which he happened to live ... the economic profession should take pride in being opportunistic in the above sense'. Idem, 'Economic Theory and Agrarian Economics', reprinted in idem, *Energy and Economic Myths*, New York, p. 200. In this way he replied to Bridgman, the Nobel laureate for physics, who argued (1950) that the major handicap of economics is the characteristic intellectual opportunism of its servants. *Reflections of a Physicist*, New York, pp.303-5.

2 Haavelmo recommends 'a little more of the "engineering approach" in the study of economic system', idem, (1968), 'The Scope for widening the scope of Economics', reprinted in S. Mitra, (1971), *Dimensions of Macroeconomics*, New York, p. 5.

3 A. Teichova, (1992), 'Interwar capital markets and south-eastern Europe', in J. R. Lampe (ed.), (1992), *Creating capital markets in eastern Europe*, Washington, DC, p. 17.

4 The line of reasoning advocated by this section can also be found in D. Daianu, (1992), 'Transformation and the legacy of backwardness', *Economies et Societies*, 44, pp. 181-206.

5 L'Emprise de la structure [the grip of structure] is a key concept used by F. Perroux, who applies it at the level of national economic entities. See idem, (1969), *Independance de la Nation*, Paris. This concept is widely used by the students of business schools, who learn about the inertia and entrenched behavioural patterns of large structures - very much in the vein of what Granovetter termed the 'embeddedness' of economic action. See idem (1985), 'Economic action and social structure: the problem of embeddedness', *American Journal of Sociology*, 19.3, pp. 481-510 but especially pp. 481-2.

6 D. North, (1981), *Structure and change in economic history*, New York.

7 After reading M. Hammer & J. Champy, (1993), *Reengineering the Corporation*, New York, I wondered why so many, presumably knowledgeable, professionals still did not seem to grasp the complexity and the complicated nature of 're-engineering' a society.

8 The overall judgement becomes even less harsher when one considers some remarkable instances of institutional modernization in that period. Thus, due to Professor Joe Tropea from George Washington University, I came across a revealing excerpt regarding the development of accounting as a profession in Romania after the turn of the century: 'Accountancy has grown rapidly, reaching great heights in 1921 when a law was passed restricting the practice of accountancy to legally

qualified accountants. Romania is the only European country aside from Italy to have restrictive legislation. The law has been successfully applied there for almost ten years (to 1930) and it is hoped that other European nations will pass similar legislation based on Romania's excellent example'. W. L. Green, (1930), *History and survey of accountancy*, New York, p. 68.

9 D. Chirot (ed.), (1992), *The origins of backwardness in eastern Europe*, Berkeley, California, p. 3.

10 I. Berend, (1994), 'Annus Mirabilis - Anni Mirabiles?' *Contention*, 8, p. 110. Similarly instructive, about the origin of the economic 'schism' between the West and the East of Europe, is Z. A. B Zeman, (1991), *The making and breaking of Communist Europe*, Oxford.

11 J. Schumpeter, (1955), *History of economic analysis*, London, p. 42.

12 See, especially, the introductory chapter to his main work, (1940), *Evolutia economiei romanesti* [The evolution of the Romanian economy], Bucharest.

13 N. Georgescu-Roegen is world famous for the application of entropy law to economic processes as well. He wrote (1976): 'an intuitive knowledge of the basic cultural traits of a community is indispensable for laying out the basis of its economic theory', 'Economic theory', loc.cit., p. 107. This may explain the difficulties of many western economists in understanding the specifics of post-communist transformation.

14 Regarding the circumstances surrounding the creation of the National Bank of Romania, see C. Kiritescu, (1964, reprinted 1971), *Sistemul Banesc at Leuli* [The monetary system of the Leu], Bucharest.

15 It may be of interest to mention that Banca Romaneasca, as a bastion of the Liberal Party, reappeared after December 1989. But it has a long way to go in order to regain its former status and prestige.

16 The major 'guru' was M. Manoilescu, whose *Theorie du Protectionisme et de l'Echange international* was published in Paris in 1929.

17 It may be incongruous with the current *Zeitgeist* of post-communist economic transformation but the fact is that what historians describe as the best economic years and the biggest industrial advance were registered after 1934 - a period characterized by pronounced state intervention in the economy and protectionism.

18 I am not referring to Manoilescu's espousal, especially during the 1930s, of corporatism and authoritarianism.

19 C. Murgescu (1987) conducts a remarkable analysis of the impact of Manoilescu's thinking and of its intellectual extraction out of a certain social prise de conscience concerning modernization via industrialization. See idem, *Mersul Ideilor Economice la Romani* [The evolution of economic ideas in Romania], Bucharest, especially chapter 13.

20 Chapter 'Commercial Banks' in P. D. Gusti (ed.), (1940), *Enciclopedia Romana*, Bucharest, p. 571.

21 Whereas the number of banks in 1919 was 486 (including those of the reunited territories), by 1928 the figure had jumped to 1,122; Gusti,

(1940), *Enciclopedia*, p. 565. It should be pointed out that the number of the major banks did not alter.

22 An interesting question is: assuming that the Great Depression could have been avoided, what would have been the, presumably, unavoidable intensity of retrenchment within Romanian banking - after the years of reckless lending during the 1920s?

23 See, for example, Chapter 'Monetary Policy' in (1940), *Enciclopedia*, p.710.

24 Thus it is argued that 'the objection that banks do not have the skills to do that right is less compelling than at first sight. The point is not that banks are good at doing this, but that they are likely to be better than anybody else.' S. van Wijnbergen, (1992), *Enterprise reform in eastern Europe*, Discussion Paper No. 738, CEPR, London, p. 14. A similar view is held by J. Corbett & C. Mayer, (1991), *Financial reform in eastern Europe*, Discussion Paper No. 603, CEPR, London.

25 As J. Rostowski remarked, (1993), 'The lack of banking skills thus introduces a fundamental instability into their monetary systems. Until this problem is resolved, macroeconomic stability will remain hard to achieve'. Idem, (1993), 'Creating stable monetary systems in Post-communist economies', mimeo, p. 5. A similar opinion can be found in R. McKinnon, (1991), *The order of economic liberalization*, Baltimore, USA and in D. H. Scott, (1993), *Revising financial sector policy in transitional socialist economies. Will universal banks prove viable?* The World Bank, WPS 1034.

26 H. Minsky, (1977), 'A theory of systemic fragility', in E. I. Altman & A. W. Semetz (eds), (1977), *Financial crises: institutions and markets in a fragile environment*, New York.

27 I. Szekely asserts that 'The model issue thus was in fact not a real issue from the very beginning', idem, (1993), 'Economic transformation and the reform of the financial system in central and eastern Europe', Discussion Paper No. 816, CEPR, London, p. 26). He continues: 'On the other hand, it is not an issue any more as the so far introduced legal regulations in each country in the region opted basically for universal banking, following the EC regulations, and the intentions in the remaining countries point to the same direction'.

28 Inter-enterprise arrears, as temporary quasi-inside money, reflect the extraordinary strain under which post-command economies function. D. Daianu, (1994), 'Inter-enterprise arrears in a post-command economy. Thoughts from a Romanian perspective', WP/94/54, Washington DC: International Monetary Fund.

29 This support was increased after the Great Depression. As it was appropriately remarked 'After 1933 industrialization proceeded at a much more rapid tempo and in a somewhat different direction. The private banks after the depression played a less important part in financing industry; the principal initiative was by the National Bank or the state itself, but through state-owned corporations and through the

growing importance of the state as consumer of industrial products'. H. L. Roberts, (1953), ***Romania. Political problems of an agrarian state***, New Haven, p. 198.

30 Like the Convention of 1925, which foresaw the termination of the extensive financing by the National Bank of the state budget deficits.

31 In 1931 the National Bank reintroduced the gold bullion standard, after the large fluctuations (devaluation) in the value of sterling; gold was deemed a more reliable reserve.

32 As against other countries, Romania did not resort to the monitoring role of the Financial Committee of the League of Nations. The Finance Minister, V. Bratianu, felt that the economic situation of the country allowed a direct negotiation with the creditors: the Banque of France, the Bank of England, and the Federal Reserve Bank of New York. For an interesting analysis of the Romanian stabilization program see R. H. Meyer, (1970), ***Bankers' diplomacy. Monetary stabilization in the Twenties***, New York.

33 Madgearu, (1940), ***Evolutia***, p.305. For a different view, see V. Slavescu, (1932), ***Curs de Moneda, Credit si Schimb*** [Treatise on money, credit and exchange], Craiova, pp. 336-76.

Bibliography

Secondary sources only

Ally, R., (1994), *Gold and empire: the Bank of England and South Africa's gold producers, 1886-1926*, Johannesburg.

Almanach československého peněžnictví [Almanac of the Czechoslovak banking system], Prague 1928.

Altman, E. I., & A. W. Semetz (eds), (1977), *Financial crises: institutions and markets in a fragile environment*, New York.

Bachinger, K., & H. Matis, (1973), 'Österreichs industrielle Entwicklung', in Wandruszka and Urbanitsch, 1973.

Bácskai, T., (ed.), (1994), *A Magyar Nemzeti Bank Története* [History of the National Bank of Hungary], 1, *Az Osztrák Nemzeti Banktól a Magyar Nemzeti Bankig 1816-1924*, Budapest.

Berend, I. T., & G. Ránki, (1960), *The development of the manufacturing industry in Hungary (1900-1944)*, Budapest.

Berend, I. T., (1994), 'Annus Mirabilis - Anni Mirabiles?' *Contention*, 8.

Borross, E. A., (1984), 'The role of the state issuing bank in the course of inflation in Hungary between 1918 and 1924', in G. Feldman (ed.).

Boyce, R. W. D., (1987), *British capitalism at the crossroads 1919-1932. A study in politics, economics, and international relations*, Cambridge.

Boyle, A., (1967), *Montagu Norman, a biography*, London.

Capie, Forrest, Charles Goodhart & Norbert Schnadt (1994), *The Development of Central Banking*, Cambridge.

Chandler, L. V., (1967), *Benjamin Strong, central banker*, New York.

Chirot, D., (ed.), (1992), *The origins of backwardness in eastern Europe*, Berkeley, California.

Clare, G., (1981) *Last Waltz in Vienna*, London.

Clarke, S. V. O., (1967), *Central bank cooperation, 1924-1931*, New York.

Clay, Sir Henry, (1957), *Lord Norman*, London.

Corbett, J. & C. Mayer, (1991), *Financial reform in eastern Europe*, Discussion Paper No. 603, CEPR, London.

Cottrell, P. L., (1994), '"Mushrooms and dinosaurs": Sieghart and the Boden-Credit-Anstalt during the 1920s', in Teichova, A., T. Gourvish & Á. Pogány (eds), 1994.

Cottrell, P. L., H. Lindgren & A. Teichova (eds), (1992), *European Industry and Banking Between the Wars. A Review of Bank-Industry Relations*, Leicester.

Daianu, D., (1992), 'Transformation and the legacy of backwardness', *Economies et Societies*, 44.

Daianu, D., (1994), 'Inter-enterprise arrears in a post-command economy. Thoughts from a Romanian perspective', WP/94/54, Washington DC: International Monetary Fund Working Paper.

de Kock, G., (1954), *A history of the South African Reserve Bank 1920-52*, Pretoria.

de Vries, J., (1989), *Geschiedenis van de Nederlandsche Bank; Vifde deel De Nederlandsche Bank van 1914 tot 1948. Visserings tijdvak 1914-1931*, The Hague.

Die Frage des Finanzkapitals in der Österreichisch-Ungarischen Monarchie 1900-1918, Bucharest, 1965.

Dulles, J. F., (1927), *Polish Stabilization Plan*, New York.

Dziennik Ustaw Rzeczypospolitej Polskiej, 1939.

Eichengreen, B., (1992), *Golden Fetters. The gold standard and the Great Depression, 1919-1939*, Oxford.

Eigner, P., (1994), 'Interlocking Directorships between Commercial Banks and Industry in Interwar Vienna', in Teichova, A., T. Gourvish & Á. Pogány (eds), 1994.

Enderle-Burcel, G., (1994), 'The Failure of Crisis Management: Banking Laws in Interwar Austria', in Teichova, A., T. Gourvish & Á. Pogány (eds), 1994.

Feldman, G. D., et al., (1984), *Die Erfahrung der Inflation im internationalen Zusammenhang und Vergleich*, [The experience of inflation: international and comparative studies], Berlin/New York.

Fink, C., (1984), *The Genoa conference. European diplomacy, 1921-1922*, Chapel Hill, NC.

Garber, P. M., & M. G. Spencer, (1992), *The dissolution of the Austro-Hungarian Empire: lessons for currency reform*, Working Paper WP/92/66, Washington DC: International Monetary Fund.

Gawith, P., (1991), 'Gencor Ltd.', in A. Hast et al. (eds), 1991.

Georgescu-Roegen, N., (1960), 'Economic Theory and Agrarian Economics', reprinted in Roegen, (1960), *Energy and Economic Myths*, New York.

Good, D. F., (1986), *Der wirtschaftliche Aufstieg des Habsburgerreiches 1750-1914*, Vienna.

Grabski, W., (1927), *Dwa lata pracy u podstaw panstwowosci naszej (1924-1925)*, Warsaw.

Green, W. L., (1930), *History and survey of accountancy*, New York.

Gruber, H., (1968), *Wspomnienia i uwagi*, London.

Günther, G., (1936), *Lebenserinnerungen*, Vienna.

Gusti, P. D., (ed.), (1940), *Enciclopedia Romana*, Bucharest.

Haavelmo, (1968), 'The Scope for widening the scope of Economics', reprinted in S. Mitra, (1971), *Dimensions of Macroeconomics*, New York.

Hammer, M., & J. Champy, (1993), *Reengineering the Corporation*, New York.

Hast, A., et al. (eds), (1991), *International directory of company histories*, IV, Chicago and London.

Hennessy, E., (1992), *A domestic history of the Bank of England, 1930-1960*, Cambridge.

Hocevar, T., (1984), 'Slovensko poslovno bančništvo, 1913-1941' [Slovene business banking, 1913-1941], *Bančni Vestnik*, 33.7-8.

Homan, B., (1916), *Magyar Penztortenet* [Hungarian Monetary History], Budapest.

Homan, B., (1921), *A magyar kiralysag penzugyei es gazdasagpolitikaja Karoly Robert koraban* [Economic policy of Carlobertus], Budapest.

Hospodářská politika, 1930 [Economic Policy].

Howson, S. W., (1974), 'The origins of dear money, 1919-20', *Economic History Review.*

Jindra, Z., (1957), 'K rozvoji českého bankovního kapitálu před první světovou válkou' [Development of Czech bank capital before World War I], *Československý časopis historický*, 5.

Johnson, E., (ed.), (1977), *Collected writings of John Maynard Keynes*, 17, *Activities 1920-22*, London.

Jonker J., & J. L. van Zander, (1992), 'Method in the Madness? Banking crises between the wars: an international comparison', in Department of Economic History, Budapest University of Economic Sciences, *20th Century Universal Banking: International Comparisons, Report from the International Conference Budapest, 2-5 September 1992*, I, Budapest.

Karpinski, Z., (1958), *Bank Polski 1924-1939. Przyczynek do historii gospodarczej okresu miedzywojennego,* Warsaw.

Kernbauer, H., & F. Weber, (1984), 'Die Wiener Großbanken in der Zeit der Kriegs- und Nachkriegsinflation (1914-1922)', in G. D. Feldman et al., 1984.

Kernbauer, H., (1988), *Das Österreichische Noteninstitut*, 3.1, *1923 bis 1938, Währungspolitik in der Zwischenkriegszeit,* Vienna.

Kiritescu, C., (1964, reprinted 1971), *Sistemul Banesc at Leuli* [The monetary system of the Leu], Bucharest.

Kola, R., (1922), *Rückblick ins Gestrige*, Vienna.

Kooker, J. L., (1976), 'French financial diplomacy: the interwar years', in B. M. Rowland (ed.), 1976.

Lacina, V., (1990), *Formování ceskoslovenské ekonomiky 1918-1923* [The formation of the Czechoslovak economy 1918-1923], Prague.

Lacina, V., (1994), 'Banking System Changes after the Establishment of the Independent Czechoslovak Republic', in Teichova, A., T. Gourvish & Á. Pogány (eds), 1994.

Lacina, V., (1994), 'Nostrifikáce podnike a bank v prvním desetiletí Československé republiky' [Nostrification of enterprises and banks during the first decade of the Czechoslovak Republic], *Česky časopis historický*, 92.

Lampe, J. R., (ed.), (1992), *Creating capital markets in eastern Europe*, Washington, DC.

Landau, Z., (1963), *Plan stabilizacyjny 1927-1930*, Warsaw.

League of Nations, (1926), *The financial reconstruction of Hungary. General survey and principal documents*, Geneva.

Madgearu, V., (1940), *Evolutia economiei romanesti* [The evolution of the Romanian economy], Bucharest.

Markowski, B., (1931), *Administracja skarbowa w Polsce*, Warsaw.

März, E., & K. Socher, (1973), 'Währung und Banken in Cisleithanien', in A. Wandruszka & P. Urbanitsch, 1973.

März, E., (1981), *Österreichische Bankpolitik in der Zeit der großen Wende 1913-1923*, Vienna.

McKinnon, R., (1991), *The order of economic liberalization*, Baltimore.

Meyer, R. H., (1970), *Bankers' diplomacy. Monetary stabilization in the Twenties*, New York.

Michel, B., (1976), *Banques et banquiers en Autriche au début du 20e siècle*, Paris.

Minsky, H., (1977), 'A theory of systemic fragility', in E. I. Altman & A. W. Semetz (eds), 1977.

Mitzakis, M., (1925), *Le relèvement financier de la Hongrie et la Société des Nations*, Paris.

Molynarski, F., (1972), *Wspomnienia*, Warsaw.

Morawitz, K., 'Der Mangel an Bankdirektoren', and 'Der Nachwuchs an Bankleitern', both in Morawitz, (1911), *Aus Arbeitstagen und Mußestunden. Neue Folge*, Vienna/Leipzig.

Mosser, A., (1980), *Die Industrieaktiengesellschaft in Österreich 1880-1913*, Vienna.

Mosser, A., (1994), 'Financing Industrial Companies in Interwar Austria: Working Capital and Liquidity', in Teichova, A., T. Gourvish & Á. Pogány (eds), 1994.

Murgescu, C., (1987), *Mersul Ideilor Economice la Romani* [The evolution of economic ideas in Romania], Bucharest.

Nečas, C., (1957), *Na prahu české kapitálové expanze* [On the threshold of Czech capital expansion], Brno, 1987.

North, D., (1981), *Structure and change in economic history*, New York.

Nötel, R., (1984), 'Money, banking and industry in interwar Austria and Hungary', *Journal of European Economic History*, 13.2.

Orde, A., (1990), *British policy and European reconstruction after the First World War*, Cambridge.

Orde, A., (1991), 'Baring Brothers, the Bank of England, the British government and the Czechoslovak state loan of 1922', *English Historical Review*, 106.

Perroux, F., (1969), *Independance de la Nation*, Paris.

Perroux, F., (1985), 'Economic action and social structure: the problem of embeddedness', *American Journal of Sociology*, 19.3.

Péteri, G., (1980) 'International liquidity and the national economy as a factor in Hungary's monetary policy 1924-1931', *Acta Historica Academiae Scientiarum Hungaricae*, 26, reprinted in Péteri, 1995.

Péteri, G., (1984), 'The inflation-proof gold standard: the foreign policy of the Riksbankschefen Victor Moll and the origins of the Swedish ban on gold imports in 1924', *Journal of European Economic History*, 13, and reprinted in Péteri, 1995.

Péteri, G., (1984), 'Tying up a loose end. British foreign economic strategy in 1924. The Hungarian stabilization', *Acta Historica*, 30.

Péteri, G., (1985), '"Montagu Norman és a Magyar szanallási mü." Az 1924-ós Magyar pénzügyi stabilizacióról', *Századok*, 1.

Péteri, G., (1995), *Revolutionary Twenties. Essays on international monetary and financial relations after World War I*, Trondheim.

Pietri, N., (1970), *La Société des Nations et la reconstruction financiere de l'Autriche 1921-1926*, Geneva.

Pimper, A., (1929), *České obchodní banky za války a po válce* [Czech commercial banks during and after the war], Prague.

Pogány, A., (1987/8), 'Két Szempont a Magyarországi infláció vizgálatához (1914-1924)', *Történelmi Szemle.*

Pohl M., & S. Freitag (eds), (1994), for the European Association for Banking History e.V., *Handbook on the History of European Banks*, Aldershot.

Ránki, G., (1983), 'Inflation in Hungary', in N. Schmukler & E. Marcus (eds), (1983), *Inflation through the ages: economic, social, pyschological and historical aspects*, New York.

Reik, W., (1932), *Die Beziehungen der österreichischen Großbanken zur Industrie*, Vienna.

Roberts, H. L., (1953), *Romania. Political problems of an agrarian state*, New Haven.

Rowland, B. M., (ed.), (1976), *Balance of power or hegemony: the interwar monetary system*, New York.

Rudolph, R. L., (1976), *Banking and Industrialisation in Austria-Hungary. The Role of Banks in Industrialisation of the Czech Crownlands, 1873-1914*, Cambridge.

Sayers, (1976), R. S., *The Bank of England 1891-1944*, Cambridge.

Schmukler N., & E. Marcus (eds), (1983), *Inflation through the ages: economic, social, pyschological and historical aspects*, New York.

Schumpeter, J., (1955), *History of economic analysis*, London.

Scott, D. H., (1993), *Revising financial sector policy in transitional socialist economies. Will universal banks prove viable?* The World Bank, WPS 1034.

Sieghart, R., (1932), *Die letzte Jahrzehnte einer Großmacht*, Berlin.

Siklos, P. L., 'Interpreting a change in monetary policy regimes: a reappraisal of the first Hungarian hyperinflation and stabilisation, 1921-28', in M. D. Bordo & F. Capie, (1994), *Monetary regimes in transition*, Cambridge.

Skidelsky, R., (1992), *John Maynard Keynes*, II, *The economist as saviour 1920-1937*, London.

Slavescu, V., (1932), *Curs de Moneda, Credit si Schimb* [Treatise on money, credit and exchange], Craiova.

Somogyi, L., (ed.), (1993), *The Political Economy of the Transition Process in Eastern Europe*, Aldershot.

Spitzmüller, A., (1955), '... *Und hat auch Ursach, es zu lieben*', Vienna.

Statistická příručka RCS [Statistical Survey of the Czechoslovak Republic], 4, Prague, 1932.

Statut Banki Polskiego, Warsaw, 1924.

Stiefel, D., (1983), 'The Reconstruction of the Credit-Anstalt', in A. Teichova & P. L. Cottrell, 1983.

Stiefel, D., (1984), 'Die österreichischen Banken am Höhepunkt von Macht und Einfluß', *Bankhistorisches Archiv. Zeitschrift für Bankengeschichte*, 1.

Stiefel, D., (1989), *Finanzdiplomatie und Weltwirtschaftskrise. Die Krise der Credit-Anstalt für Handel und Gewerbe 1931*, Frankfurt-am-Main.

Stiefel, D., (1994), '"For Better, for Worse ...": the Credit-Anstalt and its Customers in 1931', in Teichova, A., T. Gourvish & Á. Pogány (eds), 1994.

Szapáry, G., (1993), 'Transition issues as through the experience of Hungary: There is no cookbook to go by', in L. Somogyi (ed.), 1993.

Szekely, I., (1993), 'Economic transformation and the reform of the financial system in central and eastern Europe', Discussion Paper No. 816, CEPR, London.

Teichova, A., (1974), *An Economic Background to Munich. International Business and Czechoslovakia 1918-1938*, Cambridge.

Teichova, A., (1988), *Kleinstaaten im Spannungsfeld der Großmächte*, Vienna.

Teichova, A., (1992), 'Interwar capital markets and south-eastern Europe', in J. R. Lampe, 1992.

Teichova, A., (1992), 'Rivals and Partners: Reflections on Banking and Industry in Europe, 1880-1938', in P. L. Cottrell, H. Lindgren & A. Teichova (eds), 1992.

Teichova, A., & P. L. Cottrell (eds), (1983), *International Business & Central Europe, 1918-1939*, Leicester.

Teichova, A., T. Gourvish & Á. Pogány (eds), (1994), *Universal Banking in the Twentieth Century. Finance, Industry and the State in North and Central Europe*, Aldershot.

Tosti, A., (1989), *Denarni zavodi v Sloveniji po prvi svetovni vojni* [Monetary institutions in Slovenia after World War I], Ljubljana.

van Wijnbergen, S., (1992), *Enterprise reform in eastern Europe*, Discussion Paper No. 738, CEPR, London.

Wandruszka, A., & P. Urbanitsch (eds), (1973), *Die Habsburgermonarchie 1848-1918*, I, *Die wirtschaftliche Entwicklung*, Vienna.

Weber, F., (1991), *Vor dem großen Krach. Die Krise des österreichischen Bankwesens in den zwanziger Jahren*, Habilitation thesis, Vienna.

Wellhöner, V., (1989), *Großbanken und Großindustrie im Kaiserreich*, Göttingen.

Who was who, (1972), VI, *1961-1970*, London.

Williams, E. T., (1959), *The dictionary of national biography, 1941-1950*, Oxford.

Wittek-Saltzberg, L., (1970), *Die wirtschaftlichen Auswirkungen der Okkupation*, Dissertation, Vienna.

Zeman, Z. A. B., (1991), *The making and breaking of Communist Europe*, Oxford.

Zweig, F., (1944), *Poland between Two Wars. A critical study of social and economic changes*, London.

Index

For Product Safety Concerns and Information please contact our EU representative GPSR@taylorandfrancis.com
Taylor & Francis Verlag GmbH, Kaufingerstraße 24, 80331 München, Germany

www.ingramcontent.com/pod-product-compliance
Ingram Content Group UK Ltd.
Pitfield, Milton Keynes, MK11 3LW, UK
UKHW021720240926
475702UK00029BA/1669
9781138269095